How to Manage Your Accounting Practice

Taking Your Firm from
Chaos to Consensus

Jay N. Nisberg
Gary S. Shamis
Marsha Leest

CCH
a Wolters Kluwer business

Editorial Staff

Editor . . . . Holly J. Whorton
Production . . . . Christopher Zwirek; Izabel Hauser
Index . . . . Lynn Brown

ISBN 978-0-8080-2137-7

Printed in the United States of America

I would like to thank my family, Mary Ann, Ben and Melissa, and my colleagues at SS&G.
–Gary

I would like to dedicate this book to my daughter Alicia Nisberg, my wife Sally Ann Nisberg and to the memory of my son Samuel who will always be by my side.
–Jay

I would like to thank my wonderful family for their encouragement and support.
–Marsha

Preface

We believe this is a seminal moment in the future of CPA firms. Accountants are often called upon to for advice in business and personal finance situations and their work, on the whole, is excellent. But they tend to manage their own affairs rather badly. It's the classic case of the shoemaker's children going barefoot. They are their own worst clients.

Partly, the problem is because accountants spend too little time studying people—including themselves: it's not part of the coursework, and there's no time for it once work starts. That leaves many firm leaders at a loss when it comes to the so-called soft skills (which really aren't soft at all). Many think their role stops at doing their work, managing client relationships and monitoring the firm's finances. Unlike executives in other businesses, maintaining employee relations, recruiting, marketing and overseeing the firm's operations simply aren't in the curriculum. Firm leaders are expected to know them instinctively, somehow, or learn them by some kind of osmosis.

Even accountants who are aware of the need for more effective management may be baffled by the lack of management training. There are many questions: How can I find and hold good people? How can I develop profitable new client relationships? How can I compete with other firms? What do I do about old clients who are losing money for the firm? How can I delegate responsibility without losing control? Is there a way I can improve my relationship with my partners?

The number of CPA firms finding themselves in the predicament described above is the reason we wrote this book. We hope you find it useful.

Gary Shamis
Jay N. Nisberg
Marsha Leest

October 2009

About the Author

Jay N. Nisberg is an internationally recognized management consultant to the CPA community. Well known for his work in practice management, partnership issues, and business development, he is also a frequent speaker at MAP conferences and partner retreats around the world. His work encompasses consultation on the strategy development of the firm by encouraging the growth of its individual members. Jay serves as an executive coach to partners and senior firm members around the United States and is on retainer with numerous firms listed in the Top 100 CPA Firms list published by *Accounting Today*. Jay also focuses his attention on enhancing firms' marketing and communications efforts and is one of the most active consultants in helping with firm mergers and acquisitions. His expertise includes facilitating firm retreats, assisting with partnership conflict resolution, partner compensation, and conducting client satisfaction surveys. Jay has been a discussion leader and keynote speaker for the American Institute of CPAs, most state CPA Societies and associations of CPA firms, as well as numerous universities and colleges.

Jay has been quoted as an industry expert in most industry journals and magazines, including *The Wall Street Journal* and *Accounting Today*. Jay has been listed as one of the "100 Most Influential Individuals in the CPA Profession" by *Accounting Today* since the inception of their list of experts, longer than any other individual.

Presently, Jay is President of his own management consulting firm and continues his 25-year career assisting CPA firms with the growth of their practices. He works with national, regional, and local practices. His extensive experience in strengthening partnerships and helping with firm management issues makes him one of the most sought after consultants in both the United States and Europe. He has also been a consultant to numerous corporations, including General Motors Corporation, RCA Corporation, and The White House. He is the author of two nationally known business reference books published by Random House and the contributing author of the "Guide to Buying and Merging CPA Firms" section of *Practitioners Publishing Companies Strategic Practice Issues Resource Series*. Jay has also authored or co-authored over one hundred published articles on the CPA profession.

Jay is the founder of Accountants Financial Services Group and the Professional Alliance Group (PAG), an affiliation of over 65 CPA firms whose purpose is to promote the financial services niche. He has also founded two industry think-tanks in addition to the CPA industries "Million Dollar Roundtable," a unique meeting of individuals in the CPA community earning in excess of one million dollars annually in compensation. He is on the Editorial Advisory Board of numerous publications including *CPA Practice Management Forum and Wealth Management Provider*.

Gary Shamis became managing partner of SS&G Financial Services in 1985. Since then, the firm has changed dramatically. By taking an entrepreneurial approach to managing the accounting firm, he has developed SS&G Financial Services into one of the largest and fastest growing independently owned accounting/business service firms in the country. Shamis' concepts for growth and expansion are respected and emulated by both professional peers and business organizations. The firm has won eleven Weatherhead 100 Awards (Cleveland), ten Cascade CDC Growth Awards (Akron), an Achievement in Client Service Award (Cincinnati), two Accounting Today Awards for Achievement in Client Service, and has been noted as one of Bowman's Accounting Report's top ten fastest growing firms in the United States. SS&G Financial Services has also been chosen a Best Places to Work in Ohio in 2008, 2007 and 2006, and is a recipient of the Better Business Bureau Torch Awards for Business Integrity.

In addition to his management duties, Shamis is a frequent speaker, all over the world, on the management of professional service organizations. In 2000, he teamed up with three of the industry's top advisors to form The Advisory Board, a think-tank focused on assisting and developing the accounting industry within the United States. As the only practicing CPA in the group, he brings a wealth of experience and qualifications. For example, Shamis has been recognized in the *Wall Street Journal* and the *Journal of Accountancy* for creating the nation's first Employee Stock Ownership Program for an accounting firm. After completing his term as the Chairman of the AICPA Management of an Accounting Practice (MAP) committee, he was busy developing and chairing The Leading Edge Alliance, the a prominent association of CPA firms. With more than 150 member firms and collective revenues exceeding $1.7 billion, The Leading Edge Alliance has become one of the world's premier organizations for independent and entrepreneurial firms. Based upon these contributions to the industry, Shamis was named as one of Accounting Today's "Most Influential People" for the past nine years, and was chosen as the Institute of Management Accountants' 2001 Financial Executive of the Year. Shamis serves on the Advisory Board of CPA Practice Management Forum.

Marsha Leest is a nationally recognized expert in the field of accounting firm marketing. She has an extensive background in accounting and law firm marketing as well as in professional publishing. Her experience as an in-house marketing director for a top 25 accounting and business consulting firm coupled with the knowledge she gained as a consultant to the industry gives her a unique perspective of the industry, how it works and how it is evolving. Many leading experts in the industry look to her for advice and guidance.

Leest is the author of the Fourth and Fifth editions of *How to Manage Your Accounting Practice,* published by Wolters Kluwer, as well as various articles in industry publications. She is also the editor of CCH's *CPA Practice Management Forum,* a monthly journal dedicated to covering all areas of managing a CPA firm in today's complex business environment.

For several years, she served on the Executive Council of New York City's High School of Economics and Finance, and is a Board Member of the New York City Chapter of the Association for Accounting Marketing and a Member of the Communications Committee of the National Association of Accounting Marketing.

Acknowledgments

We'd like to take this opportunity to thank everyone who contributed to this book so we could provide real life examples of how firms are handling the issues that arise managing a CPA firm.

We'd also like to thank Kurt Diefenbach, who recognized the need and gave us the opportunity to write this book, and Holly Whorton and Julie Lindy, whose editing and proofreading skills were invaluable.

Table of Contents

Chapter 1
Are We in Roswell, NM or at a Partner Meeting?

¶ 101 How Times Have Changed

With all due respect to cheesy science fiction novels, managing partners at respected, successful and highly competitive accounting firms may well think they are living in an alternate universe these days. The managing partner's role, which stayed pretty much the same for decades, changed radically in a relatively short period of time due to the convergence of six distinctly different, but equally alien, forces marketing and sales; technology; Sarbanes-Oxley; consolidation; mergers and acquisitions; generational differences; and the current economic crisis.

One important thing has not changed: The managing partner is still in the buck-stops-here position. He or she must still lead the firm to growth and profitability, build its value, and preserve its long-term viability, but most things around that have been altered. Seemingly overnight, the orderly business world in which accountants operated was changed irrevocably. It was the equivalent of a white collar Industrial Revolution. The tools and skills required to achieve the end results became as foreign as if they came from outer space.

It took about 20 years for the shaping events listed above to cause the safe world of public accounting firms to morph into a quasi-corporate structure that was once unimaginable to many current managing partners. The iconic portrait of an accountant with rolled-up sleeves, a green eyeshade, and a ledger pad became the stuff of legend. The reality is an accountant with three computer screens, a BlackBerry, and a need for interpersonal skills. No green eyeshades need apply.

Ironically, many of the underlying reasons for the changes are rooted in the profession's success. Professional service firms flourished and matured in the 1980s and 1990s, largely by embracing and applying basic business concepts long practiced by their clients, such as advertising, marketing, and the segmentation of industries and practices. The crush of new technology was mind-boggling: computers and computer software made processing tax returns a somewhat routine task. No pencils or calculators needed: just plug in the numbers and a little Martian comfortably ensconced in Cyberspace (wherever that is) would do the work and spit it out. The Internet made communication instantaneous, and carbon paper gave way to IMs.

Leaders in the field recognized the opportunity for branching out and doing other work, such as consulting and asset management. Other firms quickly adopted the new business model of what a future-oriented accounting firm should look like.

The byproduct of all of these changes is that the traditional rules of order that pertain to practically every aspect of the firm can no longer be relied on to work consistently and uniformly. Now, to be successful, firm leaders need to think in terms of methods, principles, processes, and techniques. The changes are so far-reaching that keeping a bottle of extra-strength aspirin handy may be the first order of business.

Think about the changes at your firm. How have some of the systems and methods used to manage the firm have changed over the last 10 years? How many are the same? How many have gone through more than one change?

¶ 105 Effective Practice Management—Where to Begin

Today, effective practice management requires frequent reassessment of even the most basic operational functions:

- Internal communications
  — Partner to partner
  — Partner to staff
  — Staff to staff
- External communications
  — Partner to client
  — Staff to client
  — Firm to potential client
- Partner selection
- Partner training
- Staff training
- Partner and staff motivation
- Reinforcing firm culture

- Compensation structure
  - Partner
  - Staff
- Strategic planning
- Organizational nimbleness
- Recruiting
  - Lateral hires
  - New hires
- Staff retention efforts
- Risk management
- Benefits
- Niche selection and development
- New service area selection and development
- Marketing
- Fee systems/pricing for services
- Billing and collections
- Technology
  - Planning
  - Implementation
  - Training

At first, planning didn't seem to matter. Firms were swept along. They changed—and may even have been successful—simply because the business environment changed and the enhanced value of accounting was an integral part of that change.

But there is an old Mark Twain quote that says "If you don't know where you're going, any road will get you there." Managing chaos is managing using the spaghetti theory of management: throw enough against the wall and something will stick. That may work for a while, but sustained success requires excellent leadership, strategic analysis, implementation, and measurement.

Exactly how does a firm evolve to a strategic growth model? As might be expected, there is no easy answer. Perhaps a good place to start is with a brief overview of some of the major challenges the industry is facing:

1. *Future leadership/succession issues.* This is a two-pronged problem. The first issue is that many partners, including managing partners, are baby boomers who are scheduled to retire over the next 5 to 15 years. (In many cases, they will be excluded from equity partnership once they reach the retirement age stipulated in their partnership agreement. However, conventional wisdom is to expand retirement ages as high as 70.) The second part of the problem is that the pool of potential partners and managing partners in the next generation of firm leadership may be too small to effectively fill the positions vacated by partners who are retiring. Coupled with the effects of the current economic landscape, these demographics may combine to cause firms to seriously consider the possibility of mergers and acquisitions as a survival strategy. (Yes, a survival strategy—not an exit strategy. Only firms that are strong financially, have good leadership, and/or practice in a niche area are likely to be considered as viable candidates, and even then the payout terms probably will be different than the partners wish.)

2. *Retention.* It's not news that senior accountants and managers are in high demand. That is not likely to change any time soon, so firms that are looking for sustainable growth need to seriously think about how they can retain this valuable group of employees who are already trained in the firm's technology and familiar with its culture—and may not ever become an equity partner at the firm. Another barrier to retention has popped up over the last several years: firms are losing good people to the government and private sectors, where the popular perception is that the hours are shorter and the benefits are better. The generational aspects of retention are still another challenge firms are facing.

3. *Recruiting.* Recruiting is another area that is problematic. While the Big Four firms have traditionally been able to attract the best and the brightest because they are viewed as having the most comprehensive training, other firms often have trouble attracting talent. The causes vary, but location and lack of diverse assignments are two of the reasons. The current economic situation may change this scenario somewhat. The unfortunate downsizing experienced by larger firms broadens the available talent pool for downstream firms. It may seem counterintuitive, but now is a good time to look at hiring more skilled, higher priced talent so your firm is well-positioned to take advantage of the coming upturn in the economy.

4. *Talent pipeline.* The pipeline of talent flowing to firms is not likely to get stronger because our retirement, retention, and recruiting problems are being mirrored in the halls of academia. Just as partners are retiring, so are accounting professors, and they are struggling to replace themselves just as we are.

5. *Future CPAs.* A corollary to the recruiting and retention problem, firms are having difficulty motivating staff to sit for the CPA exam, so there are even fewer new CPAs than new accountants.

6. *Globalization.* The world is shrinking. Not physically, but in terms of spheres of influence, trade, and alliances. Even small accounting firms are this to be true as some of their clients move to outsource manufacturing or merge with other companies. Those clients are increasingly difficult to replace, so firms must look to other ways to restore lost business. In addition, as clients become more global, firms must be able to service them wherever they operate. CPA firm associations and networks provide the answer for many firms.

7. *Economic factors.* Many areas of the United States have been feeling the impact of hard economic times for quite a while. Areas of the Midwest, for instance, which relied so heavily on the automobile and other manufacturing industries, have been working to reinvent themselves for a number of years. Visionary firms recognized this and moved to expand their business beyond state lines. The far-reaching effects of the economic downturn will give forward thinking firms like these the ability to reinvent themselves yet again as they identify the profitable areas of the new economic reality.

8. *Cost of doing business.* Whether analyzing benefits and bonuses, adding new services, or growing a new industry niche, the cost of doing business has increased. To keep profitability up, firms have learned the benefits of marketing and business development and have adopted some of the same efficiencies of scale they have long taught their clients. Marketing and business development should be an important part of any good strategic plan regardless of outside factors such as the economy.

9. *Technology.* The business of accounting has evolved to a world of computers with multi-monitors, XBRL, and social networking. The inability to navigate through new and existing technology is not an acceptable option.

10. *Diversity.* Within the next 35 years or so, the majority of the U.S. population will be comprised of minorities as the number of Hispanic- and Asian-Americans continues to grow. This trend is already being felt in many regions. Firms need to prepare themselves for this shift. Among other things, they need to become more aware of the language and cultural differences that can impact their business and work toward having their firm demographic reflect that of the region in which they operate.

These are the major issues we see. Although they are fairly easy to enumerate, it is quickly apparent that they are even more complex and diverse than they seem at first. Scratch the surface and a Pandora's Box opens.

Chapter 2
You Can't Close or Ignore Pandora's Box, Even if You Try

¶ 201 Pandora's Box

The challenge—and the frustration—for today's firm leaders is deciding how to address these problems in a way that will allow their firms to grow and prosper well into the future. There are many options: some already proven, others more innovative and closer to the edge. Only one thing is crystal clear: Pandora's Box has been opened and can never be closed again.

¶ 205 Managing Like a Baby Boomer Doesn't Work

For the first time in history, there are four generations in the workplace, each with its own unique collective mindset about the role work plays in their lives and the nature of employer-employee relationships (see Table 2.1). The old status quo is also affected by the number of female CPAs and the changing nature of the U.S. population in general, with its shift in religious and cultural views.

Baby Boomers and their work-centric value systems dominate power positions in today's professional services firms, but they're attempting to hire, keep, and manage younger generations who have different priorities for their careers as well as different approaches for getting what they want. Generations raised on the immediate gratification rendered them by remote controls, e-mail, ATMs, the Internet, and cell phones and PDAs simply don't respond to the blueprint that Baby Boomers built their careers on: working hard and diligently for future rewards. Whereas Baby Boomers typically have a handful of employers during their entire careers, younger generations typically expect to have 10 to 12 (more by some estimates).

Table 2.1. Generations at Work

Generations	Traditionalists	Baby Boomers	Generation X	Millennials (aka Gen Y)
Birth years:	1925-1942	1943-1960	1961-1981	1982-2001
Current ages:	66-83	48-65	27-47	7-26
Events that defined them:	Great Depression, World War II, Pearl Harbor, D-Day	Vietnam War, Woodstock, touchdown on the moon, Kennedy's assassination, ERA, Watergate, Martin Luther King	Missing children on milk cartons, cable TV, mid-80s recession, computers in classrooms, space shuttle Challenger explosion, Iraq War	President Clinton/Monica Lewinsky Scandal, 9/11, Columbine school shootings, Nintendo and Sega, American Idol, reality TV
At work they value:	Security, stability, lines of authority	Collaboration, communication, innovation	Autonomy, technology, flexibility	Leadership, teamwork, social networks
Technology they grew up with:	Automobile, telephone, black and white TV	Mainframe computers, color TV, cordless phones, PDAs	Star Wars, the Internet, laptops, the Mac, Atari, CDs, DVDs, surround sound, cell phones, IM	MySpace, Facebook, YouTube, TiVo, Ipods, BlackBerrys, WiFi, Bluetooth, Xbox, Gameboys, plasma TV, satellite radio
Current leadership roles:	Partners, Emeritus Partners	Managing partner, equity partner, non-equity partner, department head, senior leadership	Equity partner, non-equity partner, manager, supervisor	Supervisor, Team Leader
Their leadership legacy or goals:	Legacy: Traditionalists invented the partnership structure that defines the public accounting profession	Goals: Re-engineer the firm's culture to attract and retain more diverse professionals, and re-align the strategy to remain profitable	Goals: Assume leadership positions that align with my family or personal goals.	Goals: Achieve a career path with a firm whose values match mine.

Adapted from *Generations* by Strauss and Howe and *Live First, Work Second* by Rebecca Ryan, Next Generation Consulting

Professional services firms with staffing policies based on Baby Boomer career paths and retention methods for younger generations don't have a chance. It's the leader's job to figure out how to run a business that relies on people who aren't committed to working for you long-term, or even, perhaps, long days. The leader can't control or change the desires and motivators of Gen X and Gen Y professionals. His or her only power is to create a system that encourages them to stay but that can also adapt when they leave.

A recent survey by the Families and Work Institute comparing the work-related value systems of Baby Boomers and Gen Xers clearly shows some of the differences that relate to each generation's view of "work-life balance" (see Table 2.2).

The term work-life balance is a buzzword in the accounting world, with many firms claiming they have found it. But the truth is that there is no such thing: the priority of each changes with the demands of the day. To put it another way, people aren't really looking for work-life balance: they are looking for work-life integration.

A sick parent or child, for example, can change the best laid plan to accomplish a work-related task. It is the job of firm leaders to recognize that one's life is the sum of all its parts and provide staff with the flexibility to meet all of their responsibilities. That may sound far too glib, but it reflects the business world in this age of two-parent earners and instant communication. It is no longer reasonable to expect that during tax season a parent who wants to attend a child's Saturday morning soccer game will simply forego that pleasure. Instead, it is firms that must adapt to the parent's need: come in later that day, work later on Monday, or telecommute.

In a sense, the workplace most of today's firm leaders are familiar with took an almost parental role toward staff, , and the unspoken mantras were effectively "speak only when you are spoken to" and "father knows best." That worked for Traditionalists and Baby Boomers. It will not work for Gen Xers or Gen Yers who were brought up from a very early age to believe their opinions matter and that questioning their parents' rules is a right.

Table 2.2. Baby Boomers vs. Gen Xers Priorities at Work

	Baby Boomers (ages 38-57)	Gen Xers (ages 23-37)
Do you put work first?	22%	13%
Do you put family first?	41%	52%
Are you dual-focused?	37%	35%
Weekly hours worked in 2002	45	44
Number of workday hours father spends with children	2.2	3.4

Source: Families and Work Institute, © 2007

¶ 210 The Pie Is Bigger: More Work Creates Demand for More People

Virtually overnight, the Sarbanes-Oxley Act of 2002 (SOX) created an unprecedented torrent of cascading new business for accountants. It is estimated that SOX created 20 percent more work for the public accounting profession, but there was no corresponding increase in available skilled professionals to perform the work. There are 16,000 public companies. If the average public company spent $3 million for implementation of SOX-mandated changes, that would generate $48 billion in revenue and require an increase in work of 15 to 20 percent over four years—all without additional staff.

In addition, SOX created a chain reaction that moved public company clients into accounting firms across the board, not only the biggest firms. The additional Fortune 500 work largely went to the Big Four, which pushed its large middle-market clients to Second Tier and large regional firms. In turn, those firms pushed their lower-end clients to mid-size firms, who pushed their lower-end clients to small firms, who pushed their lower-end clients to tiny firms. Across the board, firms took on bigger, better, more sophisticated and lucrative clients. Subspecialties and boutique firms that could tout (and deliver) unique expertise burst forth. SOX drove a virtual bulldozer across the landscape of public accounting firms, and to a somewhat lesser extent, law firms.

Firms cannot overlook the impact that Andersen's demise, which increased the workload of each of the Big Four firms by 25 percent in a single day, had on all of them. The corresponding increase in work without the increase in manpower was enormous. In addition, the difficulties of the cultural disconnect between the Big Four and smaller firms drove a number of talented professionals out of public accounting.

The accounting profession now faces the possibility of a similar tsunami of work generated by three major new challenges. First, the convergence of U.S. GAAP and the International Financial Reporting Standards (IFRS). It has been estimated that somewhere around 2011, U.S. accountants will be using the same accounting standards as the 27 European Community (EC) countries, Brazil, Canada, China, India, Japan, and many others. To date, most CPAs are unfamiliar with these standards, but they will have to learn them pretty quickly because clients will demand it. Some firms already have clients that are using IFRS for financial reporting. Even smaller firms may have foreign-owned clients who will need to comply, and potential clients are likely to ask whether a firm is IFRS capable. This change will have a far-reaching impact: university professors must be able to teach it, tax publishers will have to interpret and report on it, and so on. If talent isn't available with a particular firm, that firm will have to borrow it from a partner firm or hire it. The future may be bright as far as the availability of new work, but it is not as rosy when it comes to staffing.

Second, the differences between Wall Street and Main Street are greatly minimized by the recent global economic crisis. Just as SOX increased business over night, the fall of some of the most revered names in banking decreased it almost as substantially. For some of the largest firms, the transactional work at the core of their business is no longer there. The void is likely to be filled by other work (such as turnaround counseling, forensics, insolvency, and bankruptcy) but there is likely to be a corresponding shift in the client base of most firms. Just as SOX drove middle-market clients from the Big Four down to smaller firms, the economy may result in a further push down. This time, the shift may be based on the price sensitivity of clients who are struggling in a recovering economy. The chaos that ensued from SOX may be played out again as firms retrench.

Which leads to the last of our challenges: how fast will your firm be able to adapt to yet another volcano on the landscape of accounting firm management? Ironically, smaller firms might have the advantage here. That's because they have better, quicker access to the firm's decision makers, and the firm's staff may be well-trained to serve a number of services and industries.

Figure 2.1

Employment Screening: Best Practices

More and more professional service firms are coming to the realization that pre-employment screening makes good business sense.

Many professional service firms believe that background investigations are unnecessary due to the caliber of people they hire, but an investigation of over 100,000 candidates shows that:

- 5 percent of applicants have a criminal record.
- 27 percent will have findings in their report that are inconsistent with their resume/job application.
- 10 percent will have a negative comment from an employment reference.
- 5 percent will have an absolute disqualifier under "Best Practices" criteria. See Figure 2.2.

These statistics mean that for every 20 people receiving a job offer in the professional services industry, one will be absolutely unsuitable for employment.

Candidates lie because there is no real penalty for getting caught. A recent case proves this point. A "Big Four" accounting firm made a contingent offer to a senior manager from a large consulting practice. The consulting firm only performed a basic level criminal check in the county of residence and did not verify employment history.

The investigation revealed that the applicant had taken a job in another state prior to joining his current employer. The employment lasted only six months, during which time the candidate was convicted of sexually assaulting a co-worker. After being terminated from his job, the candidate moved back to his prior residence and stretched the employment dates for his prior employment to cover the six-month problem employment. When an individual gets caught lying on an application, he or she will not leave their profession. He or she will actively seek out a firm that does not perform any type of investigation or, alternatively, does not investigate the area where their problem lies.

A well-designed program reduces turnover and related recruiting and training costs. For professional service firms, recruiting and training are expensive line items. Proactively ensuring a "good fit" can save substantial financial and human resources.

A recent study indicated that a problem employee will cost his or her employer 125 percent of their annual salary. This figure includes: (1) amounts paid to the employee for salary and benefits, (2) recruiting and training costs, (3) management time dealing with "the problem," and (4) termination costs and replacement expenses.

Consider this example:

The Cost of a Bad Hire: Administrative Employee

- $28,000 Annual Salary
- 125% of Salary
- Cost = $35,000

The Cost of a Bad Hire: Professional Employee

- $80,000 annual salary
- 125% of salary
- Cost = $100,000

Cost of a Background Investigation Program

- $300 average cost for comprehensive investigation
- 1 in 20 disqualified
- Cost for 20 investigations, $6,000

Source: Kevin Prendergast, president of Research Associates, Inc., Cleveland, Ohio.

Note: State laws vary, especially those concerning credit checks. Consult your attorney before authorizing any checks.

Figure 2.2. ————————————————————————————————————

Best Practices at Professional Service Firms

Most leading firms use a tiered approach to investigations. The depth of the investigation depends on many factors, including the level of the position within the organization, whether the employee will have access to clients or key corporate assets, the potential exposure that could be created by the employee, and the need for integrity and trust. These packages can be tailored to meet the specific needs of a client.

Level 1: Campus Hires

- SSN trace
- Felony criminal records (1 county)
- Driver's license

Level II: Administrative and Experienced Staff through Senior

- SSN trace
- Education (highest degree)
- Credit report
- Employment (HR-7 years/limit 3)
- Felony criminal records (1 county)
- National criminal database
- Driver's license

Level III: Manager through Executive

- SSN trace
- Education (highest degree)
- Professional license
- Credit report
- Employment (7 years)
- Supervisor/reference interviews (2)
- Felony criminal (1 county)
- Civil court records (1 county)
- Federal criminal records
- Driver's license
- National criminal database
- OFAC database

Level IV: Partner/Director

- SSN trace
- Education (highest degree)
- Professional license
- Credit report
- Employment (10 years)
- Supervisory/reference interviews (3)
- Felony criminal records (1 county)

- Civil court records (1 county)

- Federal criminal/civil records

- Federal bankruptcy records

- Driver's license

- National criminal database

- National newspaper search

- OFAC database

Source: Kevin Prendergast, president of Research Associates, Inc., Cleveland, Ohio.

Note: State laws vary, especially those concerning credit checks. Consult your attorney before authorizing any checks.

¶ 215 A Flattened World Flattens Traditional Staffing Models

A decade ago, professional services firms were full of leaders who boasted that they "managed by walking around." Everybody kept similar hours, and, for the most part, worked in the same place on a fairly consistent basis. Events and meetings could be scheduled accordingly. At a certain time of the day, usually at the start or the end, a managing partner could walk around the office, see staff and partners, talk to them face to face, and observe the work and how it was being done. Today, the employees of a typical firm work in different offices, often in different time zones, on different coasts, or even on different continents. Some people go months without seeing or speaking to each other. On any given day, it's not unusual to be unable to identify two people who work identical schedules in the same place. Multiple offices, alternative work arrangements, and technology have reshaped the basic landscape of the workplace. You can't manage by walking around anymore. Instead, you must manage issues and use tools that simply didn't exist 10 years ago. Technology and outsourcing open whole new frontiers of opportunities—and corresponding challenges.

Figure 2.3

Possible Sources for Hiring Experienced Staff

- *Recruiting overseas.* Hiring from overseas was popular a few years ago when firms brought accountants from as far away as Ireland, Poland, and South Africa to the United States. The foreign accountant needs an employment authorization card from the U.S. Department of Justice, Immigration and Naturalization Services (INS), as well as a Social Security card. Both are valid for approximately one year. An immigration attorney can assist the employee in obtaining an H-1B visa from the INS, which allows the immigrant to work in the United States for an additional three years. The visa can be renewed for a second three-year term. During that time, the immigrant can apply for a green card for permanent resident status. Some firms that followed this model paid for moving expenses and offered assistance with quality of life issues like assistance getting a driver's license, finding housing, and generally helping the new employee assimilate into his or her new community. This effort might be revived as the United States moves along the path to convergence between U.S. GAAP and the IFRS.

- *Re-hiring and recruiting retirees.* Demographic realities make hiring an older work force a sensible option. For one thing, many retirees *want* to keep working. They want the money and self-esteem that comes with remaining in the work force, they're physically healthy, and they're tried-and-true experienced workers with high-value skill sets. They know how to work with clients. This practice is attracting retirees at all levels, including equity partners, who often are in a position to bring or retain clients whom they have a long history of serving. Also, there is no need to be shy about trying to recruit retired partners from other firms—including the Big Four—or those who have left positions in the private sector. Some of these retirees have wonderful connections and can be invaluable business developers. This strategy works so well in some business sectors that there are Web sites that list the best places for older workers to find employment.

- *Flex-time, telecommuting, and job-sharing.* Don't overlook the possibility of offering these options. There may be a firm alumnus who is available for a part-time job or one that doesn't require him or her to be at the office the entire work week. Ideal candidates for this include parents returning from a parental leave or those caring for an ailing family member. These people are already loyal to your firm, and they know the work you do. They will remember that you were there for them at a critical time in their lives, and you will have their devotion over the long term.

- *Outsourcing.* Evaluate your firm's staffing needs. Do you really need a full-time chief financial officer? What about a bookkeeper? Could someone perform that function on a part-time schedule? These options might not have been available just a short time ago; now there are resources for hiring high-quality employees on a part-time basis. Depending on the need, these options can be an excellent way to cut overhead costs.

Figure 2.4

McKinsey Research: A Business Case for Women

The gender gap isn't just an image problem: [McKinsey's] research suggests that it can have real implications for company performance. Some companies have taken effective steps to achieve greater parity.

Women in developed economies have made substantial gains in the workplace during recent decades. Nevertheless, it's still true that the higher up in a company you look, the lower the percentage of women.

But some companies have moved successfully to increase the hiring, retention, and promotion of female executives. Their initiatives have included efforts to ensure that HR policies aren't inadvertently biased against women or part-time workers, to encourage mentoring and networking, to establish (and consistently monitor at a senior level) targets for diversity, and to find ways of creating a better work-life balance. Changes like these have a price, but there are business advantages to making them—above and beyond the branding benefit that might accrue to companies viewed as socially progressive.

Research in Europe and the United States suggests, for example, that companies with several senior-level women tend to perform better financially. Hiring and retaining women at all levels also enlarges a company's pool of talent at a time when shortages are appearing throughout industries.

Why women matter

Few women become executives. Across the European Union, women account for only 11 percent of the membership of governing bodies such as boards of directors and supervisory boards, our research has found. In the United States, fewer than a third of the leading 1,500 companies had even a single woman among their top executives in 2006, according to research from Columbia University and the University of Maryland.[1] The numbers are even more discouraging elsewhere: in South Korea, for example, 74 percent of the companies surveyed in 2007 had no female senior executives.[2] We believe that such underrepresentation is untenable in the longer term—and not only because it's unfair . . . .

Corporate performance

In recent years, McKinsey has done extensive work on the relationship between organizational and financial performance and on the number of women who are managers at the companies we've studied. Our research has shown, first, that the companies around the world with the highest scores on nine important dimensions of organization—from leadership and direction to accountability and motivation—are likely to have higher operating margins than their lower-ranked counterparts do . . . . Second, among the companies for which information on the gender of senior managers was available,[3] those with three or more women on their senior-management teams scored higher on all nine organizational criteria than did companies with no senior-level women . . . .

These findings suggest that companies with higher numbers of women at senior levels are also companies with better organizational and financial performance. Although the analysis does not show a causal link, our research argues for greater gender diversity among corporate leaders . . . .

Rethinking HR

HR policies can inadvertently hold women back. Internal processes for identifying high-potential employees, for example, often focus on managers between the ages of 28 and 35. Broadening the parameters to include years of employment at a company—thus taking into account time spent on maternity leave, which sometimes lasts as long as two years in Europe—can ensure that the evaluation processes don't overlook qualified women.

Some companies, such as JPMorgan Chase, have organized training for recruiters and operational managers on the importance of diversity and on identifying prejudices that might affect their decisions. Together with the top team's commitment to retaining and promoting women, this training has generated a strong pipeline: in 2008, women made up 48 percent of the company's managers—and 27 percent of its most senior ones, up from 19 percent in 1996 . . . .

The role of mentors

Coaching, mentoring, and networking programs have proved quite successful in helping female executives succeed—for instance, by encouraging them to seek out new positions more aggressively. Internal research at HP showed that women apply for open jobs only if they think they meet 100 percent of the criteria listed, whereas men respond to the posting if they feel they meet 60 percent of the requirements . . . .

---

[1] http://www.mckinseyquarterly.com/Organization/Talent/A_business_case_for_women_2192

[2] http://www.mckinseyquarterly.com/Organization/Talent/A_business_case_for_women_2192

[3] http://www.mckinseyquarterly.com/Organization/Talent/A_business_case_for_women_2192

Having a life

What about retention rates? Companies can raise them by offering flexible hours, maternity and child-care leaves, and coaching to ease the return to the workforce. Such programs can have other benefits as well. Research that the Korea Labor Institute conducted in 2007 indicates that some family-friendly policies (such as allowances for child care and granting women permission to take nursing time out of their daily schedules) are correlated with higher revenues per employee: about $1,000 a year.

None of these approaches comes without cost: whether the time needed to implement change or real monetary expenditures. Yet companies reap tangible benefits, such as retaining and promoting more women, by implementing suitable policies. The other benefits—for instance, a larger talent pool and stronger financial performance—also suggest that making gender diversity a significant goal is well worth the investment.

Source: *Georges Desvaux, Sandrine Devillard-Hoellinger, and Mary C. Meaney, McKinsey and Company, September 2008.*

¶ 220 Hiring and Helicopter Parents

Most current firm management would rather chew nails than have their parents call the executive committee and ask how they are doing. But that's not necessarily the case for Gen Y. In March 2007, *The Wall Street Journal* ran an article discussing how some well-known companies, including Ernst & Young and Merrill Lynch, are reaching out to the parents of potential staffers. These super involved parents, referred to as helicopter parents, give their children career advice. According to the article, Ernst &Young distributed "parent packs" to students during information sessions at about a dozen schools. Students received memory sticks with information about benefits, the recruiting process, and the skills Ernst & Young seeks. Students were told they could email the information to parents who ask questions. Recruiters suggest that companies:

- Create a parent section in the company's career website.
- Prepare information packets about the company for parents.
- Invite parents on an office tour.
- Consider advertising in the parent section of university websites.
- Respect student wishes about how much to involve parents.

¶ 225 Lateral Hires Are on the Rise

Once the exclusive domain of law firms, lateral hires are now on the radar screen of CPA firms. There are several reasons for this, including the dearth of 7-10 year professionals, the number of accountants sitting for the CPA exam, and the availability of high visibility professionals who are either unhappy at their current firm or have retired from a partnership and are looking for work.

Hiring a lateral partner from another firm is a lot like a merger: there is a long learning curve, no guarantee that the partner will successfully integrate into your firm, and the stream of clients you envision following the partner may never materialize. As with a merger, laying the groundwork and communicating are the most likely indicators of success.

Before hiring laterally, firms should have a plan in place. Are you looking for a new niche? Do you need support for an existing niche? Can another person take on higher level work? Whatever the reason, it must be clear. Whatever promises you make must be real about what you are offering—whether that relates to the type of work, compensation, a future equity partnership—as well as about what you expect in return.

Figure 2.5 —————————————————————————————————————

Sample Introductory Letter: New Partner

[Date]

[Name]

[Co. name]

[Street address]

[City, State, Zip]

Dear _____:

As you may already know, earlier this year I joined Brady Ware, one of the region's largest CPA and business consulting firms. I wanted to take a moment to write you regarding my new position as the Tax Services Leader in our Columbus office, and to let you know how much I've appreciated working with you in the past.

Brady Ware is recognized in our markets as one of the top firms serving the closely held business client. Our office is located at 10 West Broad Street in downtown Columbus. As a regional firm, Brady Ware is uniquely positioned in the market place to provide professional services at prices in line with client value.

My primary focus will continue to be on individual and corporate taxation, including tax planning, advisory services, and compliance.

Brady Ware offers a full line of professional services, ranging from traditional tax and accounting work (including bookkeeping), to investment management, merger and acquisition planning, employee benefits consulting, and retirement plan administration.

I would like the opportunity to speak with you **again regarding** your financial needs for the coming year, especially during these turbulent economic times. I will call you within the next few weeks to touch base. In the meantime, if you would like to contact me, call me directly at (614) 384-8413.

I look forward to talking with you soon.

Sincerely,

Brady, Ware & Schoenfeld, In.

Thomas K. Munhall, CPA

Source: Brady, Ware & Schoenfeld, Inc., Dayton Ohio

¶ 230 Management Must Finesse More Constituencies

Never has politics been a bigger part of the job of managing professional services firms. As the work force becomes less homogenous and stable staffing becomes increasingly critical, leaders are forced to juggle an increasing variety of demands from increasingly diverse constituencies.

The four generations in the workplace are just one example of how the work force has become increasingly diverse. A higher number of women than men are entering professional services, and professionals with a wide variety of nationalities and ethnic backgrounds abound. Leaders and decision-makers can no longer look at employees and partners as a one-size-fits-all homogenous group and expect to have a satisfied talent pool that wants to stay at their firms and make their clients happy. Like their services, their human resources policies and retention methods must be niched and targeted. Roles that were once considered administrative or clerical—such as human resources and marketing—have become strategic and integral to a firm's future success. Conversely, computer software has relegated some tasks that were once viewed as professional, such as the preparation of certain tax returns, to a high-level clerical position.

.01 Strategic HR

The HR function has joined the long list of accounting firm functions to have an impact on the firm's strategic plan. From recordkeeping, compliance, and delivering HR services, HR professionals are taking on a more strategic role as they help firms meet their goals. According to a recent study by Mercer Human Resource Consulting, 64 percent of 1,400 HR professionals surveyed expect human capital strategy to become a key function within the next few years. Leadership development and talent management are other areas expected to become more important. Conversely, 46 percent of survey respondents listed operational excellence within the HR function as a priority today, while only 32 percent see it as a key function in the next few years.

The study also found that changing demands on HR have given rise to new challenges. The top challenges cited by HR leaders around the world are: acquiring key talent (43 percent), driving cultural and behavioral change in the organization (40 percent), and building leadership capabilities (40 percent). These challenges directly correspond with the new version of transformation and shift from a focus on process and technology to human capital strategy.

This new view of the value of the HR function clearly ties in with other corporate-based movements, including the roles played by marketing and business development as well as the non-CPA partner trend.

.02 Recognize Talent at All Levels

Business succession is one of the major sources of concern in the accounting profession, yet the concepts of identifying the next generation of "stars" and retaining staff as a priority are in their infancy. Having experienced staff—and even partners—leave is a fairly new concept for a profession that was brought up thinking in terms of "partner for life." The forces exerted on the workplace by Gen X and Gen Y are succeeding in challenging that long-held tenet.

At the beginning of the changes to our profession, firms were focused on telling clients and potential clients all about themselves; that changed as marketing campaigns shifted the emphasis to what the client would get from its association with the firm. That shift—pushed along by the collective personality of the younger generations—has moved inside the firm. Firm leaders are now looking at their staff and asking, "What are we doing to encourage our talented employees to stay with our firm?"

Holding on to talent takes a strategic effort that spans the workplace and nurtures everyone, not just those who are on the proverbial "partner track." It means finding meaningful ways to reward the stars as well as the person who has been with your firm for 10 years and never moved past senior, the receptionist who knows your important clients and greets them by name, and the secretary who works extra hours at a moment's notice. Each level needs appropriate recognition and reward; one size does not fit all.

It's also important to remember that rewards and incentives are not the same things. Rewards are awarded for a job well done. Incentives are designed to urge employees to work hard to meet a specific goal, such as a marketing goal or finishing processing all assigned tax returns by 10 AM on April 15.

Financial rewards are always appreciated, but it isn't always about the money. Most people want to know that their work is appreciated. Telling them that they are doing well, sending a handwritten note about a particularly notable event, giving them time off, presenting a commemorative plaque at a company meeting, or taking them to lunch are examples of rewards that have a personal impact. Other options include paying for classes that are interesting to the recipient. This may mean a yoga class, instruction in Mandarin, a session with a dress-for-success professional, or three sessions with a leadership coach. While these may seem wildly out of sync with the firm's core business, the yoga class promotes wellness and having an employee who is at least conversant in Mandarin can help business. A staff member's enhanced appearance benefits the firm and offering leadership training to a budding firm leader is advantageous to the entire firm.

The level of the reward will reflect how the firm views the individual's contribution, but everyone should be able to qualify for something. The keys to a successful program are: (1) clearly communicating the firm's reward policy and (2) ensuring that the rewards are tied to your firm's strategic goals.

Figure 2.6. ————————————————————————————————

Case Study: Friedman LLP/New York
Not All Partners Are (or Should Be) Created Equal

Partners are partners. Right? To the outside world that may be true but many firms realize that to be effective and efficient in today's world, not all partners can be created equal or treated equally. Nor should they be. Today's partnership may include various levels of partner, some more equal than others, and others that don't even fit the traditional definition of "partner."

Friedman LLP has devised a multi-tiered partner structure that works well for the firm. According to Michael Gaines, the firm's human resources and administrative partner:

> "Not all of these tiers are formally recognized, not all are equity positions, and some don't even include the word "partner" as part of their title. What we hoped to accomplish is letting our people know we recognize their contributions to the firm. And we've succeeded. In the last 10 years we've grown from 100 to 300 people and the number of partners, principals and directors has grown from 14 to 65."

In addition to its partner structure, the firm has worked hard to create and nurture a collaborative firm culture, and its leaders believe this has contributed to the firm's low overall turnover rate of about 14 percent for the past two years. Managing Partner Bruce Madnick points out that that this indicates a high level of contentment at the firm. Madnick, whose primary role is that of a chief executive officer charged with overseeing the firm from a strategic and marketing perspective, stated that:

> "Friedman's evolution as a leading firm in a very competitive marketplace created the need for different levels of 'partner' that allows us to reward the visionaries and leaders; identify future high performers; continue to benefit from the experience of seasoned professionals; and utilize the special talents of highly qualified practitioners. Our employees understand that the firm values their contribution."

Performance, commitment, experience, and skills are some of the attributes that dictate the "level" of success at Friedman LLP. The firm defines its upper management levels as follows:

- *Equity partners.* The highest partner level. Equity partners have a substantial interest in the firm's success. They have a base level of compensation, share in an allocated bonus pool, and share more highly in firm profits.

- *Limited equity partners.* The same concept as an equity partner but limited equity partners have a lower percentage share of firm profits.

- *Income partners.* Non-equity partners whose base compensation is guaranteed. These partners also receive a performance-based bonus, but they do not share in firm profits.

- *Retired partners.* At the discretion of the partnership, a retired partner can continue to be employed by the firm. In addition to receiving their retirement benefit and accrued capital in the firm, they receive a pro rated (dependent on days worked) portion of their base compensation. Generally, retired partners have the title of "Partner Emeritus" or "Consultant."

- *Contract partners.* Contract partners work by special arrangement. The terms of their employment, including our performance expectations, are set out in an agreement that remains in effect for a set period of time.

- *Principals.* Someone who has been identified as having partner potential or is at the partner level but is not a CPA. Principals participate in partner meetings but are excluded from discussions of financial matters.

- *Directors.* Valued professionals who are recognized for their excellent performance heading a functional area such as marketing, technology, recruiting, human resources, and finance.

For the record, many firms have "*special partners*"; these are partners who aren't retired but are working as though they were. Generally these partners are aware of the concerns of firm leadership. There are programs in place to mentor these partners and bring them to an operational level or to transition them to retirement.

The concerns and issues to consider when developing a tiered structure include the length of time people stay at a level, establishing performance criteria, managing relationship transitions, and creating a succession plan that will allow for the continuation and long-term growth of the firm. Friedman LLP also acknowledges the need to consider the philosophical issue of giving a "seat at the table" to its directors, who add significant value and want to be more involved in the decision making process.

One of the key factors creating the latest changes to Friedman's structure came as a result of understanding the importance and difficulty in recruiting and retaining talent. The firm realized that the cost of recruiting and training new employees was far greater than the cost of attending to the needs of their present staff and offering a culture and incentives that would make Friedman LLP an employer of choice. According to Madnick,

> "The firm made a conscious decision to commit to showing its employees that it is as dedicated to them and their achievements as we want them to be to our firm's future success. In addition to our strong firm culture, which promotes collegiality, teamwork, learning, a sound work ethic and commitment to client satisfaction, we wanted a tangible way to show our next generation of firm leaders how much we appreciate them."

Figure 2.7 ──

Sample Policy: Criteria To Be Considered for Future Shareholders

Future leaders in the firm must understand what they are doing, the reasons for doing it, and what the rewards are for doing it well. Therefore, the shareholders in the firm would like to give you our evaluation of what we look for as we evaluate our staff as future shareholders.

The following criteria are not listed in any special order, but as you read through them, keep in mind two specific ideas that seem to be the binding forces that we believe have molded and held our present firm together while other firms may seem to struggle. These ideas are trust and compatibility. We truly believe that our firm cannot continue to grow and improve without these two threads holding all of us together.

Technical Proficiency
- Keep abreast of current accounting and auditing pronouncements, FASBs, and other bulletins. Become a regular reader in technical areas and become an expert in your chosen field.
- Maintain strict quality control standards.

Practice Development
- A potential shareholder must show the ability to bring in new clients and expand the services offered to existing clients. This area of practice development can come naturally when "technical proficiency" is attained and exercised by you.
- Be active in professional, business, and community organizations that interest you and provide opportunities to meet potential clients or referrers (bankers, attorneys, etc).

Practice Management
- Demonstrate the ability to handle the firm's clients.
- Perform audits and other work within budget.
- Handle billing and collection on a timely basis.
- Show organization of your time and completion of jobs on a timely basis.

Staff Relations
- Develop and train staff.
- Counsel and motivate those you are supervising.
- Maintain high staff morale.

Personal Development
- Show good communication skills.
- Demonstrate the ability to delegate.
- Have good relationships with fellow shareholders.
- Show maturity.
- Maintain good general appearance.

¶230.02

Professional Development

- Be involved in activities in state societies, AICPA, local chapter, etc.
- To become a fully rounded person, join and directly participate in committees.

Community Activities

- Be involved with civic, religious, and social organizations. This helps create an awareness of the firm and the quality of its personnel.

Support of the Firm

- Show overall support of the firm's decisions.
- Demonstrate effectiveness in communicating the firm's position to other staff and in general being a team member.

Remember that none of us can fit all of the above 100 percent. But we should try our best to operate at as high a level within each of the categories as possible.

Figure 2.8

Sample Job Description: Chief Operating Officer

Summary of Duties: The Chief Operating Officer of Brady, Ware & Schoenfeld is responsible for the smooth-running, day-to-day operation of the firm. The Director is a principal in the firm and reports directly to the Managing Director. The COO works closely with the Managing Director (CEO) to formulate management goals, at least annually. The COO carries out policies made by the Board of Directors and implements procedures necessary to ensure timely completion of all client work. The COO is involved in all areas of human resources and acts as liaison between management and team members, and between accounting and administrative personnel. The COO is responsible for all firm offices and supervises office administrators in each office. The COO is ultimately responsible for:

Administration

Control workflow to regulate and maintain a balanced workload for administrative team with minimum of overtime.

Monitor client due dates to ensure all work is completed in a timely manner. Communicate deadline and workload conflicts to directors as needed to ensure timely completion of work.

Standardize office procedures, systems, and forms. Recommend system revisions and implement new forms and procedures as necessary.

Maintain master client database. Issue new client reports and assimilate new clients into firm system. Revise firm records as appropriate to reflect clients gained and lost. Report status to directors on a regular basis.

Manage and control the purchase of supplies so that adequate inventory is maintained in all areas.

Oversee the research and recommendations relating to the purchase of necessary equipment, including FAX machines, photocopiers, telephone systems, computers, and software. Deal with various vendors supplying office equipment.

Stay abreast of trends in office automation and recommend improvements to existing systems when appropriate.

Arrange for regular office equipment maintenance and negotiate appropriate service contracts.

Maintain an efficient filing system for client and administrative files.

Maintain efficient income and outgoing mail procedures.

Assist Tax and Audit & Accounting Committees with maintenance of the firm libraries.

As a director, attend all board meetings, handling any physical arrangements as needed. Work with Managing Director to prepare and distribute agendas. Serves as corporate secretary. Prepare and distribute minutes to directors.

Be responsible for all team meetings. Develop agendas and chair weekly meetings in each office.

Hold periodic administrative team meetings, keeping the administrative team informed of any management decisions relating to them. Encourage and promote team effort on the part of the entire administrative group by soliciting their input and enlisting their support relating to the efficient operation of both offices.

Attend all Tax Committee and A&A Committee meetings as a management representative. Serve as a management resource person for both committees.

Work with Tax Committee to establish forms, procedures, and guidelines to promote the efficient operation of the individual income tax area.

Maintain all firm insurance records. Provide directors with cost and coverage comparisons as needed. Recommend appropriate revisions, additions, or deletions to coverage. Firm Controller assists in this area.

Schedule and arrange all firm social events.

Personnel

Serve as human resource director for the firm, managing all hiring and recruiting activities. Be involved in key performance conferences and outplacements, when necessary.

Work with administrative manager and controller to provide new employee orientation. This includes an office tour, introductions, reviewing firm policies and procedures, and enrollment and explanation of firm benefits.

Maintain personnel files. Keep information current on each employee's personal data, status of vacation and sick leave accrued and taken, performance evaluations, professional development, and participation in benefit programs.

Annually, coordinate formal performance evaluation process for all personnel. Summarize all information relating to evaluation and provide historical information. Be involved in all administrative performance review sessions, all technology division personnel evaluations, and accounting personnel reviews when necessary.

Maintain personnel guide in accordance with applicable employment laws and guidelines. Update personnel policies and stay current on all issues. Communicate all new or revised policies to all employees.

Administer employee benefits programs. Recommend revisions to maintain a competitive compensation and benefits package. Negotiate contracts for employee insurance and benefits to provide maximum benefits at lower cost. Administer firm 401k pension plan and Flexible Benefit Plan.

Serve as trustee for the firm 401(k) pension plan.

Be responsible for the firm's CPE program. Supervise the maintenance of CPE records, file necessary reports to the state society and board of accountancy, and make seminar registrations and travel arrangements.

Be responsible for determining the number of administrative team members needed to efficiently process client engagements and support firm activities. Develop job descriptions for all administrative positions.

Serve as the director in charge of all administrative personnel, including the Dayton Office Administrator, Richmond Administrative Team Leader, and the firm Controller.

Finance

Supervise internal accounting functions, including preparation of monthly general ledgers and financial statements. Provide statistical reports reflecting each director's performance on a monthly basis.

Approve all invoices and sign accounts payable checks.

Monitor accounts receivable and cash flow. Supervise the processing and mailing of accounts receivable statements monthly. Supervise follow-up collection letters and calls when appropriate and work with attorney in collection of difficult accounts.

Supervise the preparation of firm payroll and payroll tax returns.

Monitor employee time sheets and expense reports for accuracy.

Supervise time and billing system. Monitor timely preparation of billings and distribution of management reports.

Prepare and/or review firm budget, as directed by Managing Director. Monitor budget on a monthly basis.

Practice Development

As Director, responsible for the coordination and supervision of all marketing efforts within the firm, including the supervision of Marketing Director and Marketing Assistant.

Develop and monitor a firm marketing program.

Monitor firm marketing activities for each team member, assist in development of personal marketing plans for directors and managers, hold monthly sales meetings in both offices, and provide education relating to practice development.

Responsible for all firm direct mail efforts:

> Financial Report—quarterly—coordinate client feature article
>
> Medical Report—quarterly
>
> Construction Report—quarterly
>
> Manufacturing Report—quarterly

¶230.02

Auto Dealer Report—monthly

Special mailings by various industry groups

Responsible for all firm publicity efforts. Issue news releases to local newspapers, business publications, and state society newsletters. Release, annually, a media package offering firm expertise on tax and financial issues.

Arrange, coordinate, and attend all practice development "team" meetings (auto team, manufacturing team, etc.). Carry out special projects as a result of these meetings, including special direct mail campaigns, seminars, or social events.

Responsible for coordination of all advertising efforts, including newspapers, program books in both cities, chamber of commerce publications, yellow pages, IMA membership books, etc.

Responsible for developing all firm marketing tools, such as brochures, proposal formats, and newsletters. Assist in developing tools for new services such as pension administration and technology consulting.

Responsible for firm image regarding the appearance of letterhead, logo, tax folders, financial statement covers, tax returns, financial statement style, letter style, and all printed matter going outside the firm.

Computer/System Integration

Serve as director in charge of the firm's internal technology operations, including supervision of the firm's Manager of Information Technology and other internal technology team members.

Maintain current knowledge of developments in computer hardware and software as related to CPA firm operation.

Be directly involved in hiring, supervising, and evaluating technology personnel.

Monitor technology team daily to ensure smooth and efficient computer operation for both offices.

Scheduling

Work with Scheduler in each office to effectively monitor team work schedules and keep accurate records of completed year-end engagements and all extensions.

Serve as management advisor to Scheduler and see that scheduling meetings are held in each office to guarantee better communication between team and directors.

Supervise distribution of scheduling information, current job log, and tracking information to enhance workflow.

Facilities

Supervise office maintenance to achieve a first-class, professional appearance.

Supervise the selection, purchase, and coordination of office furniture and accessories.

Analyze space utilization, office layout, and recommend revisions, as needed.

Supervise upkeep of building and grounds in Richmond.

Deal with tenants in regard to any problems or requests they may have.

Technology Consulting Division

Serve as Director-in-Charge of the firm's external technology consulting division, keeping current on trends in the industry and communicating efforts and activities to the Board of Directors.

Determine personnel requirements for the division and be involved in hiring, supervising, and evaluating technology personnel.

Work with Technology Consulting Manager to determine an annual business plan for the division and meet with technology team on a regular basis to monitor progress and set goals.

Human Resources Consulting Division

Serve as Director-in-Charge of the firm's human resources consulting division, working with HR consultants to effectively serve clients and aggressively grow the division.

Related Entities

Serve as management contact and advisor to wholly-owned or partially owned subsidiaries: Brady Ware Capital and Brady Meixner & Company.

Source: Brady, Ware & Schoenfeld, Dayton, Ohio

Figure 2.9

Sample Job Description: Firm Administrator

Experience: A minimum of three years management experience with functional emphasis on accounts receivable and collection management, financial management, personnel management, and accounting exposure.

Education: College degree or equivalent experience background. Emphasis on management, accounting, personnel, and finance. Data processing knowledge would be a plus.

Duties: Primary Function: Under the supervision of the Managing Partner, directly responsible for all administrative activities of the firm. Duties and responsibilities shall include, but are not necessarily limited to the following:

Administration

1. Administrative Manual—review and revise where necessary and develop additional sections to cover areas not presently included in the firm manual.

2. Other firm manuals—assist in the development of firm manuals for other areas and determine that all such manuals are kept current.

3. Records, filing, and retention.
   - Monitor the maintenance of client files and the operation of the filing system.
   - Maintain procedures to assure that the firm's retention policy is adhered to.
   - Assist in the formulation of retention policy for very old items presently on hand.

4. Assure adequate and optimum quantities of forms and office supplies are available.

5. Review and supervise time and expense reporting systems; recommend policy and/or systems changes where appropriate.

6. Maintain a "manpower file" of all job applicants for professional, clerical, and part-time positions.

7. The firm newsletter and bi-monthly internal newsletter
   - Control collection of input.
   - Where necessary, review technical matters with appropriate personnel.
   - Supervise and monitor above to insure timely distribution.
   - Perform the same duties for technical bulletins.

8. Library—develop and maintain a system for the orderly and supervised management of the firm library.

9. Equipment, spare assignments, and physical plant—responsible for operation and maintenance and efficient use thereof.

10. Distribution
    - Develop and manage an efficient and orderly system that insures the timely and adequate distribution of periodicals, memos, newsletters, tax bulletins, and all other similar items.
    - Approve internal memoranda.
    - Assure simultaneous dissemination to all departments and personnel.

11. Social—coordinate, schedule, and supervise all social activities.

12. Publicity—responsible for the timely and appropriate publicity of the firm and its members' activities.

Personnel

1. Recommend hiring and terminations of all administrative and clerical personnel reporting to the firm administrator.

2. Supervise and direct the work of such personnel.

3. Orient all new personnel—both professional and other.

4. Interpret staff manual.

5. Review time reports of all personnel.

6. Assist managing partner in determining employees' attitude by surveys, etc.

7. Staff evaluation summaries (professional staff)
   - Assist in revision of system and forms and firm policy.
   - Monitor and enforce firm policy; insure uniform application.
   - Accumulate completed forms for managing partner's review.

8. Assist managing partner in forecasting appropriate staff level requirements.

9. Handle all shareholder insurance matters including claims and enrollments.

¶230.02

Scheduling and Production Control

1. Schedule and staff all engagements, including *pro forma* type scheduling, 12 months in advance.

2. Approve and schedule personal time and vacations.

3. Assist CPE person in scheduling CPE.

4. Coordinate and arrange staff meetings and technical sessions.

5. Develop a job control system that ensures the timely completion and mailing of client's reports, tax returns, management letters, etc., and their processing through the office; to the maximum practical, provide an even volume of work for clerical employees.

6. Assist in the development of firm policy on the use of time budgets and monitor actual vs. budgeted time on engagements as well as the effect on future scheduling. The monitoring is to be accomplished through periodic reporting to the shareholder in charge of the engagement.

Finance

1. Accounts receivable collection—maintain system and procedures to insure control over accounts to be handled through the collection process.

2. Insurance—review adequacy of insurance coverage at least annually.

3. Expense reimbursement—approve all expense vouchers submitted for reimbursement and all petty cash disbursement requests.

4. Assist Managing Partner in budgetary forecasting, accounting, and reporting.

Figure 2.10 ———————————————————————————————

Sample Tax Department Charter

Purpose: The purpose of the tax department is to develop and maintain an effective firm-wide tax function. The department charges itself with responsibility for defining, recommending, and implementing tax procedures which will result in the highest possible standards in all tax services rendered.

Scope: The work of the department will extend to and include all functions and activities related to taxation, including: policy development, recommendations and implementation, staff training, quality control, inspection, technical assistance, and standards and procedures development.

Organization: The department shall be chaired by a director. The department will meet regularly, keep minutes and records of activities and publish, with the assistance of the Managing Partner, appropriate manuals, policies, standards, and procedures.

Service areas: The department will direct its attention to an evaluation of the existing role it plays in the organizational structure of the firm and develop recommendations for improvement in areas found deficient. The department will develop a tax manual to be used as a practical working tool. The tax manual will be designed in a manner which will communicate the concern of the firm as set forth in its policies, standards, and procedures. Concerns covered will include:

1. A technically accurate, quality product.

2. A balanced staff.

3. Standardized policies and procedures.

4. Intra-office communications.

5. Public and professional relations.

In addition, the tax department will develop practical operating procedures and make specific assignments which will enable the department to successfully meet its objectives, including:

A. A technically accurate, quality product.

    1. Adequate source information.

    2. Proper delegation to match need with resource.

    3. Adequate work paper documentation.

    4. Technical review.

    5. Professional appearance.

    6. Quality review program.

B. A balanced staff.

      1. Organizational plan which will pinpoint needs.

      2. Informing the Managing Partner of the personnel needs of the department.

      3. Technical training program.

      4. Method of responsibility assignment which will effectively utilize staff capabilities.

C. Standardized policies and procedures.

      1. Development of checklists.

      2. Development of work flow forms.

      3. Development of work paper indexing system.

      4. Development of filing procedures.

      5. Development and maintenance of a tax manual.

D. Intra-office communications.

      1. Coordination of information developed for client alerts and internal tax memoranda with all firm personnel.

      2. Development of a prime issue position file.

      3. Development of a tax research subject file.

      4. Development of a procedure for specialist consulting.

E. Public and professional relations.

      1. Develop a program of formal encouragement for participation in society committee work, speaking engagements, and writing articles.

      2. Promote adherence to ethical and technical standards.

      3. Systematic review of services offered and areas where additional services may be rendered.

Figure 2.11

Definition of the Tax Practice and Role of the Partner-in-Charge

To achieve effective management of an organization, a definition and overall philosophy should be established, specific goals should be set, and results should be measured and evaluated. The members of the organization should know the standards of measurement and consider them to be fair.

Definition and Goals of the Tax Department

The operations and goals of the tax department should include all of the following elements. Except for the development of staff, which should receive high priority, the emphasis to be placed upon each of the other elements may vary from year to year depending upon the marketplace, skills level, and mix, etc.

Development of staff: In addition to the usual items, goals can include programs for developing specialized and industry skills.

1. Service to audit clients.

2. Contribution to the audit exercise.

    • Practice development (PD) activities with client officials.

    • Profitable tax services.

    • Goals for specialized tax services from among the client mix.

3. PD activities.

    • General community.

    • Obtaining non-tax clients.

    • Developing relationships with existing clients.

4. Operations as a business unit.

5. Growth and profitability of tax related services.

6. Proper balance of tax return services.

    a. Tax related services: Plans and goals should be developed annually between the tax partner-in-charge and the managing partner in both of the following categories:

      • Tax related services performed strictly by the tax department personnel of the office.

- Tax related services for the clients of the firm, regardless of whether the services are performed by tax department personnel or personnel from other areas of the firm.

b. Tax compliance: Return preparation should continue to be viewed as an important element in the operation of a tax department and be accomplished in an efficient and profitable manner. Of greater importance than fostering growth in this area is the establishment of the purpose and philosophy for the practice. The undertaking of individual engagements should be consistent with those purposes and periodic review of the client list should be conducted.

A statement of purpose for return preparation could include but would not necessarily be limited to the following:

- PD opportunities with existing or potential clients.
- A corollary service as part of a financial planning package for individuals.
- A useful tool providing both training and productivity for younger staff.

Authority and Accountability

The partner-in-charge of the tax department has authority as a department head, accountable to the managing partner.

1. Responsible for all of the elements of the operation including quality, profitability, staff development, staff communications, recruiting goals, growth, support of the audit function, etc.
2. Performs annual evaluation of the other tax shareholders and other personnel in the department and recommends compensation adjustments to the managing partner.

Evaluation

The above statement of definition and role provides a basis for annual goal setting and evaluation of both quantitative results and contribution in the more subjective areas.

If tax is to be a cutting edge of PD, it is essential that the annual evaluation process include a review of efforts in the overall PD plan for the office and for specific contributions to the marketing of services other than tax services to both existing and new clients.

Experienced tax supervisors and managers play a vital role in the annual regeneration of tax services which in turn is the basis for the growth of a healthy tax practice. It is important to the program for the development of tax product lines that sufficient weight be given to performance in the delivery of specialized services to clients of the office.

Quantitative Data

The existing practice management computer program allows the tax department to isolate the statistics of the tax professionals. Thus, in evaluating tax department performance, charged hours to tax codes by non-tax professionals and administrative staff can be eliminated, and the charged hour contribution by tax professionals to the audit effort can be taken into account.

Figure 2.12 ——————————————————————————————

Sample Job Description: Tax Director

1. Responsible for the overall tax functions of the firm. Take directions from and report to the managing partner.
2. Develop policies and procedures to effectively carry out his area of responsibility for the firm including the effective administration of the department.
3. Develop and carry out the review functions for tax returns and tax related reports and forms and coordinate with the firm audit shareholder on review of tax accruals.
4. Develop and maintain an expertise in his area.
5. Keep all personnel in the firm informed of changes and developments in his area.
6. Plan, coordinate, and conduct, together with the staff training person, the training necessary to develop and maintain the competence of all personnel, on a need to know basis, for his area of responsibility.
7. Develop the capability of the firm in his area, to provide additional needed services for clients.
8. Establish and maintain sources of expertise outside the firm as needed to make available to our clients a full range of services they need.
9. Develop means of communicating, to clients and persons responsible for maintaining relationships with clients, the benefit of the services in his area we are qualified to perform.

10. Client service responsibility for assigned clients.

11. Supervise and utilize all assigned personnel. Obtain tax personnel from outside or by transfer from the audit and accounting departments. Review productivity and periodically evaluate and report to the managing partner.

12. Continually develop new clients.

13. Provide assistance to assigned personnel in their research of a tax problem.

Figure 2.13 ——

Sample Job Description: Accounting and Audit Director

1. Responsible for the overall auditing and accounting functions of the firm. Take direction from and report to the managing partner.

2. Develop policies and procedures to effectively carry out his area of responsibility for the firm.

3. Develop and carry out the review functions for audit programs, audit reports, financial statements, and special reports and coordinate with the firm MAS Shareholder on review of management service.

4. Develop and maintain an expertise in his area.

5. Keep all personnel in the firm informed of changes and developments in his area.

6. Plan, coordinate, and conduct, together with the staff training person, the training necessary to develop and maintain the competence of all personnel, on a need to know basis, for his area of responsibility.

7. Develop the capability of the firm in his area, to provide additional needed services for clients.

8. Develop areas of specialization by industry when practical.

9. Establish and maintain sources of expertise outside the firm as needed to make available to our clients a full range of services they need.

10. Develop means of communicating, to clients and persons responsible for maintaining relationships with clients, the benefit of the services in his area we are qualified to perform.

11. Client service responsibility for assigned clients.

12. Supervise and utilize all assigned personnel.

13. Continually develop new clients.

14. Assist shareholders and staff in their research of an accounting or auditing problem.

Figure 2.14 ——

Sample Accounting and Audit Committee Charter

Purpose: The purpose of the committee is to insure that accounting and auditing functions are conducted in accordance with accepted standards and to the highest quality level.

Scope: The work of the committee will extend to and include all functions and activities related to accounting and auditing, including: (1) standards and procedures development, (2) policy development and implementation, (3) quality control, and (4) technical assistance.

Organization: The committee shall be chaired by a shareholder and three other members. The committee may assign special projects to personnel outside the committee.

Service Areas

- Develop, implement, and communicate policies and procedures to assure that all accounting and auditing work is adequately supervised and reviewed; that reports issued by the firm are in accordance with generally accepted accounting principles (or any deviation from such is properly disclosed); that independence in fact and in appearance is maintained in connection with audit clients; and that proper criteria are used in making decisions concerning the acceptance and continuation of services to audited and unaudited statement clients.

- Assist in implementing staff training programs in the audit and accounting areas. Programs utilized will include AICPA and CFCPA programs, supplemented by in-house programs as appropriate. Publish frequent bulletins for internal distribution regarding current developments in the audit and accounting areas.

- Maintain a Report Manual and such other guides requested by the managing partner or as this committee deems appropriate. The guides should be a reference source for all personnel and should be effective in helping to standardize many of the recurring items which are a part of all engagements.

- Develop and maintain a system whereby technical assistance can be supplied as the need arises. The assistance would be provided from within the firm if possible and would include both review and consultation services.

- Develop and maintain a program for periodic technical review to determine if firm policies are being followed. The committee shall assist the managing partner in the implementation of such technical reviews.

- Establish liaison and effective channels of communication with other technical departments and the managing partner.

Figure 2.15 ———

Sample Management Advisory Services Department Charter

Purpose: The primary purpose of the Management Advisory Services (MAS) department is to provide competent and diverse consulting capability to all clients of the firm. The Management Advisory Services department will set procedures and standards to act as consultants in assisting client management to develop more effective and more profitable operations through improved organization and controls, and the application of appropriate procedures and techniques.

Scope: Management Advisory Services is the consulting activity of our profession, which is directed to providing investigative and analytical talents with respect to the operation of enterprises, for the purpose of evaluating and suggesting improvements in the use of money, people, and other resources. The possible range of services we might provide is obviously quite broad and could conceivably include most management areas. However, the scope of our services is determined by applying criteria of competence that are considered to be consistent with our role of independent Certified Public Accountants. Accordingly, it is our policy to offer a reasonable range of management related services and to demonstrate a high degree of competence in what we undertake. We will undertake only those types of engagements for which we have someone at the review level who is qualified to evaluate the quality of work.

Our work as accountants and as consultants within the broad fields of administration and management controls takes us into practically all function areas of business. However, our concern will be primarily with the organization, policy and planning, management performance measurement, accounting, and reporting aspects rather than with specialized techniques such as those inherent in advertising, market strategy, product and equipment design, tooling and machine operations, etc. We will adopt a consulting approach in the Management Advisory Services work, and on most engagements, a small staff will work closely with the client. It is our policy, wherever practicable, to have client personnel contribute their knowledge and ideas. We acknowledge our responsibility for the results of an engagement, but our emphasis will be in providing know-how rather than manpower. Accordingly, we do not propose to furnish services which the client can provide as well at the same or at less cost.

Organization: A shareholder will direct the Management Advisory Services practice. When deemed necessary, we will utilize the individual skills of our audit, tax, and other staff as a firm-wide staff pool. The Management Advisory Services staff functions as a firm-wide staff.

The Management Advisory Services shareholder is responsible for the conduct of the Management Advisory Services practice including practice development, negotiation, and execution of the MAS engagement. In carrying out his function, he is subject to the review and concurrence of the Managing Partner. From the firm-wide staff pool, the person with the greatest expertise in the field of a particular Management Advisory Services engagement will be drafted to assist on the engagement. He will be involved in planning an engagement as well as in the development of recommendations. It is not practicable to assign the necessary complement of disciplines and capabilities to all personnel. Thus, the Management Advisory Services department may utilize a pool of personnel with diverse consulting competence.

Service Areas

1. To provide competent consulting capability to each client.
2. To define and continuously update the philosophy, role, and scope of the firm's Management Advisory Services activities.
3. To establish Management Advisory Services standards and procedures and evaluate performance.
4. To assure that a schedule is maintained of the skills and qualifications our staff and shareholders have in the Management Advisory Services area.
5. To organize and administer a Continuing Professional Education Program in the Management Advisory Services area.
6. To prepare and have available information advising of our specialized abilities and qualifications in the Management Advisory Services area.

7. To provide for and encourage the training of audit and tax personnel in the recognition of potential Management Advisory Services engagements.

Figure 2.16

Sample Criteria for Advancement: Senior

Advancement to the senior level is considered a significant step in an individual's career development. It is at this level when the person first assumes "in-charge" field responsibility. The senior is responsible for the day-to-day conduct of the field engagement, supervision of staff, and review of work papers. It is at this level where the first one-to-one contact with key client management personnel begins.

Promotion to this level will be made when it is clear that an individual has developed sufficiently to the degree where the firm's management is confident of the individual's technical proficiency and supervisory capability. In the case of the audit and accounting personnel, the candidate for promotion would be well accomplished in the audit techniques of all balance sheet sections and on several occasions would have successfully handled senior responsibility on a number of small engagements.

Some specific responsibilities of the senior position would include the following:

Job Management:

- Preparation of engagement budgets for submission to management.
- Preparation of engagement letter.
- Preparation of work program.

Engagement Supervision:

- Effectively supervise staff in all areas of the field work.
- Provide adequate on-the-job training, including staff performance evaluation.
- Keep supervisors informed of job progress.
- Interface on a day-to-day basis with appropriate client personnel.
- Responsible for the completion of all work papers in accordance with firm standards.
- Accountable to engagement budget guidelines.
- Responsible for preparation of a draft report.

Each individual progresses at a different pace, and the firm recognizes that it is possible for so-called "fast track" persons to advance to a certain level and reach their potential while another individual may acquire skills at a slower pace yet reach shareholdership potential. It is for this reason that there are no hard and fast guidelines for promotion to senior. A promotion will only be undertaken when it is felt that the staff person has attained a strong foundation in his or her technical skills, is confident of his abilities, and appears capable of developing and directing the work of staff assistants.

Figure 2.17

Sample Criteria for Advancement: Management

The firm's middle management group consists of supervisors and managers. Responsibilities of each of these classifications are as follows:

Supervisor

The promotion to supervisor represents the first introduction to the firm's management group. To be eligible for promotion, the staff person must be a Certified Public Accountant. Through demonstrated performance at the senior level, the candidate for supervisor would have clearly exhibited a high degree of accomplishment in technical, administrative, and organizational skills. In addition, the individual's interpersonal skills would have developed at least to the level of efficient and effective interaction with all professional levels within the firm and, at a minimum, with client's middle-management personnel.

It would be impossible to define precisely the responsibilities of a supervisor. To a degree they would vary depending on job assignments. At this level, additional field engagement responsibilities are assumed. Specific duties normally would include the planning, scope setting, and staffing of assigned engagements. The individual would also begin to establish on-going business relationships with key client personnel. Under usual circumstances, a supervisor should have primary responsibility for assuring that the engagement is completed in accordance with firm standards and guidelines.

Other specific job responsibilities relating to engagement management would include the following:

- Monthly analysis of client time charges and submission of pro forma invoices for shareholder approval.

- Coordinate the report processing procedures from draft report to final issuance to client (assuming responsibility for completion of all quality control procedures prior to report issuance).

- Responsibility for completion of engagement time control summary and analysis of variances between actual and budgeted time.

- Responsibility that proper on-the-job training was conducted on the engagement.

- Responsibility for preparation of client engagement letter and participation in fee proposals.

At this level, an individual's participation in the administrative matters of the firm increases. The person becomes more involved in determining firm personnel needs and actively participates in recruitment and counseling of staff personnel. At the supervision level, the individual becomes more involved in engagement profitability and client responsibilities broaden to a point of significant involvement in a client's forward business planning and greater participation in ongoing business decisions. It is expected that an individual's community involvement will broaden and will thus become more actively involved in the firm's practice development efforts. Frequency of client contact is increased as the individual's advisory role to clients is expanded. Advancement guidelines to this level are difficult to quantify since such skills develop at a different level for each individual. However, for the purpose of providing a norm, consideration for advancement to this level would normally occur after an individual has performed to the senior level for three years.

Manager

The promotion to manager will be undertaken when there is a consensus of opinion that the candidate will proceed to the director level. In addition to evidencing clear potential to director, the candidate would have attained a proven "track record" in handling the responsibilities of supervisor. Performance at the supervisor level would have been such that the candidate has clearly demonstrated the ability to handle complex situations, both from a technical and administrative aspect. The individual's interest and accomplishments in the practice development function of the firm would have broadened.

At the manager level, the individual becomes more deeply involved in the administrative and financial aspects of firm management. Normally, a manager will assume complete in charge responsibility for one or several administrative functions such as scheduling, recruitment, or counseling. Upon promotion, the person will become more deeply involved in personnel decisions such as promotions, establishing compensation level, etc. The individual becomes more exposed to operating budgets and financial results of the firm. A manager is capable of handling a number of engagements simultaneously and on certain engagements may have the primary client relationship with top management.

Figure 2.18 ———

Sample Executive Committee Charter

The Executive Committee (the Committee), the governing body of the firm, is responsible to the partners for the overall operations of the practice. Decisions and actions of the Committee shall be for the benefit of the partnership and the mutual well-being of all its members. Provisions of this charter include:

Membership

The Committee shall consist originally of three partners, the managing partner and two members elected by the partnership, serving rotating two-year terms. A member may succeed himself for one two-year term, then be eligible for re-election after not serving one term. The initial committee will be composed of_____ whose term shall be for one year (and may be elected to serve for one additional year); _____, who shall serve for two years; and _____, Managing Partner. The managing partner shall serve as Chair of the Executive Committee. To insure its own successful operation, the Committee shall develop, endorse, and subscribe to rules of operations, including:

Operations

The Committee shall develop and communicate such policies and procedures concerning its activities as will insure continuity and successful operation. The Committee shall maintain minutes and other historical records of its operations and those of the partnership. The managing partner shall be the custodian of the official copies of these documents. Written reports of Committee activities shall be distributed to the partners as soon thereafter as practical.

The Committee normally shall implement its decisions and actions through the managing partner. The Committee may seek information directly as it deems necessary to fulfill its responsibilities to the partnership.

Regular Committee meetings shall be held at least once each month, at such time when all three members can attend.

The Chair of the Executive Committee shall call special meetings at the request of the other Committee members or any other partner. A quorum to transact business, at a special meeting, shall consist of two members of the Committee. A vote of two voting Committee members shall be necessary to pass or adopt. Actions shall not be approved when all three members are not present unless required by time constraints. The Committee may vest in the managing partner the authority to act on its behalf in specific situations.

The partnership, within 30 days, will elect a partner to fill the unexpired term created by a vacating Committee member.

A majority vote of the partnership shall be required for the removal of a Committee member, in addition to any changes, deletions, etc. to the Charter. The Committee shall be vested by the partnership with the necessary authority to accomplish its responsibilities. Authority shall include:

FUNCTIONS

Organization

- Develop procedures to monitor and enforce policies adopted by the partnership and Executive Committee, and other actions implemented by the managing partner.
- Approve the appointment of all members of the firm and CPA Association technical committees.
- Review and monitor firm Technical Committee activities and programs.
- Make nominations to the partnership for the position of managing partner, and act on recommendations of the managing partner for positions of the partner-in-charge of each technical area (tax, audit, and MAS).
- Receive drafts of Technical Committee reports and recommendations and act upon them.
- Review and approve personnel assignment recommendations made by the managing partner.
- Develop annual firm goals, budgets, time tables, and results for acceptance by the partnership.
- Recommend to the partnership actions concerning acquisitions, mergers, opening of new offices, or the closing of an office.

Finance

- Recommend to the partnership for approval, changes in the system of partner compensation.
- Define and recommend to the partnership for approval, compensation, and billing rate guidelines and formulae for staff.
- Recommend compensation for staff in accordance with approved guidelines and formulae.
- Review, monitor, and enforce firm budgets, including capital expenditures, debt structure, and cash flow.
- Approve unbudgeted capital expenditures, rent or lease agreements, and increases in debt structure not to exceed $50,000 in the aggregate within any fiscal year.

Administration

- Approve and endorse all necessary administrative policies. Make available to the partnership its policies, decisions, and actions by publishing and maintaining a section in a Partners' Manual (to be developed and maintained by the Executive Committee).
- Establish reporting systems to be maintained by the managing partner for communicating financial data, policy decisions, and performance results.
- Charge the managing partner with specific responsibilities and authority for the management of the practice, including standards, manuals, policies, fiscal management, goals, and other functions and programs as set forth in the managing partner position description.
- Review and evaluate the performance of the managing partner.

Partnership

- Define and recommend profit distribution guidelines to the partnership for approval.
- Make recommendations to the partnership regarding changes in the Partnership Agreement.
- Recommend, review, and evaluate firm-wide and individual goals programs and performance.
- Determine and recommend actions to the partnership concerning withdrawal, incapacity, and involuntary retirement of partners consistent with the provisions of the Partnership Agreement.
- Design and implement programs which will encourage the development of future partners.
- Recommend admission of new partners to the partnership.

¶230.02

- The Executive Committee shall perform such other acts, not specifically prohibited, to implement decisions and take actions for the welfare of the partnership and its members.

- The Executive Committee shall continuously be aware that it serves at the pleasure of the partnership, and therefore must function in accordance with sound business practices in a prudent manner and for the benefit of the firm.

.03 Good Security Is a Requirement

A few short years ago, locking file cabinets and shredding selected papers was the requisite level of security in most firms. Now that is almost laughable. Nearly every process associated with running a firm is computerized, bringing a new level of vulnerability to the confidentiality of the work you do. Firewalls, spam filters, and passwords protect you from goodness knows what may be lurking in cyberspace. Storing prior years' tax returns at a storage facility has given way to back-up servers and companies that come to your offices to shred tons of paper.

Not to overwork our initial analogy, but it is all alien to most firm leaders today. That will not always be true: the next generation of leadership was brought up with technology. (There are other issues around this, such as privacy, social networking, and company-bashing websites, but we'll get to that later.)

Another aspect of this issue relates to the retention of electronic data. The Federal Rules of Civil Procedure were recently amended to require companies to be able to access a variety of electronically-stored data in the event of litigation. The penalties for noncompliance range from sanctions to obstruction of justice charges, depending on the severity of the noncompliance (e.g., if records were knowingly destroyed). Because the amount of data stored on firm servers and outside servers, compliance is quite complex. The problem is so far-reaching that it has given birth to a cottage industry. For instance, there are companies that can examine American International Group's (AIG's) e-mails for the past six years to find those that refer to the sale of derivatives.

.04 Privacy Risks

Accounting has become a very mobile profession, bringing laptops and printers to clients' offices, working from home or other remote locations, and communicating through various wireless devices. Along with the benefits of portability comes the very real risk of the loss of sensitive information. Having personnel policies in place to prevent this, such as requiring employees to handle all client-related work on a firm-supplied computer and only allowing software provided by the firm to be downloaded onto the computer, is beneficial.

It may sound like George Orwell's *1984*, but a popup should appear each time the laptop is turned on warning that the employee should have no expectation of privacy on the computer. Keep in mind that firewalls only work on computers that are networked to the firm's server.

.05 Don't Forget About Disaster/Business Continuity Planning

The importance of disaster recovery planning was one of the lessons of Hurricane Katrina. What would your firm do if there was some kind of disaster in your area? How long would it take for your firm to be up and running again? How would you contact your partners, employees, and clients?

Figure 2.19 ───────────────────────────────────────

Case Study: Disaster Planning
PKF Texas/Houston Meets Hurricane Ike

Hurricane Ike caused more than 85 percent of the Houston area to lose power. Over 2,500 traffic signals were non-operational, creating a huge problem for transit. While mobile phone service never went down, most communication was via texting since the circuits were too busy and voice connections were not always available. According to Kenneth Guidry, the firm's president, of PKF Texas, "We could have required our team to report to the office, but since we're paperless they can work from anywhere, as long as they had power. But there was nothing for them to do in most cases because the clients we're dealing with the recovery as well. Any projects scheduled for that week were deferred as a result. The exception was the tax department, which had most of the client information they needed in anticipation of the October 15, 2008 tax filing deadline."

This is the communication the firm sent to all employees once it became obvious that Houston was going to take a direct hit from Ike:

Our offices will be closed tomorrow to allow everyone to take whatever actions are necessary for your personal safety. Today we should remain calm and focused on client service and taking care of business. This email explains certain actions that should be taken before you leave the office today. If you are receiving this email remotely (i.e.) if you are not in the office, contact your departmental administrative assistant to request their assistance in accomplishing these measures ASAP this afternoon.

In offices with exterior windows, take these actions prior to leaving the premises:

1. Remove all client workpapers and files from the tops of the desks, credenzas, cabinets, shelves and window ledges. These should be returned to the file rooms, placed in empty cubicles or stacked in the interior hallway near your office. If you need boxes see Melissa Estrada.

2. Put the blinds down and turn slats to shut position.

3. Disconnect all electrical office equipment (see more specific instructions on this below).

4. Close all doors to exterior offices.

This evening when you leave, please turn off all computer equipment (computer and monitor) and unplug it/them from the wall. If you have a laptop, take it (and the power cord!) with you when you leave the office. Monitors and printers in the outer offices need to be moved to the interior hallway outside your office or in a cube to protect them from the unlikely event of a window being blown out. Colin, Greg, Tom and Weylon will be here to assist if necessary.

As for the network, all backups are being performed as planned. All servers will be up and running to allow for firm wide communications—assuming the power stays on. If you plan on working on something from home, grab what you need before you leave today. Your Practice Leaders or project leaders will provide you with any department specific communications that may be applicable.

Stay tuned to the local news channels, especially 740 KTRH, for current and up to the minute weather information. Building management will continue to update Annabella, Kenneth and Tom on the buildings status and we will get that to you as quickly as possible via email (if possible) and on the phone message listed below.

We have setup an information number for you to call for any information regarding the building, closing of the office, etc . . . You will be able to connect to this number regardless of whether we have power in the building. The number is 877.753.4855 or 877.PKFIT.55 (this is the same number we have for after hours IT support). Press 2 for information and listen to the prompts for information from PKF Texas. Please take a minute to program this number into your mobile phone for easy access. If necessary we will post periodic updates.

If you are unable to access voicemail or email, it is unlikely that it is safe to return to the office following the storm. A copy of our firm directory is in Outlook which can be printed or you can access the folder without being online. If you haven't already done so, please take a minute to make sure your information in the directory is accurate and complete. Please take this with you so that you can check with your friends via cell phone or otherwise. Previous experience tells us that electrical power will likely be lost for some period of time. When your power is restored you may be able to offer assistance to others who may be without power for an extended period of time.

If you have questions on something that you are unclear on, please ask. Stay tuned for any additional instructions.

Please stay safe and take good care. I look forward to seeing you all next week!

Kenneth

P.S. Payroll is being transmitted today!!!!!!!!!

Here is the communication that went out once the hurricane passed:

I hope everyone is doing OK and recovering from Hurricane Ike? Please contact your Practice Leader, Annabella [Firm Administrator]or me if there is any information you need to share with us or any assistance or support we may be able to provide for you and your family.

As you are obviously aware Houston and the surrounding area took a major hit from Ike. Recovery will take some time. I suspect many of you are still without power to your homes (as I am), or your home has sustained some damage. We understand that attending to your home and family will take some time and attention over the next few days.

Power to the office building has been restored and the building is now open for business, however at the moment the power in the garage is out and the lights and elevators are not working.

All PKF Texas file and phone servers are operational and up and running. We expect to be in "transition" for the next several days until we are able to return to more normal business operations at the office.

If you have power and are able to work remotely, please feel free to do so. On my drive to the office I observed that two out of three traffic signals are not working and gas is in short supply. Until power is restored to our area gas will continue to be hard to come by. These conditions should steadily improve over the next few days (hopefully). Monitor travel conditions in your area to determine if you are able to find gas and if you choose to come to the office, we will look forwarding to seeing you. Over the next several weeks we will monitor due dates, deadlines and projects as we may need to adjust our work schedules and hours to make up for the time lost due to the storm and recovery.

If you come to the office, be aware that a few offices suffered minor water damage and restoration crews will be on site for the next few days to dry out the offices and make any necessary repairs.

Please check with your Practice Leader ASAP to report your status and workload and to receive any further instructions. You will also need to communicate and coordinate with your Practice Leaders and project leaders since our clients have been similarly impacted and are likely to be in transition in their business operations.

If you have not already done so, please reach our to your PKF Texas friends to share this message and offer your assistance where needed. **We will continue to update you via email and the 877.753.4855 number periodically.**

Kenneth

.06 Losing a Key Client: Another Type of Disaster

Natural and IT disasters aren't the only crises a firm can face. What happens if a key client is acquired, leaves for a competitor, or goes out of business? Such transitions have such a negative effect on your firm's bottom line that it can be deemed a disaster. The most obvious ways to avoid this particular disaster are simple: (1) don't rely too heavily on a small number of highly profitable clients who represent a disproportionate percentage of your firm's income and (2) nurture your top clients as though your business depended on them. Develop systems for contacting these clients regularly and scheduling off-the-clock meetings to listen to their issues and show your concern for their success. Clients will be less inclined to leave if they feel they are getting value added services.

¶ 235 Firm Management Models Are Morphing

We already mentioned that some roles, such as firm administration, human resources, and marketing, have become strategic. The concept of strategic planning and strategic initiatives extends to the managing partner as well. In many firms of all sizes, the managing partner has taken on a role comparable to that of a Chief Executive Officer (CEO) or company president in private industry. This model was considered heresy a few short years ago. Now, adopting some form of this model may be a key element of a firm's survival.

Chapter 3
Your Firm Into Infinity?

¶ 301 Control Your Future

Now, more than ever, your firm's future depends on having a comprehensive strategy for growth. Arguably, a reliable staffing model with minimal disruptions should be the linchpin of the plan since the historical succession model, wherein one generation of partners buys out the next, is broken. Basic demographics, along with the value systems of Gen X and Gen Y professionals, combine to make it obsolete. The numbers game doesn't work when the number of people retiring or otherwise leaving the profession is greater than the number entering it.

The American Institute of Certified Public Accountants (AICPA) predicts that in the next 15 years, 75 percent (247,500) of its 330,000 existing members will be approaching retirement age. So, if you want your firm to survive over the long term, you need to be sure your future leaders are identified and nurtured. Firms that formulate and implement strong succession and growth strategies are likely to have unprecedented opportunities.

Even firms that decide they want to be merger candidates need to take steps to insure their viability. The number of firms that may opt (or be forced) to follow this course will find the value of their firms reduced. As succession issues heat up, there will be more sellers than buyers, which means that buyers can be very choosy about their criteria for purchasing a firm and the price they're willing to pay. In addition, the resources required to run and grow a firm have become so vast that the capitalization demands can be prohibitive.

¶ 305 The Changing Management Paradigm

Power in this business traditionally has little relationship to leadership ability. Historically, a firm's managing partner has either the biggest ownership stake or the biggest book of business. He or she sits at the top and rules the fiefdom in the valley below.

That model no longer works for the same reasons that Mom & Pop convenience stores have such a tough time competing in a 7-Eleven world: there are too many complex variables in modern business, and the ability to thrive requires skills that aren't necessarily related to ownership shares or the ability to win or service accounts.

Many firms now grasp the realities that come with additional size, including larger staff, more complex client demands, technological changes and advances, and the other factors that complicate operation of a modern practice. The skill set required to lead a professional services firm today is completely different from those required five years ago.

These firms either are turning to professional CEOs and COOs with corporate backgrounds and relatively little experience working in CPA firms or transitioning their managing partners to exclusively executive roles with no billable hours. They often use consultants to formulate and implement the strategic initiatives inherent in these changes. They also use them to help partners adapt to the changes in the way the firm is being managed, which may include changes in the way partners are compensated. Using an outside party to help with these very sensitive matters can be beneficial. People—even partners—are much more likely to share their true feelings, both positive and negative, when they feel there is a buffer between them and the source of their discomfort. The process of communicating the changes to the firm is critical to the success of the transition. This is true for partners, who may be giving up some of their perceived "power," as well as for the entire staff.

The change in the managing partner's focus from managing a book of business to overseeing the firm's strategic direction is a seismic shift. Instead of the "do this because I said so" model firms are accustomed to, future leaders need to embrace the empowerment of others, the delegation of responsibility, and the openness to find creative—and perhaps even groundbreaking—solutions to thorny problems. This is a different leadership philosophy, and it requires a different set of skills.

Figure 3.1

Case Study: Business Succession

Kahn, Litwin, Renza & Co., Ltd./Providence, R.I.

There has been plenty of talk about business succession. And rightly so, the leaders of many firms are approaching retirement. The statistics have been well-reported, but the practicalities of developing a workable succession plan have received a lot less attention. Kahn, Litwin, Renza & Co., Ltd. (KLR) has put a workable succession plan in place. The firm has three offices, 10 shareholders, 15 principals, and 160 employees. Twelve of the firm's 25 firm leaders, four are likely to consider retiring from their current roles over the next five to seven years.

That puts the firm in the same position as many others, with one very important difference: Co-Managing Partner Larry Kahn started thinking about the problem of succession soon after the firm was formed.

Over the past 10 years, the firm completed five mergers, and, as of January 1, 2009, accomplished its goal of moving into the Boston market. KLR takes its mergers very seriously. The firm believes it is easier to have a culture evolve than to make drastic changes. Consequently, the firm's merger integration process takes a long time, generally 18 to 24 months, and involves a lot of hands-on teaching and mentoring. Achieving a one-culture firm takes effort. It can be a tough balancing act, but the firm has become good at it.

Although the firm has retained clients through generational changes in leadership, nothing is a given. Today's clients are looking for the firm that can best serve their needs a global economy with specific and detailed tax and accounting regulations. Firms need to be able to provide higher level work, which, unlike lower-level tax and accounting work, is not being commoditized.

KLR sees itself as having a strong presence in the marketplace for the foreseeable future.

Nurturing Future Leaders

The firm has a multi-faceted approach to identifying and nurturing its future leaders. For example:

- It holds monthly senior management meetings, at which leaders discuss the firm's goals. They believe everyone needs to be continually educated about what KLR is doing because so much is going on. Part of the discussion centers on the firm's sales pipeline. The meetings are viewed as a way to gain the strategic involvement of the shareholders and principals.

- Two years ago, KLR hired a consultant to come on a bimonthly basis to meet with six to eight people and coach them in what it takes to be a leader in today's accounting firm. Those involved have found the program has enhanced their skills.

- To provide incentives for younger shareholders, there is a cap on the goodwill portion of the older shareholders' buyouts. This levels the playing field somewhat for the newer and younger shareholders. It also allows them to see that the firm's capital will not disappear when shareholders retire.

- The firm continues to work on the curriculum at its internal learning center, KLR University, which is geared toward developing employees at all levels. Its courses provide technical training and CPE, as well as leadership training and soft skills, developments. Experts are invited to teach specific courses; the expense of outside experts is simply a part of the budget, and the benefit to the employees is immeasurable.

The firm also advocates plans and programs that are important to younger workers. Benefits that were not on the radar screen of CPA firms a few years ago, such as flextime, are routine. Also, the firm's community service program is attractive to younger staff.

Schedule for Retiring Partners

KLR's partnership agreement allows shareholders to retire at any time between the ages of 55 and 65, as long as they give two years notice. Once they give up their stock, these shareholders are welcome to continue at the firm at the pleasure of the firm's leadership as long as they add value to the firm. The two-year window allows the shareholder to implement his or her plan for transitioning clients to younger professionals.

The firm has noticed that this transition can be multi-layered. For instance, many physician practices are led by doctors who also are approaching retirement. This may complicate the transition process because younger professionals must impress both the outgoing doctor and the incoming physician practice leader. It is not the kind of straight switch the firm generally sees in, say, an automobile dealership or a manufacturing business. This is where the firm's investment in educating and mentoring younger staff in soft skills pays off. The concepts of relationship-building and discerning what the client really needs, wants, or is concerned about have been ingrained in young leaders at the firm. The transition period is the time for them to live the lessons they have learned.

When shareholders retire, they are paid out over a 10-year period using this fomula: [100% of firm revenue X percent ownership in company]+ [tangible net worth of company (i.e., receivables and WIP) X percent of ownership].

Figure 3.2 ——

Case Study: A Retired CEO's Reflections on Being a CPA Firm Owner—A Right or a Privilege?/Tim Michel

As I was preparing for my final shareholders meeting during the last few days of my tenure as CEO and Shareholder of Rea Associates, Inc., I found myself reflecting on how important it was to me to have been an owner in our firm. It was a position I held for nearly 30 of my 35 years with the firm.

Upon graduating from college in 1974, I had the good fortune of being hired by a small multi-office firm in Ohio that believed in growth and good management. The firm's founder and managing partner was a practice management guru. Richard C. Rea was also editor of the Practitioners' Forum section of *The Journal of Accountancy* and had developed a well-known workshop titled, "Founding and Maintaining an Accounting Practice." He told me that if I worked hard and did the things that would help grow the firm, I could make a place for myself and become an owner. I bought into what he said and tried to practice what he preached.

The firm grew rapidly and, sure enough, after four years I was promoted to "resident partner," the first of three levels of ownership we had at the time. It was about then that I was talking with a CPA who had just made partner with the national firm he worked for. He told me that making partner at his firm was like getting to heaven and finding out there is no God. He was probably being facetious, but I knew I was much happier with my situation than he was of his.

During my career, I had the opportunity to manage engagement teams, small and large practice offices, serve on the firm's management committee and eventually to serve as the firm's CEO/president, a position I held for my last 10 years with the firm. Being an owner was one of the most meaningful opportunities in my life. Each time I said, "I am a partner in our firm," internally I was beaming with pride. And to be able to introduce a member of our firm as a fellow partner was, in my mind, second only to saying he or she was a family member. I tried to never take it for granted.

So, as I was preparing for this final shareholders meeting, I found myself thinking about how to tell my fellow shareholders how important being an owner in the firm had been to me, and perhaps more importantly, how each of us needs to continue to earn that title every day.

Generally, people are promoted to an ownership position because they have achieved a certain level of performance and demonstrated their unique value to the firm. But, I wondered, once a person earns his or her ticket to the dance, should that person be an owner for the balance of his or her career? That is, once obtained, is the position a right or a privilege?

Being an owner carries many responsibilities. Mostly, it means thinking like an owner. By my definition, an owner is an ambassador for the firm requiring honesty and integrity at all times and setting a high standard of performance and behavior for other members of the firm to witness and emulate. A CPA firm owner is a person of influence at the firm, at home, and in the community. The firm's interests must supersede his or her self-interests. As a steward of the firm, an owner is obligated to safeguard its assets and take care of the goose that lays the golden eggs. Among other things, this means nurturing the firm's most important assets—its people—by delegating tasks and responsibilities that challenge staff and help them grow while focusing their own efforts on activities that bring value to the firm. Another responsibility of ownership is training and coaching other firm members to excel so as to raise up future leaders. It is much more than a job: it is an integral part of one's very being. Our shareholder group often discussed the importance of performing at a high level. We believe that the whole is equal to, and possibly can exceed, the sum of its parts. Therefore, the strength and success of a CPA firm is determined by the collective strength and success of the owner group. For a few moments, think how the performance of professional football players determines the success of the team. What is the effect on the team when:

- The offensive lineman misses the block or moves before the ball is snapped?
- The quarterback holds onto the ball too long and gets sacked?
- The flashy wide receiver continually drops pass after pass?
- The linebacker misses making the tackle?
- The defensive lineman roughs the quarterback?

The team suffers. And if it happens often enough, the player is cut or traded from the team. So is playing professional football a right or a privilege?

Now, think about a professional accounting firm. What happens to the success of the firm when an owner:

- Takes on low realization work?
- Lets a client's accounts receivable get out of control?
- Doesn't manage their responsibilities well?

- Sets a bad example in the office with a poor attitude or inappropriate actions?
- Doesn't respond timely to the needs of the staff?
- Doesn't bring new business to the firm?
- Just doesn't seem to bring value to the firm or perform at the owner level?

The firm suffers. What if it happens too often?

Well, performing and highly successful firms deal with under-performing owners by holding them accountable, providing feedback, coaching, and counseling. In the end, however, it is up to the owner to see that they earn their ticket to the dance every day. After all, being an owner is a great honor and a great privilege.

Source: Timothy I. Michel, CPA/Michel Consulting Group LLC, New Philadelphia, Ohio

¶ 310 The FACE Principle

Managing a firm in this climate of chaos can be overwhelming, exasperating, frustrating, and depressing for seasoned veterans who wake up every day to a work environment they don't understand on a visceral level. That's a lot of negative feeling to negotiate on a daily basis while trying to grasp a new management style and a higher level of competition.

The worst thing a firm can do is stand still and allow the negativity to overtake the firm. In business, as in other areas of life, change is the only constant—and all change, whether positive or negative, is difficult. Things never will go back to the old comfortable ways, and moving forward is the only path to success. Only firms that embrace that truth can make thoughtful change a positive part of their overall strategy will be able to survive over the long term.

We believe in a management philosophy that embodies this fact and provides the foundation for living it. Instead of wishing things were the same as they used to be—a futile wish—a more productive way to lead your firm into the future is to adopt the FACE principle:

- *Flexibility*
- *Adaptability*
- *Communication*
- *Experience*

.01 Flexibility and Adaptability

Flexibility and adaptability are closely related. Both need to be core values of every firm's culture. That may sound trite. You may be wondering how flexibility and adaptability can be part of a viable strategy. Perhaps that depends on your definition, as shown in the following examples:

Example 1: You've had a successful real estate niche for years. You even started a cost segregation practice to enhance your service offerings to your clients. Real estate generated 20 percent of your firm's net revenue. Then the mortgage crisis happened and business wasn't as good as it had been. What do you do? A flexible strategy would allow you to adapt by looking at other options, such as developing debt restructuring strategies, that allow you to leverage your existing contacts and service your clients' needs.

Example 2: Your firm is located in an area that is 100 miles from the nearest sizeable city, which makes hiring experienced professionals more difficult. You are creative, though, and were able to attract a number of women accountants to your firm. How did you do it? You offered the options of flextime or telecommuting. These options, which are antithetical to the standard CPA firm model that requires a hands-on supervisor, allow your firm to flourish in its market.

Example 3: Gen Xers and Gen Yers value philanthropy. So, historically, does your firm. You always donate to the local community, and your new hires should recognize that. They don't though. You brainstorm with your partners, human resources director, and marketing director and come up with a solution: in addition to your usual donation, you will encourage staff to volunteer at a local soup kitchen on Sunday mornings. The team effort results in a boost in firm morale.

Flexibility and adaptability are primary survival skills. Implementing a set strategy is simply more difficult in a global business environment populated by a high-value, skilled work force that's wired, mobile, and more committed to their own goals than to your firm's future. Secondary and tertiary plans become more important, because the unexpected is to be expected.

.02 Communication

Open communication channels are critical in this instant message world. Forward-thinking firms operate in a team environment rather than the old silo model, where one held on to his or her Rolodex as though it contained the code to the universe. Today, shared databases are the norm, computerized processes are in place for monitoring WIP, teams use instant messaging to communicate with each other, and the Internet provides immediate access to world events happening outside of the firm.

Firm leaders need to know what's going on throughout the firm. To be effective, part of the leader's job is to keep all the cogs greased through effective communication on all fronts: partner to partner, partner to professional and administrative staff, leader to leader, and so on. Each of these communication channels must be considered in terms of goals, security, and what needs to be told to each level of staff and when.

.03 Experience

Experience remains one of your most precious assets, and one that compounds in value. While today's leaders may feel like dinosaurs unable to evolve at the lightning speed of the changes around us, the fact is that experience is one of the most indispensable weapons in your arsenal of management tools. In today's business environment, plans and strategies serve more as a guiding light rather than a road map.

Your experience is most valuable when you have to detour from your plan and as you make contingencies for detours in future plans. Implementation of a plan is no longer a straight road from Point A to Point B, but rather, it's predictably zigzagged in today's business climate, where more fires ignite along the way and have to be extinguished.

Adopting FACE as a key part of your firm's strategy, getting all of the partners to buy into it even though it goes against their long-standing management styles, and developing plans and programs that educate firm employees and getting them to believe that you believe in this new management model can be a daunting task. But taking the first step and recognizing that the world of CPA firms has changed irrevocably is the most important thing you can do to secure your firm's future.

No matter how the management model for CPA firms has changed or may evolve going forward, the firm's leadership remains responsible for making the right decisions that will guide the firm to profitability. There is no logical reason for our profession's leaders to fail to properly read and adapt to the change in our world.

Figure 3.3

Five Helpful Hints That Can Make a Difference

1. *Hiring new college graduates don't always pay off.* New college graduates generally don't begin to pay off until they have a few years of experience under their belts. In fact, they are encouraged to try several, if not many, job experiences early in their careers. Many times, you hire and train them, and then they leave. It may be better to be their second or third employer. An experienced hire is more likely to stay long term and will contribute more to your practice.

2. *Hold an annual firmwide retreat.* Retreats provide time for social and professional interaction for your staff and help your valued professionals develop relationships that they'll invest in and that can, in the long run, help keep them invested in your firm. It will also reinforce the firm's culture. Make the event fun and informative. And be sure to feature a "State of the Firm" address that updates everybody on how the firm is doing and the vision for what lies ahead.

3. *Don't mix reviews and raises.* It's a big mistake to combine annual performance reviews with compensation adjustments, because your employees will not focus on the review. The compensation adjustment will grab their attention rather than the assessment of their performance.

4. *Empower your people—but have a system of checks and balances in place.* A feeling of empowerment is a key element employees look for in their employer. Yet, to paraphrase Harry Truman, "the buck stops with you." Be sure you have a system in place that monitors what your staff is allowed to do or say. Some examples of situations where this is critical include limiting who may speak to the press on the firm's behalf, having a strict approval process in place for what may be posted on the firm's Web site and providing soft skills training for staff that interact with clients or visits their facilities.

5. *Don't let your firm become arrogant or complacent.* These principles should be ingrained in your firm's culture. Park your ego at the door and be open to suggestions about how your firm could be better, more efficient, and more profitable. There are many firm leaders now who have mentors in the older (or peer) generation as well as the younger one. Each sees things differently, and each viewpoint has value.

Figure 3.4

Positive Firm Culture Is Even More Important in Tough Economic Times

A combination of widespread layoffs and high levels of job stress is causing many workers to experience what is being called post-downsizing stress syndrome as they adjust to a new organizational culture and management style. In *The Economist,* Barry Shore, professor of decision sciences at the University of New Hampshire's Whittemore School of Business and Economics elaborates on the new culture:

> "It is a culture that shifts the focus from motivation and collaboration to delegation and compliance. It is also a culture that expects those who remain to take over responsibility for the work done by those who have left.

Certainly, those who still hold their jobs feel grateful for being spared, but many also feel threatened, abandoned, burdened with more work, and subject to overall greater job stress."

This stress differs from traditional job stress because it generally results from deteriorating business conditions that are beyond the immediate control of management. Employees become obsessed with their plight—it dominates informal discussions in the organization, and, as a result, employees turn their focus inward and worry about job security rather than focusing outward on job performance. According to Shore, employers can help by doing the following:

- Lead with humility and professional will. A command-and-control environment can work in the short run, but over the long term, it stifles individual initiative, commitment, and contribution.

- Communicate frequently, sending a strong message that a firm cares about the plight of its workers.

  — Acknowledge the insecurities and fears of the work force. Bring current concerns into the open, talk about them with employees, and acknowledge their concerns.

  — Hold meetings to discuss the problems faced by the firm. Ask employees what is on their mind. Start a blog. Create a new page in your newsletter devoted to the issues the company faces during the recession.

- Share the complexities of management decisions. Help employees understand the tradeoff between survival and job cuts. Ask for their suggestions; employees can offer useful responses during the economic downturn.

- Develop a questionnaire to study employee morale. Before taking steps to improve morale, management should understand current attitudes toward the company, management, and the job.

- Encourage collaboration. Schedule team-building workshops and invite groups to plan their own workplace strategies that may include setting their own budgets and timetables.

- Improve trust. Trust is one of the most important human resource assets, but it is often undermined by cut jobs and a command-and-control culture. Management must do what it can to maintain trust. Trust starts with honesty, even when it means warning employees that bad news may be coming. Trust also requires fairness, even when it means explaining what criterion was used to furlough workers, and even when this explanation leads to significant criticism from employees. Finally, trust is doing one's best to keep promises, even when these promises are tough to keep.

- Recognize contributions. Celebrate accomplishments. Everyone likes to be appreciated, but few take the time to show appreciation.

- Start new projects. Understandably, some projects were delayed as the economic crisis forced the organization to circle the wagons. But that doesn't mean there should be a moratorium on new projects. Initiate studies of the competitive market environment. What opportunities now exist because competitors have left the market? How have customer needs changed in response to the expectation that this slowdown will be prolonged? The answers to these and other questions may suggest new products, services, and projects. It's important to keep in mind that people are energized by new ideas and fresh starts.

- Involve the work force in developing new ways to improve old products and processes. The economic crisis provides an opportunity to change processes that have resisted change for many years. Involve employees to make the change effective and to help build morale.

Source: Newswise

¶ 315   Empowering Others Is Powerful

One of the core skills to success today is the ability to empower others by delegating decision-making and responsibility effectively. Here's a fairly typical scenario and how it would be handled under the traditional business model and the strategic model:

> **_Traditional firm model:_** You ask a veteran principal to head up a practice group, but he has a busy family life. He believes the extra hours will be impossible for him and reluctantly turns down the offer. When someone else takes the job, he becomes resentful, and conflicts arise on a regular basis. Finally, you move him to a different practice area. He doesn't have as much experience in that area, though, so he continues to receive the pay of a principal but performs the job function of a lower-level employee. Eventually, he gives his notice and goes to work elsewhere.

Overall, it's been a bad situation, but it's no better when he leaves. How do you replace him? How do you handle his clients? How do you address the bad feelings that have arisen throughout the firm as the result of the situation? These situations are now the rule rather than exception and contribute to the chaos.

Strategic firm model: You talk to the principal in detail about his concerns, which you address by coming up with productive solutions. In the case of this principal, perhaps you allow him to telecommute. This gives him the flexibility to fulfill his new role as practice leader while still meeting his family obligations.

By coming up with a creative plan, you've accomplished two important goals: hired the best person for the job and reinforced the principal's loyalty to the firm. (You've also opened another Pandora's Box, because there is no doubt that other employees will want the same treatment. But what's wrong with that if, at the end of the day, the work gets done with the same level quality and client service you've always demanded?)

The No. 1 reason firms have this kind of problem in the first place is because they haven't created a firm culture that empowers people to create job enrichment and self-actualization. It is, in fact, a part of the new firm paradigm, which responds to the new cultural influences of Gen X and Gen Y by striving to be much more employee-centric than former firm structures.

¶ 320 Leadership Must Delegate

The ability to delegate to others effectively is one of the key skills for managing a professional services firm in the 21st Century—not only to lighten the load of the firm's executives, but also because professionals today won't work in an environment where they do not feel job-enriched and challenged by new skills. To them, the ideal job is one in which they are involved in the assignment from beginning to end and over which they have as much decision-making control as possible, with immediate and direct feedback from both supervisors and clients.

In some firms that follow the traditional firm model, staff members aren't even allowed to meet and speak with clients until they become managers. Such environments generate a revolving door culture. Instead of reducing chaos, they foster it. In order to survive and flourish, the firm's culture must allow capable staff to make decisions, handle increasingly difficult work assignments, and have relationships with clients long before the historic norms.

This is a huge leap for veteran leaders who are accustomed to having ultimate control at their firms. It is a skill that needs to be learned, and the learning process can be painful.

There are four primary ingredients to empowering people:

1. *Training and education.* Be sure you have top-notch training programs in place for both technical skills and soft skills (e.g., marketing) to create a continuous learning environment. If you cannot handle this in-house, hire consultants who have the requisite expertise. Don't be afraid to establish a training budget; whatever you spend will come back in increased business and employee job satisfaction. In some larger firms, there is a trend toward hiring a director of training who is responsible for keeping track of all training activities and requirements. Hiring a training director may be impractical for smaller firms, but the lesson is there: training is an increasingly important factor in retaining talented staff.

2. *Trust.* Trust your instincts. Once you are reasonably confident a staff member has had enough training to handle a particular task, let them try. Don't only look at the length of time they've been in the profession or with the firm. Send them out with a supervisor the first few times to test their readiness. You may have identified a rising star who will evolve into a firm leader.

3. *Allow for mistakes.* Keep in mind that you were once a new employee at your firm, and when you were, you probably made your share of mistakes. Making mistakes is an important part of the learning process. Treat them as learning experiences rather then catastrophes or proof that the old system works better. Chances are that if you have a good training program in place, the errors will not be serious ones. Deal with them and move on.

4. *Run interference with others who think individuals should not be empowered.* Even if you, as managing partner, think empowering others is a good idea, other leaders at your firm may be harder to convince. Empowering others is a change in the fundamental culture of the firm. Just as employees must be trained before they can be empowered, the firm's leadership must be taught the value of endorsing the new firm policy. The truth is this strategy is less likely to succeed if it doesn't filter through the firm from the top down.

Figure 3.5

Case Study: Core Values: Know What You Stand For
Sobel & Co., LLC/Livingston, N.J.

According to Alan Sobel, managing member of the 15-member firm, Living core values means embracing a series of valued characteristics and finding ways to exemplify these in everything. The firm took that idea to the next level when we created the acronym "ENCOURAGE" to assist in identifying what we are committed to as a firm:

E thical and trustworthy behavior

N o compromise on quality

C are about your people

O utstanding client service

U nderstand diversity

R each for responsibility

A llow yourself to be passionate about your career

G rowth and learning

E ncourage each other to fulfill these core values

The firm's leadership team spends a significant amount of time finding ways to incorporate the firm's values into its culture so that they become a daily routine. The firm's core values are a part of its mission statement as well as its development and evaluation process.

Tri-annually, the staff is asked to nominate fellow colleagues for the firm's "True Professional Award." This employee recognition opportunity asks fellow workers to identify instances of work behavior that go above and beyond the call of duty, whether in client service, helping a fellow colleague, service to the community, or personal achievement. Nominators are asked to link the events that led to the nomination of the core values. Sobel selects each "True Professional" winner reads every nomination out loud at a staff meeting.

When the branding of ENCOURAGE was launched, the firm held a design-a-logo contest. Many staff participated with submissions and everyone got to vote on the submission they wanted to represent the firm's values. The winner was an apple core.

By singling out special initiatives, daily, weekly, monthly, quarterly, and annually, the firm integrates its values into everything it does. No one said this would be easy. There are far simpler ways to manage a CPA firm than spending one's time watching for prime examples in the firm's daily behavior just to illustrate how important it is to uphold core values. There may be a simpler way, but Sobel is not convinced there is any better way to help the firm stick to its core values.

¶ 325 The X and Y Factor: Find the Sweet Spot

There is no getting around the fact that every day firms come closer to being controlled by the values and demands of the next generations of professionals—Gen X and Gen Y. We've said it before, but if you're a Baby Boomer or a Traditionalist in executive management at a CPA firm, you are looking at a radical change in how the work place is viewed.

Members of Gen X and Gen Y perceive risks and rewards differently than Baby Boomers do. Their time is currency to them, and they're not willing to let you control it in exchange for a paycheck. Personal time is one of their core values, and they expect more return on the time they do invest at work than the generations before them did. Their loyalty is to people, not companies, and their decisions to leave an employer are based solely on what's best for them.

You can't blame them for this. They spent their childhood in a world where, in the words of one senior, "companies were willing to lay off our parents with little regard for the impact dad's or mom's job loss had on our family, so if a better opportunity comes along for me, I won't worry about the impact it has on my employer. If the tables were turned, they'd do the same to me."

It's as if they have a pre-programmed chip in their brain that's morphed the old do unto others adage into a new one: "do unto others" *before* they do unto you. In addition, they've learned to boldly ask for what they want.

We know of one large regional firm where a group of three- and four-year partners united, almost like a labor union, to tell management how much their raises had to be if the firm wanted them to stay. The firm was in no position to negotiate: it gave them the raise they demanded. Each of those partners could have a new job within hours, but it would take the firm months to replace them, wreaking havoc on schedules, workload management, client relations, staff morale, and recruiting budgets. According to the managing partner, "We did what we had to do, but it really drove home the question of how loyal our employee base really is." (This type of attitude may have changed somewhat due to the economy—but that doesn't mean you can forget about generational difference.)

This audaciousness is astounding to parental model-oriented Baby Boomers. It's no wonder they feel they are dealing with a group of aliens. Nevertheless, firms that don't adapt will not be able to survive.

When you find professionals who are stable and have the values you cherish in an employee, it is critical that you get into their psyche to find ways to win their commitment to your firm. Where is their sweet spot? Is it greater compensation? Little or no travel? A predictable schedule? A continuous learning environment? Something else? Managing partners must now add "psychologist" to their job description.

As the firm leader, you must step out of your comfort zone to try and accommodate the needs and wants of your staff and give them a reason to stay. It can be a balancing act. Your firm can't offer the above-par compensation, state-of-the-art benefits, and personalized perks that make it an employer of choice without the corresponding level of profitability necessary to pay for the costs of such programs. Nor can you wave a magic wand to develop the new niches and services areas that create the challenging career paths that today's best and brightest young talent demands. You can, however, do things like speed the track to partnership, offer ongoing training in areas that matter to talented team members and their futures, make sure their compensation is above the norm in your area, allow to telecommuting or job sharing, or any of a number of other creative and innovative solutions that fit your firm's profile.

Figure 3.6 ————————————————————————————————————

Annual Compensation Summary

Employee name_____ Year ended_____

Compensation

Salary/wages	_____
Overtime compensation	_____
Bonuses (holiday, merit, finders' fees, etc.)	_____
Total base compensation	$_____

Taxes

Unemployment	_____
Social security	_____
Total taxes	$_____

Insurance

Workers' compensation	_____
Health	_____
Dental	_____
Life	_____
Disability	_____
Other	_____
Total insurance	$_____

Profit sharing/retirement contributions $_____

Education and professional costs

Continuing professional education (CPE) and related costs	_____
Professional membership dues	_____
License renewal fees	_____
CPA examination fees	_____
Tuition reimbursement	_____
Total education and professional costs	$_____
Total compensation for the year Ended [date]	$_____

———

The price of finding and keeping good people at all levels goes deep into the firm's psyche—as well as its pocket. But the financial cost is offset by a low turnover rate. It is estimated that the cost of training a new employee can be tens of thousands of dollars. And that does not even consider the costs of disruption to ongoing projects, the time it takes for teams to forge the bonds needed to make them perform at an optimum level, the unrest other employees might feel as a result of a well-liked employee leaving, or the possibility that the level of dissatisfaction at your firm is so great that others might follow.

Figure 3.7 ——

2008 Annual EDGE Survey Shows Both Employees and Employers Face Challenges in Tough Economy

Key Findings:

- More than half of employers said it is challenging to find skilled professionals today; Generation Y workers are the most difficult to recruit.

- Closely mirroring responses from employers, more than half of workers said it is challenging to find a job today.

- Nearly two-thirds of workers are more likely to try to negotiate a better compensation package today than last year.

- A lack of qualified workers and the higher cost of gas/commuting were among the top factors impacting companies' ability to recruit skilled labor.

- Many employers are likely to offer reduced work schedules, "bridge" jobs, and consulting arrangements as an alternative to retirement.

- The time to fill open positions ranges from four to 14 weeks, with senior-level roles demanding the most time.

- Six in 10 employers estimate at least a quarter of applicants who contact them are not qualified.

While many workers are having a tough time finding suitable employment in today's uncertain economy, companies also face challenges finding highly skilled people. Employees rated the level of challenge in finding a job at 3.56 on a one-to-five sliding scale; similarly, employers rated the level of challenge in finding qualified candidates at 3.47.

The Challenge of Recruiting Qualified Staff

The shortage of qualified workers has grown more acute, with 59 percent of hiring managers citing it as their primary recruiting challenge, up from 52 percent in 2007. Six out of 10 employers estimate that at least a quarter of the applicants who contact them are not qualified. Thirty-one percent report more than half of applicants are not qualified.

Complicating the task of finding qualified talent are spiraling energy costs, hiring managers said. Twenty-nine percent said the rise in fuel prices and commuting expenses has negatively impacted their ability to attract skilled candidates who may want to limit their travel distance to and from the office.

As employers manage through these challenges, recruiting has become time consuming, taking anywhere from four to 14 weeks to fill open positions. More than half of hiring managers (56 percent) said Generation Y employees (those born between 1979 and 1999) are the most difficult to recruit, perhaps because of high expectations around pay, career advancement, flexible schedules, and overall work environment.

The Compensation Question

When they find qualified professionals, firms appear anxious to win them over. Nearly two-thirds (65 percent) of hiring managers said they are willing to negotiate compensation for top candidates; 19 percent are very willing.

Despite not feeling overly confident in job prospects, professionals are increasingly inclined to negotiate better compensation levels as fuel, food, healthcare, and other expenses grow. Sixty-three percent said they are more likely to try to negotiate a better compensation package with a new employer compared to 12 months ago. This contrasts with 58 percent in 2007.

"Businesses are operating on leaner resources and are competing to secure the intellectual capital that will drive productivity and new revenue streams. Companies are also replacing lower-performing employees to strengthen their talent bench to prepare for a time when the economy shifts into higher gear," said Matt Ferguson, CEO of CareerBuilder.com. "Recruiting highly skilled professionals may require a greater financial commitment or special perks that provide a more attractive work environment, however. Nearly three-quarters of employees surveyed said the availability of flexible schedules may cause them to choose one job over another."

Holding on to Top Performers

While employee retention may be less of a concern in a tougher economy, many employers have nonetheless taken measures to prevent good workers from leaving their organizations, including:

- Allowing flexible work schedules - 63%

- Providing funding for additional training/certification -62%

- Increasing salaries - 56%

- Instituting telecommuting options - 29%

Companies also expressed an interest in retaining employees nearing retirement age to manage through the exodus of the baby boomers from the workforce. Forty-seven percent are likely to offer reduced work schedules as an alternative to retirement. Thirty-nine percent are likely to offer "bridge" jobs, while 37 percent are likely to offer consulting arrangements.

Source: 2008 Annual *Employment Dynamics and Growth Expectations (EDGE) Report* by Robert Half International and CareerBuilder.com. The survey includes responses from more than 500 hiring managers and 500 workers, and was conducted from May 7 to June 1, 2008, by International Communications Research in Media, Pa.

¶ 330 Positive Firm Culture Is Essential

There's a lot of talk about "positive firm culture." It is another theme that indicates a firm that is headed for success.

Firm culture is easy to define, but the words tend to sound like platitudes. A good firm culture might be defined as one that reinforces the firm's integrity, honesty, ethics, trustworthiness, and compassion. Every firm uses these adjectives (just read their brochures). They "live" these ideals when they deal with paying clients, but it just isn't the same when it comes to the firm's internal clients—their employees. Firm leaders need to rethink their priorities in this area and begin to treat their employees as they treat their best external clients. The truth is that a firm's employees are their greatest assets.

Whether you call it firm culture, something else, or don't give it a name, your firm does have a culture. It comes from the managing partner and works its way through the ranks. Here are some examples:

Example 1: Partner A is the managing partner of a 100-person firm. He comes in early every morning and is the last one to leave at night. When he comes in, he nods to anyone who might be in the hallways, continues to his office, and closes the door. Anyone who needs to see him must make an appointment with his secretary. If he leaves his desk to go out to lunch, he eats with referral sources. When he is obligated to attend a charity event on behalf of the firm, he takes the partners with whom he's worked the longest.

Example 2: Partner B also manages a 100-person firm, but his style is completely different. B also comes in early, but usually isn't the last one out the door. He knows the names of virtually everyone at the firm. At the very least, he knows their faces and the job they do. He greets people freely and asks them about their work and if they are satisfied. He frequently takes managers to lunch, sometimes with a senior. Partners attend charity functions with others on their team.

Each of these partners is living his firm's culture. Think about it: which firm would you rather be at?

If the managing partner does not believe in the firm's core values, the message will filter down to everyone at the firm. Although it would be hard for Partner A to change the culture at his firm, it can be done, as long as he believes that the change is needed and is committed to taking the necessary steps to make them happen.

There are many ways to reinforce a positive culture, including:

- formulating a mission statement that summarizes the firm's core values.
- clearly and consistently communicating the values throughout the firm.
- publicly recognizing employees who demonstrate the stated values.
- asking employees to nominate their colleagues for such recognition.
- including them as a component of performance evaluations, including partner evaluations.

For Partner A, the change process should be viewed as a strategic initiative. (This is another instance where getting input from an experienced consultant might be helpful.) He also needs to remember that the changes will not happen overnight. He will need to work hard, day after day, to get people to believe that the changes are real. If he does this, then, over time, he will get buy-in and begin to see incremental changes toward a positive firm culture.

Figure 3.8 ———

Employee Loyalty

According to a 2008 CareerBuilder survey of 2,500 HR professionals and 7,000 employees nationwide, one in four workers doesn't feel loyal to their current employer:

61%—Don't feel my employer values me

52%—My efforts are not recognized or appreciated

51%—Employer doesn't pay enough

44%—Not enough career advancement opportunities

33%—Don't like the work culture

32%—Benefits are not good enough

23%—Don't like my boss

21%—Employer doesn't provide enough ongoing training or education

19%—Work is not challenging enough

.01 Creating a Continuous Learning Culture

Learning is a powerful motivator, and fostering it should be a part of a firm's culture. Creating a continuous learning culture is essential to empowering others and teaching them how to be empowered.

Unlike corporate America, the professional services environment has historically viewed continuing professional education as a regulatory requirement rather than as a tool to aid in their long-term growth and profitability. But the firms that have taken the giant step of creating a learning culture have shown phenomenal success getting people to work for them.

Don't discount the idea of allotting a certain amount of the training budget to seemingly unrelated courses. Allowing someone to study Mandarin Chinese might lead to a lucrative niche for the firm; teaching someone to dress better can enhance the firm's image; paying for a yoga course can increase health-consciousness.

Figure 3.9

Case Study: M&K University

As accounting firm Marcum & Kliegman of New York snowballed in growth and its work force topped 200 employees, its leaders realized that an environment of continuous learning opportunities was becoming increasingly important to attracting and retaining top talent. Historically, the firm offered training through procedural manuals and courses given by outside providers. Department heads often organized technical training sessions for their respective staffs that were led by a department supervisor or manager.

The firm's leaders recognized a need to formalize programs that would keep staff invested at the firm and help them visualize long-term career paths there. "As we've grown, we're able to offer better long-term career opportunities to our staff, and we want them to be aware of those opportunities," says Managing Partner Jeffrey Weiner. "We don't want our people coming in and trying to figure out how to move up the career ladder or even if there *is* a career ladder for them."

The goal of the program was to demonstrate to its non-partner professional staff that the firm offers them long-term career and growth options. M&K University was created in 2003 as an in-house training and continuing education system to support the staff's long-term professional and personal growth.

It fosters an environment for technical and professional growth that helps bond professionals to each other at all levels, from entry-level to partner. The firm recruits approximately 25 new graduates every year, and the continuing education program creates an avenue for them to grow and socialize throughout their work lives.

"The motivation isn't CPE, although professionals earn continuing professional education credit through M&K University," Weiner says. "The goal is to develop a learning culture so that our people see that we want to help them become better personally and professionally, and that we're willing to invest time and money in it."

Like at any university, some courses are required, while others are elective. Core classes are determined by the participant's area of expertise and career track. Technical classes include audit; tax; valuation/litigation support; various niche practice areas, such as hedge funds, investment partnerships, and SEC practices; and technology topics such as Epace and Microsoft Office. The course catalogue also includes training in non-technical skills such as public speaking, business writing, interviewing techniques, and sales. Supervisors, managers, and partners teach most of the courses. M&K University is headed by a partner and administered by the human resources department. Courses conform to regulatory and educational requirements for continuing professional education.

A firmwide intranet site is dedicated to M&K University. Employees can browse available courses on the intranet and sign up for them from their desktop. The intranet access also allows the human resources department to track who is taking which course and record the accumulation of CPE credits and general progress. Participants receive an M&K University sweatshirt upon enrollment.

"Accountants are educated people. They don't go to college for four years and then stop learning technical and soft skills. We wanted to package and organize continuing education for our people in a way that we could integrate a learning environment into our culture, and it really has created a learning culture at our firm," Weiner says.

Although the impact of M&K University on staff retention is difficult to quantify, Weiner believes it's one of many factors that plays a significant role in minimizing professional staff turnover at his firm. "Everything you can do to create an environment that people want to work in can make a difference," he says. Other benefits include greater control over the quality of employee training and improving the cost efficiency of staff training. Participants can use unassigned or non-billable time to take their courses, maximizing the use of their "down time." The use of in-house experts to teach classes right at the firm's offices saves money otherwise spent on course fees and travel for outside instruction. But most significantly, M&K University positions the firm to offer its employees clear career paths and to demonstrate that it offers them a variety of opportunities for professional and intellectual growth.

Figure 3.10

One In Five Employers Use Social Networking Sites to Research Job Candidates

According to a recent survey conducted by Careerbuilder.com, one in five employers use social networking sites to research job candidates. Twenty-two percent of hiring managers said they use social networking sites to research job candidates, up from 11 percent in 2006, according to a nationwide survey of more than 3,100 employers from CareerBuilder.com. An additional nine percent said they don't currently use social networking sites to screen potential employees but plan to start.

Of those hiring managers who have screened job candidates via social networking profiles, one-third (34 percent) reported they found content that caused them to dismiss the candidate from consideration. Top areas for concern among these hiring managers included:

- Candidate posted information about them drinking or using drugs (41 percent);
- Candidate posted provocative or inappropriate photographs or information (40 percent);
- Candidate had poor communication skills (29 percent);
- Candidate bad-mouthed their previous company or fellow employee (28 percent);
- Candidate lied about qualifications (27 percent);
- Candidate used discriminatory remarks related to race, gender, religion, etc. (22 percent);
- Candidate's screen name was unprofessional (22 percent);
- Candidate was linked to criminal behavior (21 percent); and
- Candidate shared confidential information from previous employers (19 percent).

On the other hand, social networking profiles gave some job seekers an edge over the competition. Twenty-four percent of hiring managers who researched job candidates via social networking sites said they found content that helped to solidify their decision to hire the candidate. Top factors that influenced their hiring decision included:

- Candidate's background supported their qualifications for the job (48 percent);
- Candidate had great communication skills (43 percent);
- Candidate was a good fit for the company's culture (40 percent);
- Candidate's site conveyed a professional image (36 percent);
- Candidate had great references posted about them by others (31 percent);
- Candidate showed a wide range of interests (30 percent);
- Candidate received awards and accolades (29 percent); and
- Candidate's profile was creative (24 percent).

"Hiring managers are using the Internet to get a more well-rounded view of job candidates in terms of their skills, accomplishments and overall fit within the company," said Rosemary Haefner, vice president of human resources at CareerBuilder.com. "As a result, more job seekers are taking action to make their social networking profiles employer-friendly. Sixteen percent of workers who have social networking pages said they modified the content on their profile to convey a more professional image to potential employers."

Source: *CareerBuilder.com,* September 2008

¶ 335 Corporate Social Responsibility

Corporate social responsibility is an area that has slowly gained prominence over the past several years, due in part to the emphasis Gen Y places on it. A number of initiatives fall under this umbrella, including green offices, community involvement, and firm ethics. If the headlines are any indication, the ethics and dealings of our clients also matter, as evidenced by the public outcry against awarding bonuses to failing companies. This relates back to your firm's client acceptance and retention policies procedures.

.01 Going Green

It's everywhere, from gurus like author and *New York Times* columnist Thomas Friedman saying environmental industries will rescue the economy to the local supermarket selling reusable bags for groceries, and your firm should be thinking of going green as well. Many, if not most firms, are already paperless (although that is somewhat of a misnomer since there is still plenty of paper around the office). Not nearly as many have instituted formal green policies that include activities such as:

- Recycling newspapers, other print media, bottles, and cans.
- Recycling toner cartridges.
- Banning styrofoam containers.
- Encouraging the use of washable ceramic mugs, plates, and silverware rather than paper and plastic goods.
- Using water coolers rather than bottled water.
- Using environmentally friendly light bulbs.
- Instituting a lights-off policy at the end of the workday.
- Offering clients:
  — Their tax returns in DVD format.
  — Newsletters and other communications in electronic format.

There are instances when some of these policies are impractical, such as when lease terms make replacing overhead lighting the landlord's responsibility or when an office building hasn't contracted with a recycler for pick-up. In those circumstances, you can ask for volunteers to bring recyclables to a facility. The money the firm gets can be donated to a charity.

Figure 3.11

How to Green Your Engagement—Green Team Reminders

Weiser's Green initiative extends past the walls of our four offices. As professionals demonstrating model responsible environmental behavior, we should try to lessen our impact on the environment whenever possible. It is understood that once the firm enters into its busiest time of year, a lot of our green efforts are overlooked in order to save time and get as much work done as possible. As we get busier during the next few months, we should maintain our green practices and let our green ideals trickle down to our clients whether we are in their offices, or our own. Our biggest resource that we are the most wasteful with is paper. With this handbook as your guide, we wanted to bring to light some easy ways to make a big impact by conserving resources when we travel and reducing the amount of paper we use (approximately 17.5 million sheets used in a year) as a firm.

Please take this guide, read it through and save it somewhere on your computer. We hope you take these tips, along with those that you get e-mailed to you weekly, and apply them to your life both at work and at home.

Table of Contents:

Green Manifesto

As a Weiser employee, I will demonstrate model responsible environmental behavior by:

- Recycling more of the waste generated by my daily activities;
- Conserving resources by consuming less;
- Using recycled products in place of non-recycled products;
- Participating in Green events in my community; and
- Applying the tools provided by the Green Team to make environmentally conscious decisions at work and beyond.

.02 Community Involvement

Pro bono work has long been an established practice at law firms. In fact, many firms are assigning pro bono cases to attorneys they would otherwise consider laying off during the current economic downturn. CPA firms don't have the same tradition, but giving back to the community is gaining traction at firms across the country.

Figure 3.12 ——————————————————————————————————————

Corporate Volunteerism—It's Up to Each of Us!

> *"A lot of people are waiting for Martin Luther King or Mahatma Gandhi to come back—but they are gone. We are it. It is up to us. It is up to you."*

—Marian Wright Edelman

These words are the driving force behind a program at Amper, Politziner & Mattia. Called Amper CARES (an acronym for <u>C</u>ommunity <u>A</u>ction <u>R</u>esource), the program encourages and supports the volunteer efforts of the firm's employees in the community.

Though corporate volunteerism isn't new, it may be less than common at accounting firms, where the billable hour is king. But founding partner Alfonse Mattia sees it differently. "Clearly, we do worthwhile work, helping businesses succeed. But it's very important to have a well-rounded life, and that includes giving back to the communities in which we work and live. I had been hearing more and more about the individual volunteer efforts of various employees, and thought it was time the firm played a leadership role in encouraging them and others to get involved."

Amper CARES is designed to be employee-driven, and each of the firm's seven offices have team leaders who coordinate events and recruit volunteers. Amper CARES is purely sweat equity; we don't give money as a firm and no one is required to participate nor rewarded for participating. However, while most of the projects take place after hours or on weekends, Amper gives each employee one full paid day annually to volunteer. The days off are in the line budget.

To promote the firm's efforts and create an identity, a logo was designed and T-shirts and ball caps are distributed to the volunteers.

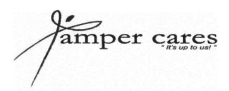

Volunteer programs reflect the varied interests of the firm's 650 employees. The only types of programs Amper CARES doesn't support are religious or political, although a church-sponsored food drive, for example, probably would fall into the permitted category. Each office team leader has the authority to decide. Approximately 85 percent of the firm's employees volunteer for Amper CARES.

Source: Amper Politziner & Mattia, Edison, NJ

.03 Firm Ethics

As trusted advisors to the world's businesses, CPAs have a duty to perform their engagements using the highest ethical standards, standards even more stringent than those mandated by the government and the AICPA. This is an opportunity for firms to provide a level of client service that indicates to clients that their CPA firm will be there for them to guide them through the rough patches as well as the boom times. CPAs have to be living proof that any CPA who violates the honor of the profession is the exception that proves the rule.

¶ 340 Performance Evaluations Count

Feedback on performance is one of the measures employees value. In addition to ongoing feedback at the time a task is performed well (or badly), many firms conduct annual performance evaluations that rely on individual employee performance plans, and some firms are moving toward semi-annual or even quarterly reviews. That approach is very ambitious, and out of the realm of possibility for most. Still, firm leaders should plan for at least one formal review annually.

How performance evaluations are conducted is part of the firm's culture. Software is available from a number of vendors for online surveys that require first the employee and then the employer to perform specific tasks related to evaluating job performance and goal setting. In smaller firms, the managing partner may be responsible for discussing the review with managers and above. That system is simply not possible in larger firms, and the evaluation is delegated to the employee's direct report.

But staff are not the only ones who should be reviewed. Contrary to the traditional firm model, successful firms encourage firmwide reviews for partners, including the managing partner. These reviews generally follow one of these formats:

- Upward evaluations, which provide an opportunity for staff to share their thoughts and feelings on each various leadership criteria as they relate to each individual partner and the firm.
- Peer evaluations, which provide partners with the opportunity to rate each other in terms of their contribution to the firm and their value as a partner.
- 360 degree evaluations, which gather feedback on the leadership skills of a partner from subordinates, peers, and superiors.

In each case, the review is divided into seven broad categories:

1. Relationships
2. Leadership
3. Adaptability
4. Communication
5. Personal development
6. Development of others
7. Productivity

Figure 3.13 ———————————————————————————————

Sample Partner Self-Evaluation Form: Online Format

Partner Performance Form

Name:_____

Period Covered: _____

Rate each item 1-5:

1 -   Needs Significant Improvement
2 -   Below Average
3 -   Average
4 -   Good Performance
5 -   Excels

Practice Efforts:	Development	Rating	Comments
New Clients (see attached)		[Click Here]	[Click to Fill In]
Outside Activities		[Click Here]	[Click to Fill In]
Cross Selling		[Click Here]	[Click to Fill In]

Financial Performance:	Rating	Value	Comments
Managed Book of Business	[Click Here]		[Click to Fill In]
Managing Your Accounts Receivable	[Click Here]		[Click to Fill In]
WIP Charges	[Click Here]	[WIP_CHARGES]	[Click to Fill In]
WIP Write-Offs	[Click Here]	[WRITE_OFFS]	[Click to Fill In]
Billings	[Click Here]	[BILLINGS]	[Click to Fill In]
Realization %	[Click Here]	[REALIZATION]	[Click to Fill In]
Accounts Receivable Write-Offs	[Click Here]	[AR_WRITE_OFFS]	[Click to Fill In]
Bad Debt Occurrences	[Click Here]	[BAD_DEBT]	[Click to Fill In]
Collections	[Click Here]	[COLLECTIONS]	[Click to Fill In]
Collections %	[Click Here]	[COLLECTIONS_]	[Click to Fill In]
Trade Outs	[Click Here]	[TRADE_OUTS]	[Click to Fill In]

Hours:	Rating	Value	Comments
Total	[Click Here]	**[TOTAL_HOURS]**	[Click to Fill In]
Chargeable	[Click Here]	**[CHARGE_HOURS]**	[Click to Fill In]
Budget	[Click Here]	**[BUDGET_HOURS]**	[Click to Fill In]
Utilization Rate (Chargeable/Budgeted Hrs)	[Click Here]	**[UTILIZATION]**	[Click to Fill In]

Management Performance:	Rating	Comments
Staff Training	[Click Here]	[Click to Fill In]
Staff Supervision	[Click Here]	[Click to Fill In]
Mentoring	[Click Here]	[Click to Fill In]
Leadership Qualities	[Click Here]	[Click to Fill In]

Client Performance:	Rating	Comments
Acceptance	[Click Here]	[Click to Fill In]
Lost Clients (low turnover earns the higher rating)	[Click Here]	[Click to Fill In]
Technical Competence	[Click Here]	[Click to Fill In]

Other Performance:	Rating	Comments
Attracting New Employees	[Click Here]	[Click to Fill In]
Adhere to Admin. Requirements	[Click Here]	[Click to Fill In]
Participate in Prof. Associations	[Click Here]	[Click to Fill In]
Firm Technical Leader/Resource	[Click Here]	[Click to Fill In]

List the three items (with explanation, if necessary) that you believe the Compensation Committee should take into consideration evaluating your compensation:
1. [Click to Fill In]
2. [Click to Fill In]
3. [Click to Fill In]

List three goals (with explanation, if necessary) for the coming year that will increase your value to the firm:
1. [Click to Fill In]
2. [Click to Fill In]
3. [Click to Fill In]

If you believe your compensation was unjustified in the prior year, please let us know why and what you believed to be the appropriate compensation:
[Click to Fill In]

Figure 3.14

Sample Upward Evaluation

Name of Partner, Director or Manager: _____

Period covered: _____

Name of Evaluator (optional): _____

Rate each item 1-5 or N/A

1 -Needs significant improvement

2 - Below average

3 - Average

4 - Good performance

5 - Excels

N/A - Not applicable

Organization

    1. Demonstrates ability to plan and organize individual jobs

    2. Clearly explains each assignment

    3. Sets out timeline for completion

    4. Points out potential problems

    5. Understands the technical aspects of the assignment

    6. Shows ongoing interest in how the assignment is proceeding

Comments:

Communication

    1. Is available for discussions

    2. Explains reasons for his/her decisions

    3. Clearly communicates and explains new firm policies and procedures

    4. Solicits feedback

    5. Communicates good business judgment

Comments:

Relationship with Staff

    1. Has a positive attitude about his/her work

    2. Is knowledgeable about technical issues

    3. Willingly shares knowledge with staff

    4. Encourages staff to express opinions

    5. Encourages staff to express ideas

    6. Gives valuable feedback when opinions and ideas are shared

    7. Listens to staff

    8. Proposes resolutions to staff concerns

    9. Motivates staff

    10. Handles any conflicts that arise fairly and impartially

    11. Respects staff

    12. Receives respect from staff

Comments:

Staff Development

    1. Makes an effort to develop staff

    2. Meets individually with staff to set goals

    3. Meets individually with staff to discuss professional development

    4. Provides opportunities for staff to improve skills

    5. Provides constructive criticism

Comments:

Personal Characteristics

    1. Is trustworthy and conscientious

    2. Demonstrates integrity

    3. Demonstrates fairness

    4. Appears professional

    5. Is committed to personal success

6. Is committed to firm's success

7. Is committed to success of direct reports

Comments:

Major strengths:

Areas needing improvement:

Comments:

¶ 345 When the Conversation Becomes Difficult

Inevitably, the day will come when a partner has to hold a difficult conversation regarding another partner's performance. When they do, it is important to hold these talks privately. If possible, the discussion should be scheduled at the end of the day so your partner has time to reflect on your comments before he or she interacts with others at the firm. Be braced for the rumor mill to start if the partner decides to tell others about your talk. Never underestimate the power of the grapevine.

- *Use a soft entry*. As much as you want to get it over with, don't jump in with the negative feedback. It is fine to say that you have to provide feedback that is difficult to share and that the conversation is difficult for you.

- *Don't embellish*. Simply say what you have to and allow the partner to respond. The one thing you don't want to do is pretend to only be the messenger. You're not: you represent the consensus opinion of the firm's leaders.

- *Be straightforward*. Tell the partner you are speaking with him or her because you value him/her and want him/her to succeed. Lay out the parameters the partner needs to meet to enhance his/her career, and tell him/her that doing nothing will have a negative effect.

- *Set a time frame to review progress*. Set up a schedule of meetings to discuss the partner's progress. If it is appropriate, arrange for coaching and training that will help the partner achieve the goals that were set.

Figure 3.15

Case Study: Conflict Management

Most people go to great lengths to avoid conflict, yet conflict is an integral part of all relationships. In a business environment, all firm leaders need to develop a method of dealing with conflict effectively and with as little negative fallout as possible.

As difficult as it may be, confronting the issues as directly as possible is the best course of action. Tom Marino, CEO of J.H. Cohn LLP strongly believes in this philosophy. At his firm, problem partners are invited to his office for a meeting where, as he describes it, he is "candid to blunt" about the situation. Using a direct approach isn't intended to be confrontational; it is geared toward getting to the crux of the problem and, ultimately, creating an atmosphere of trust. Generally, Marino can get to the heart of the matter "within about 30 seconds." By acting immediately and with no equivocation, the partner quickly understands that help is available for the asking. A self-improvement plan is developed, complete with a time frame and other measures of accountability. Coaching and/or counseling are provided as needed. No partner has ever been fired during Marino's tenure, which he credits to the firm's conflict resolution process:

> "I've gotten better at these meetings over time, but they're never easy. I need to prepare for each one, so I have the facts at my fingertips and can cut to the chase with a minimum of politically correct banter. The partner has every opportunity to talk about his or her perspective on the issue. That's a critical part of all this. It's not about getting raked over the coals. It's more like, 'This is what we see. We're behind you; we're a team. We want to know how we can work together to fix the problem.' The first couple of times, partners probably thought the worst, but now we've proven that we live our philosophy.

> "It's been a long time since firms—at least those with a strategic view of the firm of the future—have thought of themselves as anything but an entity that's in business to make money. For a firm's leaders, that sometimes means doing things that you'd rather not do and making hard choices. But it's not about you. It's about the good of the firm."

Figure 3.16

Communication Essential to Leading Workers Through Current Economic Crisis

To maintain employee morale during times of financial crisis, senior leaders can allay employee fears by communicating clearly on topics such as pensions, 401(k) investments, and even job security, according to communication experts at Watson Wyatt.

According to Richard Guinn, senior communication consultant at Watson Wyatt, "the current turmoil in financial markets is obviously a distraction to workers. While companies cannot advise their employees about their investments, they can reassure them about the security of their defined benefit pensions, which are government-backed. Employers can also help their workers understand the implications of their 401(k) investment strategy, including the importance of saving, diversifying portfolios and taking a long-term perspective."

Guinn suggests that senior executives should keep basic communication tenets in mind:

- *Be a leader.* Leaders don't have to have all the answers. Tell employees what you know and what you don't. Explain the steps the organization is taking to identify issues and resolve problems. Knowing senior executives are there to lead through uncertain economic times is crucial to your people.

- *Show your strengths.* Reinforce the core competencies and values that make your organization successful. Talk about how they will help the organization thrive in the future.

- *Be visible.* Credibility, conviction, and passion are important messages that only actual presence can convey. Employees can benefit from seeing engaged and informed senior leaders through Webcasts or other interactive vehicles.

- *Use your team.* Make sure the management team knows how and what to communicate, and that no one is a bystander. Limit potential damage from leaders' informal conversations that are overheard and ripple through every organization.

- *Be coordinated.* Coordinate your internal and external messages. Employees should hear company news from the company first.

- *Share responsibility.* Be clear about what you want your managers and your work force to do. People want to help—tell them how. It's never a bad time to reinforce customer focus.

- *Give up the myth of message control.* Find ways to listen to what is on employees' minds. Monitor the press and social media for what is being said about your firm and your profession. Have a process for quickly developing and distributing answers to rumors, such as possible layoffs, and for clarifying inaccurate statements.

- *Be humane.* Some employees are experiencing personal trauma from falling 401(k) account balances and home prices. Acknowledge their pain and make them aware of the resources at their disposal, such as the company's employee assistance plan.

Source: Watson Wyatt; *www.watsonwyatt.com.*

Chapter 4
Regulation: The Runaway Train

¶ 401 The Post-Enron Firm

The post-Enron world engendered a new universe of regulation that had a colossal effect on the management of accounting firms. The result was chaos filled with paradox:

- Accounting firms became more profitable despite the biggest accounting scandals in U.S. history, the implosion of the largest accounting firm, and the enactment of the most monumental accounting legislation in a century.
- The resulting publicity attracted more (but not enough) young people into university accounting programs, because the accompanying publicity showcased the profession's enormous significance to stock markets, shareholder value, Wall Street, and the business world in general.
- The scandals and subsequent legislation spawned a demand for new specialties and subspecialties of expertise as diverse as those in the medical profession.

In the immediate aftermath, the management teams at Main Street accounting firms faced an eruption of new paradigms for practice management. Historically accustomed to peer-based accountability and regulation, they now were accountable to the regulations of a chain of bureaucracies; accustomed to local markets, they now had access to high-end business opportunities worldwide; accustomed to incremental increases in volume, they faced windfalls of new work; accustomed to broad-based practices, they faced a business world that demands specialization and niche expertise.

The Sarbanes-Oxley Act of 2002 (commonly known as SOX) was enacted in direct response to the Enron scandal and other corporate debacles that occurred at about the same time (think Tyco, Adelphia, and WorldCom). SOX was intended to calm the public's confidence in the nation's securities markets by imposing new checks and balances on how companies report their balance sheets. Although private companies weren't directly affected, many thought the law would eventually reach further and touch them.

There was another little publicized aspect of SOX that viscerally affected how firms across the spectrum operated:—in order to maintain their independence, firms could no longer advocate for their clients in the same way. So, if you know an electrical contractor or plumber who can help your property management clients, that knowledge cannot be shared. This shift has impacted the profession in a subtle but very real way. The relationships at the core of a firm's business have shifted from that of advocate to that of collegial business associate.

Currently, firms are staring at even more far-reaching changes. The Wall Street meltdown that resulted in the demise of Lehman Brothers, the takeover of Merrill Lynch, the federal government's bailout of Freddie Mac, Fannie Mae, and American International Group, Inc. (AIG), and the numerous other bank takeovers and buyouts is almost certain to result in new regulations. While any new regulations most likely will affect publicly traded companies, there surely will be a trickledown effect similar to the one created by SOX.

In addition, the convergence of FASB and the IASB have been systematically working together to remove substantial differences between U.S. GAAP and IFRS. The process, which began in 2002, is expected to be complete in 2014. No one is sure quite how this final convergence will look, but there is no doubt that firms' leaders will have to be prepared for a gigantic educational and training initiative.

Profitability at most CPA firms went way up as the result of SOX. But some of the thorniest problems—most importantly staff shortages and the weakening of the bonds of "partner-for-life"—have been exacerbated. This exacerbation does not bode well for the future of firms that aren't well prepared when the coming volcano of new regulations, and the resulting high demand for audit, tax, and consulting services, occurs.

¶ 405 From Self-Regulation to "Shock and Awe"

The accounting profession has gone through several phases of regulatory focus in recent history. In the 1970s and 1980s, the accounting profession was a self-regulating environment that basically managed and oversaw itself. The AICPA was actively involved, and the profession monitored itself. There were regulatory blips, but they were few and far between. For example, 1972 brought a major regulatory shift in allowing CPAs to market and advertise. In 1986, the accounting profession saw a technical regulatory shift toward tax reform. Since then, tax reform has been a continuous conversation point by Congress. In 1997, the regulatory environment changed to allow the accounting profession to involve itself in commissions and contingency fees through financial services.

But the 1990s and early 2000s brought shock and awe that wasn't limited to military maneuvers or Saddam Hussein. Within seven months, Enron filed for bankruptcy, Arthur Andersen was convicted of obstructing justice (the conviction was later overturned by the Supreme Court of the United States), and Congress enacted SOX. The environment of self-regulation evaporated amazingly fast. In its place, government took a Big Brother role to the accounting profession, and the impact was seismic.

.01 SOX

As a result of SOX, the audit business now is regulated by government agencies such as the SEC, the U.S. Treasury Department, state boards, the U.S. Government Accountability Office (GAO), and the Public Company Accounting Oversight Board (PCAOB). Legislative and international bodies also have their hands in the regulatory pot. Individual disciplines have their own unique standards. Firms with clients in multiple states must deal with regulatory issues in each respective state, which complicates engagements, licensing, and training. In Ohio, for example, the state changed its personal property tax and corporate income tax system to a Commercial Activity Tax (CAT). This is a stand-alone state regulation that is not related to SOX, but every business in the state must implement the CAT tax instead of using the system that's been in place for the last 30 years. The other change that needs to be mentioned is SOX's protection of employees who complain of financial or other specific wrongdoing related to shareholder fraud, and/or mail, wire, or bank fraud. This so-called "whistleblower provision," which is overseen by the Department of Labor, added another layer of complexity to an already complicated regulatory environment.

¶ 410 More to Come

Accounting hasn't seen the end of new laws and regulations. A storm of new legislation and regulation is a probable result of the stories we're reading about in the headlines:

- The mark-to-market rules still are a topic of discussion, and there may be changes.
- New tax legislation is a given as the Obama Administration struggles to correct the economy.
- The scandals surrounding Bernie Madoff's $64 million Ponzi scheme, as well as the other notable Ponzi schemes making the news, are likely to trigger an additional layer of oversight to the SEC and new accounting rules.
- The possibility that the so-called Red-Flag Rules will affect CPA firms. (This seems unlikely as of this writing.)
- The convergence of IFRS and GAAP, which was on a fast track under former SEC Commissioner Christopher Cox, has slowed down considerably under Commissioner Mary Schapiro. Although she supports the objective of a single set of globally accepted accounting standards, she hasn't set an agenda for the shift from a rules-based process to one that is principles-based.

And these are the changes and potential changes on the federal level. State laws are changing as well. New York state provides a notable example. On January 27, 2009, Governor David A. Patterson signed into law a bill that made sweeping changes to the accounting profession in the state. Among other things, the new state law requires out-of-state CPAs whose principal place of business is New York state must be licensed in New York.

While we don't know exactly what the coming changes are or when they will occur, we are sure of one thing: firms that have visionary leaders, that are structured to react to change quickly, and that are well-positioned in the marketplace will come out stronger and healthier than they were before.

Figure 4.1 ——————————————————————————————

The Likely Implications of IFRS/Bob Bunting Chair, Moss Adams LLP International Services Group; President, International Federation of Accounting (IFAC)

One of the first questions most CPAs ask is how IFRS differs from U.S. GAAP. One might think that after several years of convergence between the IASB and the FASB, there would not be many differences left. Certainly the gap is closing, but significant differences still remain.

One way to understand the magnitude of the differences would be to look at the SEC's Form 20-F reconciliations of IFRS to U.S. GAAP filed in 2006 by foreign private issuers. For example, the reconciliation filed by a large foreign publishing company resulted in the movement of net income of 55 million euros under IFRS to a net loss of 199 million euros under U.S. GAAP. The same company saw its shareholders' equity change from 2.2 billion Euros under IFRS to 1.3 billion euros under the U.S. GAAP. Common reconciling items resulting in large potential differences include accounting for business combinations, pensions, taxation, financial instruments, provisions, and contingencies. Other differences commonly occur in impairment, inventories, leases, and capitalization reporting. These are a few of many areas of outright or subtle differences between the standards as they are applied today.

Readers who would like a detailed comparison of the differences in the standards can find high-level side-by-side comparisons on the web sites of the six largest firms.

What Should Firms Do Today to Prepare for Convergence?

Whether your firm is planning for convergence or trying to figure out how to respond to current inquires, the time to begin is now. Here are a few suggestions for getting started:

- *Assign an IFRS leader or team.* In most mid-size firms, the senior auditing or quality control partner should get this task. His or her role is to lead the process of assessing what and how the firm will respond to the IFRS issue.

- *Complete an assessment of needs.* My firm needs dedicated IFRS experts today to serve current and prospective client needs. Smaller firms may not have a need for in-house expertise in the near term but may need to build that expertise over time. The needs assessment should consider the current and future needs of current clients and those you are targeting for future growth.

- *Develop a plan.* The plan should address how short-term needs for expertise and assistance will be met. It should also address how the firm's internal capability will be built up as convergence closes in on us or as more clients demand dual U.S. GAAP and IFRS expertise from their CPAs.

- *Buy, Borrow, or Build.* Most firms in the current environment will have to "buy or borrow" expertise to bridge the gap between their current capability and the knowledge and experience they will need to be self-sufficient in the IFRS world. If activity levels are expected to be modest in the near term, the buy decision may not make sense. If your firm is a member of an international association, you may be able to make arrangements to borrow expertise and experience from one of the European members of your association. Most European auditors now have three years of experience with IFRS. The other borrow alternative is to set up an arrangement with a larger U.S. regional or national firm. Many of us have been helping clients with IFRS reporting for a while and have already built or bought some of the talent we need.

Source: Excerpted from an article in the September 2008 issue of CCH's *CPA Practice Management Forum.*

.01 The AICPA

The AICPA may soon replace its loss of oversight over the public company realm with new authority over standards for financial reporting for private companies. The institute lost the authority to set and regulate audit standards for public companies when SOX was enacted and the SEC took on that authority and created the PCAOB to administer it.

Now, the AICPA is trying to regain its lost power by establishing and regulating standards for privately owned companies. The organization has a lot of support as it tries to re-engineer its power, but it also has plenty of critics. Many believe the institute was blindsided by the quick passage of SOX, and that it served as an impotent and hapless advocate for the accounting profession as Congress wrote, debated, and enacted the most significant accounting legislation since the ratification of the 16th Amendment to the Constitution in 1913. The AICPA's meekness in taking a lead role in writing SOX, combined with other dubious and controversial initiatives in its recent history (such as its drive for the failed "Cognitor" credential, the controversy surrounding its CPA2biz Web portal, the change to the S Corporation year end, and the changes to Code Sec. 7216 and its accompanying regulations), raises doubts among many of its members regarding the organization's competence to lead and act in the best interest of the accounting profession. They believe that the AICPA should take a more forceful and influential leadership role in *reducing* the regulatory demands on accounting firms, not in *adding* to them.

In addition, as the world flattens, international standards come to the forefront. Suddenly clients have international reach and must comply with international guidelines, which are also evolving and snowballing. Accounting firms suddenly find themselves plodding through a regulatory swamp that erupted in the last decade and that shows no signs of draining.

¶ 415 Specialize or Die

One of the most significant results of the new regulatory environment is the increasing obsolescence of the general practice. Historically, accountants could practice in a lot of different areas using multiple and diverse skills, and most of them did. They could also be good at all of them, and most of them were. It was relatively easy to be a generalist.

Now firms are segmented by niches, specialists, and teams. The amount of regulation and body of knowledge required to comply with standards make the viability of a general practice incredibly difficult, because it's almost impossible to attain the level of education and expertise on multiple fronts that's necessary to maintain professional standards of competence and to serve clients adequately. Larger firms are segregated into specialty areas, which are often further divided into sub-specialties. For example, assurance specialists may concentrate on specialized industries such as financial institutions, automobile dealerships, or retail. Taxation, estate planning and succession planning, retirement administration services, business valuation, litigation and litigation support, and payroll are other examples. There's an overwhelming amount of knowledge required in each of these areas to justify the spin-off of multiple sub-specialties ripe for specialization.

General practices still exist in some smaller firms, but even they must be focused. They are forced to concentrate on a smaller amount of territory than they were in past. Perhaps they abandon their audit practices, for example. As a result, clients are shuffled. Because SOX creates up to 20 percent more work without creating the workforce to perform it, firms focus on larger clients who can pay higher fees. Consequently, smaller clients aren't serviced as well or are deliberately transitioned to smaller firms.

Adding fuel to the fire of specialization is the fact that public companies frequently run into obstacles when working with their primary auditors, because SOX limits which services the primary auditor can perform. On top of that, most companies' audit committees became very cautious in the wake of SOX and prohibited the companies from hiring the primary auditor for ancillary services without the committee's prior approval. But audit committees generally don't meet often enough to approve those types of projects on a timely basis. To avoid the need for approval from their audit committees, companies began hiring firms that don't handle their primary audit engagements for jobs like tax planning, Section 404 compliance, valuation, internal audit work, 401(k) audit work, and outside partnerships. Large public companies typically use a national firm for their primary audit, and to avoid conflicts with SOX and their audit committees, they typically turned to large local or regional firms. The bottom line is that SOX and other regulatory issues caused work to be pushed down across the board and drove up demand for expertise.

The regulatory environment also encourages firms to structure engagements so that their staff works in teams rather than as individuals. Typical clients now have multiple service providers: benefits specialists, tax specialists, audit specialists, specialists for LIFO, and specialists for depreciation. Specialists who provide these services to a client usually work for the same firm. When they don't, the firms they work for often have alliances through strategic relationships with other firms, and the work tends to stay within these relationships. These types of relationships evolved both formally and informally as a result of increased regulation. Pre-SOX, such alliances between traditional competitors were rare, but now, they're common. Local and regional firms frequently work with Big Four firms through alliances—a practice virtually unheard of a decade ago. SOX and other regulations set the demand for specialization on fire and continue to fuel it.

.01 Training

This regulatory environment presents stunning training challenges. Like practice areas, training can no longer be targeted to a general practice. Training must be specific and tailored for different levels of experience. At one time, a large firm could bring in one speaker to address everybody, but one speaker won't apply to everybody at a large firm anymore. Now, large firms may need 10 different speakers, which significantly increases the costs of training.

Regulations are being passed on an unreal pace of change in all areas. From a management perspective, the never-ending regulatory upheaval creates a whole new universe of chaos to manage. It also forces professional services firms to question the type of work they're willing to perform, and in many cases, to re-engineer their traditional practice areas as they angle for ancillary work. They must analyze the staffing implications of the work they accept, their ability to service the client effectively, and their ability to staff engagements appropriately. They must ask themselves which clients they'll keep and which clients they'll drop. They must continually assess the skills they deploy to react and think strategically.

The regulatory environment demands strategic management for firms of all sizes. The magnitude of regulation on all fronts makes generalization too overwhelming and too risky. The effect on sole proprietors with general practices has been especially dramatic. Eventually, most such practices are likely to become extinct.

Practitioners must strategically identify what specialties they can focus on, how to acquire the knowledge required, and how to develop expertise. The eruption of new regulation continues at a never-ending pace.

¶ 420 The Threat to Entrepreneurship

In the years leading up to the accounting scandals and the passage of SOX, accounting firms were becoming more and more entrepreneurial. CPAs were uncovering seemingly limitless opportunities to offer broader and expanded services to their clients and prospects. Mortgages, insurance products, employee benefits, telephone systems, electronic payroll systems, and reselling software were just a few of the nontraditional products and services that accounting firms were now offering. Many of these services complemented existing practices and brought profitable work to not-so-profitable firms.

As the scandals erupted, the bubble began to lose air. Federal and state governments entered the regulatory arena, and the bubble deflated even faster. As SOX and GAO changes leave little, if any, room for entrepreneurship in the largest firms, the progressive trickle-down effect to smaller firms is beginning to limit business opportunities to them. The direction and model for accounting firms is changing from an entrepreneurial environment back to the days of heavy compliance. This profound change back to the staid accounting profession raises many questions about what the future holds:

- Is regulation turning the clock back and forcing us to practice in a more traditional model?
- Will the traditional model attract new and much-needed talent to the profession?
- Will accounting firms be able to capitalize on the newfound importance of the audit?
- Has the entrepreneurial spirit become part of our firms' cultures, and if so, how will this spirit manifest itself in our future?

Professional services firms are at a crossroads regarding their future business models and their focus. Practitioners must make decisions today that will direct their firms in the years to come. The 1990s were a time of entrepreneurship, but because of the proliferation of regulation and other factors fueling a chaos in professional services firms, we are now significantly limited as we try to move forward, and the future may very well bring more restrictions. Going forward, we will find ourselves in a controlled environment with less flexibility and fewer options.

¶ 425 The Phoenix Factor

Professional services firms, and accounting firms in particular, have long demonstrated a venerable resilience and ability to thrive in spite of obstacles. Although the accounting scandals and SOX ushered in a new era of regulatory chaos, they also stimulated some indisputably positive changes. The scandals brought an institutionalized fear and horror within the accounting profession, but most of the tarnish fell upon Arthur Andersen and the remaining Big Four firms. Nobody could have predicted how the 44,700 remaining firms would emerge like a phoenix from the ashes.

Few local and regional firms lost a client due to the accounting scandals that wrought such chaos on the profession, and the CPA image emerged not only relatively unscathed, but prospering. The audit was soon recognized as a valuable service, not just a routine ritual of compliance. Because of the scandals and the subsequent government attention, more young people were attracted to careers in public accounting. Individuals, families, and corporate businesses rely on their CPAs, and accountants are now the most influential and trusted business advisors and consultants. In their clients' eyes, they supersede lawyers, bankers, brokers, and insurance agents as the professionals they turn to in times of crisis and in times where they seek advisors they most trust. The level of sophistication of skills provided to clients is significantly increased, and accountants make more money than ever. Practices are better run and better managed, and leadership is valued at a premium. The accounting scandals were tragic in many ways, but some good did come out of them.

Figure 4.2 ——

Section 7216 Rules: Compliance Master Checklist

This master checklist may be used to help the practitioner to comply with all aspects of the new law:

- Create and maintain a database for different types of consents to use and consents to disclose.
- Ensure that each consent form includes the mandatory language and warnings set forth in Rev. Proc. 2008-35 and Reg. § 301.7216. Each consent form must include the following, which is mandatory:
    — The name of the tax return preparer and the name of the taxpayer;
    — The intended purpose of the disclosure and the specific recipient(s) of the tax return information; and
    — A specific description of the tax return information to be disclosed or used by the preparer.
    — Any applicable mandatory language set forth in section 4.04(a)-(c) of Rev. Proc. 2008-35 that informs the client that he or she is not required to sign the consent form and that if he or she signs the consent, he or she can set a time period for the duration of the consent;
    — Any mandatory language set forth in section 4.04(d) of Rev. Proc. 2008-35 that refers the client to the Treasury Inspector General for Tax Administration (TIGTA) if he or she believes that his or her tax return information has been disclosed or used improperly.
    — If in paper form, it must be in 12 point type font, on 8 ½ × 11 inch paper.
    — Make sure electronic consents are in the same type as the website's standard text.
- Ensure that forms for multiple consents to use are not included on the same form as multiple consents to disclose, and vice versa.
- Make sure clients sign and date forms before you receive any tax return information.
- Make sure that disclosure authorization forms for other services such as financing planning, insurance, investment advising, etc., are signed by the client before receiving any tax return information.
- Make sure all tax return information is not disclosed outside the United States without the proper advance consent from the taxpayer and redaction or other masking of the taxpayer's Social Security number (SSN).
- Ensure sure that lists for solicitation of tax return business are compiled and maintained separately; and that they only contain the names, addresses, email addresses, and phone numbers of taxpayers whose return you have prepared or processed.
- Create and maintain a database to manage when consents expire and need to be re-signed by clients. Under the law, unless a client has explicitly established on the signed consent form a different time for the consent to expire, consents lapse one year after the day after the client signs the form.

Source: *©2009 CCH. All Rights Reserved.*

Figure 4.3

Section 7216 Rules: Sample Client Letter

This client letter may be sent to clients to update them on the new rules that practitioners now must follow to keep their clients' tax return information private.

Dear Client:

With tax filing season in full swing and April 15 around the corner, many newspapers have of late been reporting on the confidentiality of taxpayer returns and privacy of taxpayer information. We want to reassure you that we hold all your tax and financial information in the strictest confidence.

Federal law requires us to obtain your consent before we use or disclose your tax return information for purposes other than preparing your return. We are well aware of the rules and restrictions involving the use and/or disclosure of your return information, and we take our obligations extremely seriously. This letter is to bring you up to date on the rules that we must follow when handling your tax return information.

Client Disclosure and Consent

The IRS has recently added provisions to the Tax Code designed to provide added safeguards regarding the transfer and use of your personal tax return information. The new rules reaffirm that you control your tax return information, not us or the IRS. The rules ensure that you know who your tax return information may be shared with, with and without your consent, and when it may be shared with and without your consent.

These new rules give you even greater control over the use of your tax return information. Unless the law allows us otherwise (in very limited circumstances), we can not disclose, without your signed permission, your tax return information to third parties for purposes other than for the purposes of preparing your tax return.

What is "Tax Return Information?"

Tax return information is all the information we obtain from you or other sources in any form or manner that is used to prepare your income tax return or is obtained in connection with the preparation of your return. It also includes all computations, worksheets, and printouts preparers create; correspondence from IRS during the preparation, filing, and correction of returns; statistical compilations of tax return information; and tax return preparation software registration information.

The rules allow us to make two types of disclosures:
- Certain disclosures *requiring* your consent, and
- Certain permissible disclosures *without* your consent.

Disclosures/Uses That Do Not Require Your Consent

The only disclosures of your tax return information that we can make without your consent are to:
- Other U.S.-based tax return preparers assisting in the preparation of your return.
- The IRS and other taxing jurisdictions.
- Disclosures permitted under another provision of the Tax Code.
- The courts.
- Disclosures for the purpose of obtaining legal advice.

Disclosures/Uses Requiring Your Consent

We must obtain your consent to disclose or use your return information to any third party who is not a U.S. return preparer assisting in the preparation of your return. For example, if your mortgage lender, attorney, or bank contacts our office for information about your return, or asks for information from it, we must obtain your written consent beforehand. Moreover, you can establish the time at which you would like the consent to expire in the form itself. If you do not provide a specific date, your consent will lapse one year after the day you signed the form.

Consents to disclose or use your tax return information—paper or electronic—must contain certain specific information. Every consent form must include:
- The tax preparer's name and the taxpayer's name.
- The nature of the disclosure(s).
- To whom the disclosures will be made.
- Details on the information being disclosed.
- The particular use authorized.
- The product or service for which the tax return information will be used.

If you have any questions about the rules regarding use and disclosure of your tax return information, please contact us as we'd be happy to address any concerns you may have.

Sincerely yours,

Source: *©2009 CCH. All Rights Reserved.*

Chapter 5
The Chaos of Practice Development

¶ 501 Grow or Die

The old stereotype of an accountant as a nerd with few social skills, no entrepreneurial skills, little self-confidence, no understanding of the value of his expertise, and little desire to be rich is long gone. Beginning in the 1980s, CPAs started to realize that their expertise was valuable and well worth paying for. Government restrictions on the ability of accountants to market their services eased away, and so did the stigma associated with promoting professional services. By the late 1990s, practice development activities were accepted as a normal part of a professional services practice and CPAs began to understand that their firms were in business not only to practice accounting, but to make money. They embraced their own value and began charging for their services accordingly. The Age of CPA Entrepreneurship was born, and in spite of some blips, accounting practices continue to morph into accounting businesses whose professionals are regarded as experts and indispensable members of any business's team.

We are now in the Age of Opportunity. We are questioning the right things: the billable hour, time sheets, value billing, and our roles in the community and with clients. Practices are consolidating into extremely strong organizational entities, developing professional leadership, and generating even more influence. Managing partners truly are becoming their firm's top strategists. They are following their own management advice and developing strategic plans for their future, whether that means mergers or acquisitions or organic growth. They are partnering with other firms to service clients located in geographic areas in which they don't have offices. They are hiring lateral partners, learning to price engagements more efficiently, and taking on leadership roles with their clients.

The shift in management style is startling. Managing partners are viewing themselves as CEOs and following a corporate leadership model. They are surrounding themselves with C-suite executives, and it is not unusual for firms to have a management committee that includes a chief operating officer (COO), chief marketing officer (CMO), and a chief information officer (CIO). As CEOs, they are expanding their roles in their communities, spending significantly less time on client matters (often under 400 hours per year for firms with $10 million in revenue), and investing more time in strategically managing their firms. As a result, the so-called soft skills—leadership, communications, and management—have taken on added importance. Their role in creating a vision for their firm's future has been recognized, and managing partners, partners, and staff all participate in various training programs.

But the path to growth is not smooth, and firms need to have strategies ready to meet the known and unknown challenges they will face along the way. The Wall Street crisis is clear evidence. Most transactional work has dried up. While there may be other work for a time, perhaps even a long while, the accounting and law firms who counted Lehman Brothers, Merrill Lynch, AIG, and others among their best clients need to have a Plan B so they can replace them when the smoke clears.

Most firms across the country don't have such large clients, but even they may be dealing with the fallout of a weak economy. What is a firm to do when it needs to attract new business? The only given is that new business is gained using a long-term strategy. Only rarely does a large client or an unexpected piece of new business land at the firm's door on some sort of fluke.

Firms of all sizes realize this and have addressed the issue of practice development head-on. In 1981, most firms invested 0 percent of gross revenues in marketing. Today, approximately three percent to five percent of gross revenue goes to marketing activities. Even firms that don't have on-staff marketers understand the benefit of marketing and have earmarked some funds for this purpose. From stock newsletters to part-time marketers to consultants and off-site training, accounting firms have embraced the need to promote themselves in the marketplace. All of these things can be helpful, but they are only Band-Aids unless they are part of a strategic plan and the culture of the firm.

¶ 505 Strategic Planning Defined

It has been estimated that about 60 percent of mid-sized and large firms have written strategic plans. Articulating a strategic plan for your firm is a process that begins with a certain amount of soul searching. We say that because the first thing you need to determine is what you are planning for: do you want the firm to remain an independent entity long into the future or do you think that your eventual goal is to be acquired by another firm? Finding the answer to this question can be gut wrenching because it means examining your firm critically and without emotion. Is it feasible to remain independent? Do you have the depth of next generation leadership? Do you have a mix for vertical and horizontal growth strategies that will enable your firm to remain competitive?

A good place to start is with an analysis of your firm's Strengths, Weaknesses, Opportunities, and Threats. Commonly called a SWOT analysis or SWOT audit, these analyses can provide detailed information about your firm and provide insights into diverse areas. To be most effective, a cross-section of the firm's staff should be asked to participate, from support staff to managing partner. The results of the analysis will reveal a picture of where staff perceives its strengths to be as well as their perceptions about how well management functions, among other things. A SWOT analysis can be administered in discrete sections, so questions can be designed to probe for information in the areas in which you are most interested.

These audits should be conducted anonymously and individually, either in person or online using either the firm's intranet or a service such as Survey Monkey (*www.SurveyMonkey.com,* or Zoomerang (*www.Zoomerang.com*). (In-person interviews are more interactive. No matter how carefully the questions in the survey are crafted, nothing will give the same kind of feedback as a conversation.)

To encourage openness and honesty, the process works best if the managing partner is held at arm's length, and participants should be assured that their anonymity will be preserved. No one wants to feel as though there will be repercussions if they report something that can be interpreted as negative.

We are aware of firms that do not honor their promise of anonymity. They tell staff the results are anonymous and then ask to see individual comments. It is predictable that such behavior fosters a firm culture that is likely to have a lot of staff paranoia and turnover.

The answers should be reviewed and quantified by either an outside consultant or in-house marketer who should be charged with writing a report and presenting it to the managing partner and/or the executive committee. The sample SWOT analysis shows questions that might be included in a typical marketing audit.

Figure 5.1 —————————————————————————————

Vision and Mission Defined

- Vision statements create an image of the future the firm wants to create.

- Mission statements define who the firm is and what they do.

Figure 5.2 —————————————————————————————

Sample SWOT Analysis

The XXX Group, LLC

SWOT Audit

The Practice

1. If I met you at a social event and asked you what you do, how would you describe:
    a. The firm?
    b. Your practice?
2. Tell me about how you developed your practice.
3. Tell me about your background—how and where did you get your experience?
4. What would you consider to be the firm's premier areas of practice and why?
5. Over the years, how have you gotten new clients?
6. If referral sources, when was the last time you found a new source?
7. Are these sources all in the same industry/area?
8. Generally, do your clients come to you for the same type of work or do their needs vary?
9. What aspects of the firm would you like to see carried over to the newly merged firm?
10. What changes would you like to see made?

Reputation and Competitive Position

11. How would you describe The XXX Group's reputation?

12. What is the geographic and/or industry range of that reputation (in what communities does the firm have this reputation)?

13. Does the firm have other reputations in other communities?

14. What are the things that you think contribute to the firm's reputation?

15. How would you prioritize them?

16. Do you have any recommendations on how the firm can capitalize on its reputation(s)?

17. Who are the firm's competitors? (E.g., to whom do you lose business that you would like to have; what kind of firms are your competitors and where are they located?)

18. Can you identify any firms or describe the profile of the types of firms that get the kind of work you would like?

19. Do any firms refer work to your firm?

    a. If so, what is the basis of the referral (i.e., why was your firm selected?)

    b. What feedback did you get?

20. Name your five best referral sources.

21. What is the basis of the referral (personal relationship, service, niche)?

22. Have you ever referred business back to these sources and on what basis did you make the selection for the referral?

23. When was the last time a referral was made by each of these sources?

24. Are you the only person in touch with these referral sources?

25. How often do you get in touch with these sources?

26. What system do you use to track referrals?

Name Your Top 10 Clients

Give the following information for each of these clients:

27. What were the initial services you performed for the client?

28. What year was that?

29. Were additional services ever added to the basic/initial services?

30. Comparative billing: What is the dollar amount billed for each of the past three years?

31. How many times a year do you contact these clients? What is the nature of these contacts?

32. Do you ever meet with these clients for a nonbillable event, such as lunch or dinner?

33. How do you track client information, such as life changes (e.g., marriage, birth, death, divorce)? How do you disseminate this information to others in the firm?

34. Is there a single firm database (or employee) who keeps track of firm-wide information, or does each person have his/her own Rolodex?

35. Do you note opportunities for cross-selling services to clients?

36. Do you ever ask clients or referral sources for referrals?

    a. Why/why not?

    b. Would you feel comfortable/uncomfortable doing that?

37. How does the firm respond to requests for formal RFPs?

38. How do you think accountants in other accounting firms would describe your firm?

39. Are there any aspects or practices of other firms that you admire or would like to see emulated at XXX?

Expectations

40. What do you expect to come out of a marketing and business development plan?

    a. For the firm?

    b. For your own practice?

41. Do you think increased general visibility and name recognition of the firm will produce new business? If so, why?

42. How have marketing and business development been handled within the firm?

43. What is your responsibility for developing your practice?

44. For bringing business into the firm?

¶505

45. Who decides what should be done and by whom?

46. Are there any standards or measurements to determine who is spending what on marketing and whether the efforts are successful?

47. Have you ever thought about the things you already do as marketing/business development?

48. Do you ever take clients to lunch, dinner, or golf and other social activities?

49. Do you purchase ads in business/charitable journals?

50. How much did you spend on these activities in 2005 and 2006?

51. What is the firm's budget for marketing-related activities (if no budget, what do you think the firm spent on marketing activities in 2006 and 2007)?

52. What kinds of activities do you consider marketing?

53. What do you do that you consider marketing or business development?

54. Do you ever attend meetings of organizations for exposure and networking (in addition to education) and what are they?

55. Do you set any kind of goals for yourself or have any kind of a personal business development plan? If so, please summarize your goals.

56. What do you think you can do to better market yourself?

57. What do you think the firm can do better in marketing itself?

58. Do you have any suggestions on how the firm can increase its visibility and name recognition?

59. What ideas do you have that you think would be helpful and/or practicable for the firm to initiate that would increase its visibility?

60. How important is the firm's Web site?

    a. For existing clients?

    b. For prospective clients?

    c. For recruiting?

    d. As a general public relations tool?

61. How important is a firm brochure or other printed materials?

    a. For existing clients?

    b. For prospective clients?

    c. For recruiting?

62. Are there other materials explaining the firm or its areas of expertise that the firm should have? If so, what?

Current Activities

63. What professional/business/social organizations do you belong to?

64. Are you a member of any committees of any of those organizations?

65. Other than committees, how else do you participate in these organizations?

66. Does the firm pay for these activities?

67. Describe any business development or marketing activities you currently participate in or have participated in within the last several years?

68. Did you do so on your own?

69. Did you do so with any firm members? (Please be specific as to which activities and firm members.)

70. Approximately how many hours a week/month do you devote to business development/marketing activities?

71. Would you characterize your participation in business development activities as relatively consistent or irregular (i.e., widely variable depending on your schedule and mood)?

72. When and under what circumstances have you introduced someone else in the firm with a different area of practice from yours to one of your clients? Did the introduction result in additional business? Why do you think it did or didn't?

73. Which if any of the following are you willing to do to support a marketing and visibility enhancement program?

    a. Speaking (Where? Business groups, industry organizations, bar associations, law school or business school, other?).

       b. Writing (scholarly or practical). If so, do you have any topics in mind?

       c. Managing a project.

       d. Other.

Managers and Staff Only

74. From whom do you directly receive your work assignments? Indicate approximate percentages for the following categories:

       a. A partner (indicate if primarily from a single partner).

       b. Other managers or staff.

       c. Directly from clients of the firm.

       d. Your own clients.

75. Has any partner ever discussed with you the firm's view of business development? What were you told?

76. Do you believe that business development is an activity that should be expected of managers and staff?

77. Do you think that the amount of new business a manager has generated is an element that is considered in the decision to make new partners?

78. What is your understanding of the way the firm currently treats time spent on business development?

79. Do you believe that the time a manager spends on client development should be recognized in determining your total billable hours? Why or why not?

80. Other than your salary, are you compensated separately for bringing in new business to the firm?

¶ 510 New Lessons in the Geography of Firm Management: The World Is Flat

There's no question that Thomas Friedman is right: the world is getting smaller and flatter. Until the last decade, a firm's clientele more or less mirrored where it was located geographically: firms in larger cities, for instance, tended to have larger clients than those located in more rural areas. Occasionally, a client would move and the firm would keep the client because the client liked the firm, but that was the exception rather than the rule. Today, geography is no barrier to client retention. Technology, firm affiliations, and the like make it possible for firms to service national and international clients. The client's physical location no longer matters. Whole new frontiers of opportunity have opened up. There was a tradeoff, though: instead of performing a wide range of services for diverse clients across a range of industries, firms were forced to narrow their focus to a smaller list of niches and specialties.

This is a radical change on many levels, and it took time for many firms to adjust. Firms began to streamline their practices, cutting unprofitable services or industries—just as they advise their clients to do. The business efficiencies used by public and private companies to enhance their bottom lines spilled over into the somewhat cloistered world of professional services. Professional service firms began to merge and become bigger and more focused. These changes, along with those discussed in other chapters of this book, rocked the very foundation upon which most accounting practices were built.

The result was a new firm profile. The new paradigm for success, and one that is still evolving, is a firm that is decentralized, niched, and well-connected to other firms and centers of influence in their most successful areas. As firms began to live and breathe in this alien environment, they started attracting business across the country and even around the world. And a whole new range of issues emerged.

¶ 515 The Geography of Networks, Associations, and Alliances

Historically, professional services firms within a given city or geographic location rarely interacted with each other when seeking creative ideas for running their practices. Instead, they started talking to firms outside their geographic arenas, because those firms weren't their competitors. Professional associations and alliances evolved from these relationships, and as the relationships became stronger, these firms started to share more with each other. Gradually, they developed into formal associations. Traditionally, these alliances, associations, and networks tended to restrict and define each member's geographic boundaries, and members were granted exclusive territorial rights. This attempt to allay member firms' fear of direct competition was a key selling point of associations in the 1980s and 1990s. It is a good illustration of how warily firms within the same geographic boundaries viewed each other, and how strongly competition was confined within specific geographic borders. That geocentric attitude is evaporating, and it will change even more over time as firms and their leaders learn to better manage their firms, the boundaries of practical service delivery shrink, and the laws of competition adapt. Already, member firms share far more information than they once did in the areas of human resources, technology, marketing, and training. Through associations, member firms often find new and practical twists on solutions to common problems. For example, a firm based in Detroit may have clients in Houston. The Detroit firm may outsource its staffing needs for the Houston engagements to its association's member firm in Houston. That arrangement would save the Detroit's firm travel costs, time, and other resources while opening a new revenue stream for the Houston firm, as well as the potential for positive word of mouth and development of relationships within its home territory.

Because the changing nature of geography's importance has evolved over the last decade, we see some major regional firms with unusual territorial configurations. One Top 100 firm has multiple locations in the metropolitan New York area and on the West Coast, and another location in the Caribbean, but no locations in middle America. Another has offices in New York, Connecticut, New Jersey, Michigan, Ohio, Illinois, Missouri, Louisiana, Texas, Massachusetts, Georgia, the District of Columbia, and California. A third has offices in Georgia, North Carolina, Texas, Illinois, the Washington-Baltimore corridor, and California. These odd physical configurations are reflections of how these respective firms are capitalizing on niche strengths and technological advances. Technology and niche expertise invalidate the traditional common sense of geography and allow traditional territorial boundaries and issues to become less important.

¶ 520　CPA Firm Associations and Networks: Abandoning the Silo

Part of the shift in management style is a willingness to share knowledge and expertise. That, along with the globalization of businesses across the spectrum of size and geography, has led to the formation and growth of CPA firm associations and networks. These entities vary in size and specialization, but all of them have the same goals at their core: to help the growth and profitability of their member firms. Often, they host meetings that allow member firms to share their experiences, and perhaps even get valuable insight and advice. Some provide marketing training or materials.

Member firms may consist of independently owned local, regional, national, and international accounting, consulting, and service firms with similar client service goals. Membership allows firms to share resources and expand their services to clients. Figure 5.3 contains a list of major associations and their contact information.

Figure 5.3 ———

CPA Firm Associations and Networks

CPA PRACTICE
MANAGEMENT FORUM EXTRA

February 2009   Part 2   Volume 5, No. 2

2009 Annual Directory of CPA Firm Associations and Networks

In challenging economic times, public accounting firms can find strength and enhanced value in the resources of CPA firm associations and networks. Across the country and the globe, in such cities as Las Vegas, Phoenix, Seattle, Sacramento, Denver, Detroit and Cleveland (to name a few), associations and networks are looking for a few good members to add to their teams. CCH's *Annual Directory of CPA Firm Associations and Networks* details 41 associations and networks—taking a look at what they offer, what they're looking for, how much it costs to participate and more! This year's survey adds new information on the geographic distribution of member firms, the association/network distinction, and whether associations and networks are providing member education regarding the anticipated convergence of GAAP with IFAS. Enjoy!

February 2009

.CCH
a Wolters Kluwer business

¶520

Service Codes:

A. Member conferences/meetings (frequency)
B. Networking/information exchange within specific peer groups (e.g., MPs, marketing, COOs/firm administrators) in person, at conferences or elsewhere
C. Networking/information exchange within specific peer groups (e.g., MPs, marketing, COOs/firm administrators) via Webcast or teleconference
D. CPE for technical proficiency
E. CPE for "soft" skills (e.g., leadership, marketing)
F. CPE via remote medium such as DVD or intranet
G. International referrals
H. Technical manuals, software and other tools
I. Assistance with marketing collateral templates
J. Assistance with Web site development and/or hosting and maintenance
K. Assistance in development of niche practices
L. General client newsletters/mailings (print)
M. General client newsletters/mailings (electronic)
N. Niche client newsletters/mailings (print)
O. Niche client newsletters/mailings (electronic)
P. Newsletter distribution facilitated (print)
Q. Newsletter distribution facilitated (electronic)
R. Recruiting and human resources programs/assistance
S. Vendor/consultant discounts
T. Members only intranet
U. Podcasts/web casts/teleconferences
V. Proprietary research and/or surveys that generate publicity for association or member firms
W. International staff exchanges
X. Formal peer review program

1 Extra fee charged
Utilizes a management organization
* BDO Seidman's firm revenues, 7/28/08
** Gross revenue, $M; net revenue figure N/A
† For period ending 12/31/07
†† North American revenue figure; global revenue, including North America, $284.5 M
††† Firm Foundation and RSM McGladrey Network share staff.

Note: Revenue figures generally between 10/1/07 and 10/1/08 unless otherwise noted. Exchange rates to U.S. dollars based on currency rates, Jan. 12, 2009: U.S. dollar/British pound 1.49553/1; U.S. dollar/Euro 1.33939/1.

Association/Network Headquarters Contact Other (U.S. Or Int'l) Contact	U.S. Association Staff (FT/PT)	Int'l Staff (FT)	U.S. Member Firms	Non-U.S. North American Firms	Non-North American Firms	U.S. CPA Firms	U.S. CPA Firms Joining/Leaving*	Non-CPA Firms	Median Rev. ($M), U.S. Member Firms	Total Assoc. Net Rev. (N. America Only)	Details
AGN International-North America Rita J. Hood, Executive Director 2851 S. Parker Road, Suite 850 Aurora, CO 80014 303-743-7880 Fax: 303-743-7660 E-mail: rhood@agn.org Charlie McGimsey, U.S. Chair 404-898-2000 Fax: 404-898-2010 E-mail: cmcgimsey@winhambrannon.com Web: www.agn-na.org	6/0	4	46	6	152	46	1/0	106	11.8	$625.68 M	**Reporting As:** Int'l association based abroad, listing its information through U.S. or "Americas" regional entity **Largest U.S. Firm:** Rothstein, Kass & Co./New York **Smallest U.S. Firm:** Kane & Co./Miami **International Affiliate:** AGN International-North America is a region of AGN International **Fees Initial/Annual:** $5,000/$15,000 plus percentage of revenues **Membership Requirements:** Growing firms with young, aggressive partners and revenue of $2 million otherwise, prefer firms with revenues of $4 million; not likely to consider firms in smaller metro areas with existing AGN members **Seeking Representation In:** Salt Lake City; Las Vegas; Phoenix; Nashville; Calgary, Edmonton, Canada; Oklahoma City; Little Rock; Billings, Mont. **Quality Control Program:** Reports from AICPA peer review **Referrals Expected Between Members?:** No **Does Association Track Referrals?:** Not intra-U.S.; internationally, between countries **If Yes, Tracking Criteria:** Twice a year, members receive request for referrals given/rec'd, if any **How Is Tracking Info Used?:** For internal information purposes only **Services Provided:** A1 (annual), B1, C, D1, E1, F, G, I1, L1, M1, N1, O, R, S, T, U, W **Other Services:** Online anonymous upward evaluation services; quarterly teleconferences for A&A, tax, HR, IT, marketing, business valuations, not-for-profit, SALT; working moms listserve; online knowledge, expertise banks; Beta Alpha Psi Advisory Forum membership; Plain English Accounting membership; predictive index surveys; staff, partner training; video library **Niche Practices:** Construction; healthcare; SALT; employee benefit plan administration; pension plan audits; not-for-profit; manufacturing; business valuation; SEC clients, family office practices; small business practices **Education for Convergence of GAAP and IFAS?:** Yes **Needs Assessment of Member Firms?:** No **Plan to Meet Members' Potential Needs for Expertise, Assistance?** Yes **Network or Association?** Association

Alliott Group North America

Jon A. Meyer, Executive Director
642 South Fourth Avenue, Suite 300
Louisville, KY 40202
502-583-0248
Fax: 502-589-1680
E-mail: jon@agna.org
John Jones, U.S. Chair
707-546-0272
Fax: 707-546-5642
jjones@linkcpa.com
Web: www.alliottgroup.net

0/2 | 4 | 23 | 1 | DNP | 23 | DNP | DNP | 3.3 | DNP

Reporting As: Int'l association based abroad, listing its information through U.S. or "Americas" regional entity
Largest U.S. Firm: DiSanto Priest & Co./Warwick, R.I.
Smallest U.S. Firm: DNP
International Affiliate: Alliott Group North America is a region of Alliott Group
Fees Initial/Annual: $3,000/$9,000
Membership Requirements: $2 million – $12 million revenue, core services (A&A, tax, consulting), independent, active participation in Alliott Group
Seeking Representation In: New York; Tampa; Washington, D.C.; Denver; Dallas; Seattle
Quality Control Program: Proprietary peer review; reports from AICPA peer review, other AICPA quality centers
Referrals Expected Between Members: Yes
Does Association Tracks Referrals?: No
Services Provided: A1 (three/year), B, C, D1, E, F1, G, I, J, S, T, U, W, X
Other Services: Technology; tax credit services; cost segregations studies; annual member surveys
Needs Assessment of Member Firms? No
Education for Convergence of GAAP and IFAS? No
Plan to Meet Members' Potential Needs for Expertise, Assistance? No
Network or Association? Association

Baker Tilly North America

Samuel F. Wholley
80 City Square
Boston, MA 02129
617-241-6400
Fax: 617-241-6421
E-mail: samuel.wholley@bakertillyusa.com
Robert J. Ciaruffoli, North American Regional Chair
215-972-3349
E-Mail: rciaruffoli@parentenet.com
Web: www.bakertillyinternational.com

2/4 | 11 | 23 | 11 | DNP | 23 | 0/1 | 0 | 43.5 | $1.5 E

Reporting As: Int'l network based abroad, listing its information through U.S. or "Americas" regional entity
Largest U.S. Firm: Virchow, Krause & Co./Madison, Wis.
Smallest U.S. Firm: Hansen, Barnett & Maxwell/Salt Lake City
International Affiliate: Baker Tilly North America is a region of Baker Tilly International
Fees Initial/Annual: Commensurate with firm revenues
Membership Requirements: Reputation; quality; growth of practice; national and/or int'l clients; strategic U.S. location
Seeking Representation In: Seattle; Phoenix; Denver
Quality Control Program: Reports from AICPA peer review, PCAOB
Referrals Expected Between Members?: Yes
Does Association Track Referrals?: Yes
If Yes, Tracking Criteria: Referring firm, receiving firm, net fees resulting from referral
How Is Tracking Info Used?: Used by int'l ~IQ to determine income generated at the association level from referrals
Services Provided: A1 (annual regiona_ world), B1, C1, F1, G, H, I, Q, R, T, W
Education for Convergence of GAAP and IFAS? No
Needs Assessment of Member Firms? No
Plan to Meet Members' Potential Needs for Expertise, Assistance? No
Network or Association? Network

BDO Seidman Alliance

Michael G. O'Hare, Executive Director
One Prudential Plaza
130 E. Randolph, Suite 2800
Chicago, IL 60601
312-240-1236
Fax: 312-240-0213
E-Mail: mohare@bdo.com
Web: www.bdo.com

17/DNP | DNP | DNP | DNP | DNP | 153 | 10/9 | 60 | 6.0 | $659 M*

Reporting As: A U.S. association with int'l affiliates
Largest U.S. Firm: bmo/Reading, Pa.
Smallest U.S. Firm: Ashby & Assoc./Tupelo, Miss.
International Affiliate: Members have access to international BDO member firms
Fees Initial/Annual: None/1% of first $10 million in net accrued fees (min. $30,000, max. $100,000)
Membership Requirements: Membership in AICPA Division for Firms; peer review; professional liability insurance; other due diligence
Seeking Representation In: DNP
Quality Control Program: DNP
Referrals Expected Between Members?: Referrals often take place, but not required
Does Association Track Referrals?: DNP
How Is Tracking Info Used?: DNP
Services Provided: A1 (national, local, fee varies), B, C, D, E, F, G, H, I1, J1, K, L, M, N, O, S, T, U
Niche Practices: Financial services; IT; real estate; construction; healthcare; dealerships; energy, business valuations; risk advisory services; gov't; others
Education for Convergence of GAAP and IFAS?: Yes
Plan to Meet Members' Potential Needs for Expertise, Assistance? DNP
Needs Assessment of Member Firms? DNP
Network or Association? DNP

Association/Network Headquarters Contact Other (U.S. Or Int'l) Contact	U.S. Association Staff (FT/PT)	Int'l Staff (FT)	U.S. Member Firms	Non-U.S. North American Firms	Non-North American Firms	U.S. CPA Firms	U.S. CPA Firms Joining/Leaving*	Non-CPA Firms	Median Rev. ($M), U.S. Member Firms	Total Assoc. Net Rev. (N. America Only)	Details
BKR International Maureen Schwartz, Executive Director 19 Fulton Street, Suite 306 New York, NY 10038 212-964-2115 Fax: 212-964-2133 E-Mail: bkr@dbr.com Donald Timmins, Americas Regional Chairman 613-236-9191 Fax 613-236-8258 E-mail: dtimmins@welchllp.com Web: www.bkr.com	3/4	1	46	11	6	46	1/1	0	8.1	$1.33 B	**Reporting As:** Int'l association based in the U.S. **Largest U.S. Firm:** Tofias/Boston **Smallest U.S. Firm:** DNP **Fees Initial/Annual:** $5,000/$10,000-$22,000, based on firm revenue **Membership Requirements:** In target city (see below), leader in market area, willing to participate in association activities **Seeking Representation In:** Sacramento; Delaware; Indianapolis; Las Vegas; New Mexico; New York (Albany, Buffalo, Syracuse); Nashville; Texas (Austin, El Paso, San Antonio); Richmond, Va.; Milwaukee **Quality Control Program:** Reports from AICPA peer review **Referrals Expected Between Members?:** Yes **Does Association Track Referrals?:** Yes **If Yes, Tracking Criteria:** DNP **How Is Tracking Info Used?:** DNP **Services Provided:** A (annual global; quarterly regional, subregional, niche); B, C, D, E, F1, G, H, I, K, L, M, N, O, P, Q, R, S, T, U, V, W, X **Other Services:** Comprehensive marketing tools, programs; interactive Web site; unlimited access to First Research and ProfitCents; Doing Business brochures series for 39 countries; The BKR Leadership Institute; strategic alliances for financial services; document mgt. software:cost segregation studies, R&D credits, lead generation, media relations, document management and review program for CPA candidates **Niche Practices:** Americas region: business valuation and forensic accounting; emerging leaders; financial services; firm administrators; gov't/not-for-profit accounting/auditing; healthcare accounting/tax; advisement and consulting; high net worth families/estate planning; HR; Leading Edge Technology; others **Education for Convergence of GAAP and IFAS?:** Yes **Needs Assessment of Member Firms?** Yes **Plan to Meet Members' Potential Needs for Expertise, Assistance?** Yes **Network or Association?** Association
CADCA (CPA Auto Dealer Consultants Association) Patrick Pruett, Executive Director 624 Grassmere Park Drive, Suite 15 Nashville, TN 37211 615-377-3392 Fax: 615-377-7092 E-Mail: info@autodealercpas.net Ira Silver, U.S. Chair E-Mail: isilver@mbafcpa.com Web: www.autodealercpas.net	3/1	DNP	21	DNP	DNP	21	2/DNP	DNP	DNP	DNP	**Reporting As:** Niche-specific U.S. association **Largest U.S. Firm:** DNP **Smallest U.S. Firm:** DNP **Fees Initial/Annual:** $1,500/$1,800 **Membership Requirements:** DNP **Seeking Representation In:** DNP **Quality Control Program:** DNP **Referrals Expected Between Members?:** Don't know **Does Association Track Referrals?:** No **Services Provided:** A1 (annual), B, D, E, K, M, S, T **Other Services:** Listservs **Niche Practices:** Auto dealers **Education for Convergence of GAAP and IFAS?:** DNP **Needs Assessment of Member Firms?** DNP **Plan to Meet Members' Potential Needs for Expertise, Assistance?** DNP **Network or Association?** DNP
CBAN (Community Banking Advisory Network) Patrick Pruett, Executive Director 624 Grassmere Park Drive, Suite 15 Nashville, TN 37211 615-377-3392 Fax: 615-377-7092 E-Mail: info@bankingcpas.com Web: www.bankingcpas.com	3/1	DNP	19	DNP	DNP	19	1/0	DNP	DNP	DNP	**Reporting As:** Niche-specific U.S. association **Largest U.S. Firm:** DNP **Smallest U.S. Firm:** DNP **Fees Initial/Annual:** $1,500/$1,650 **Membership Requirements:** DNP **Seeking Representation In:** DNP **Quality Control Program:** Client reference; executive committee oversight; member references **Referrals Expected Between Members?:** Don't know **Does Association Track Referrals?:** No **Services Provided:** A1 (annual), B, D, E, J, K, M, N1, O1, S, T **Other Services:** Listservs **Niche Practices:** Community banking **Education for Convergence of GAAP and IFAS?:** DNP **Needs Assessment of Member Firms?** DNP **Plan to Meet Members' Potential Needs for Expertise, Assistance?** DNP **Network or Association?** DNP

¶520

CPA Associates International

James Flynn, President
301 Route 17 North
Rutherford, NJ 07070
201-804-8686
Fax: 201-804-9222
E-Mail: jlflynn@cpaai.com
Raymond Strothman, U.S. Chair
502-585-1600
Fax: 502-585-1601
E-Mail: rstrothman@strothman.com
Web: www.cpaai.com

| 4/0 | 4 | 48 | 3 | 101 | 48 | 4/1 | 0 | 4.5 | DNF |

Reporting As: Int'l association based in the U.S.
Largest U.S. Firm: Margolin, Winer & Evens/Garden City, N.Y.
Smallest U.S. Firm: DNP
Fees Initial/Annual: $2,200/based on annual revenue
Membership Requirements: Territorial exclusivity, full-service practice; member, AICPA PCPS; market leader; high quality firm
Seeking Representation In: Alabama; Arizona; Arkansas; Iowa; Kansas; Nebraska; New Hampshire; New Mexico; Washington; Wyoming
Quality Control Program: Reports from AICPA peer review
Referrals Expected Between Members?: Yes
Does Association Track Referrals?: Yes
If Yes, Tracking Criteria: Part of our peer review program
How Is Tracking Info Used?: Informally
Services Provided: A1 (many), B, C1, C1, E1, G, I, J, K, L1, M1, N1, O1, R1, S, T, U1, W, X1
Other Services: Member services; leadership program; staff training; practice consultants; management assistance program; tax practice assistance program; regional meetings; member directory
Niche Practices: Auto dealers; business valuations; litigation services and forensic accounting; construction; employee benefits; family business; financial institutions; gov't/not-for-profit; IT; medical professionals, more
Education for Convergence of GAAP and IFAS?: Not yet
Needs Assessment of Member Firms?: Yes
Plan to Meet Members' Potential Needs for Expertise, Assistance?: Yes
Network or Association? Yes

CPAConnect

Douglas H. Thompson, Jr., Chief Executive Officer
11801 Research Drive
Alachua, FL 32615
386-418-4001
Fax: 386-418-4002
E-Mail: dthompson@cpamerica.org
David A. Deeter, U.S. Chair
404-253-7501
Fax: 404-253-7501
Web: www.cpamerica.org

| 27/4 | 0 | 252 | DNP | DNP | 252 | 41/11 | 0 | 0.6 | DNP |

Reporting As: U.S. association with int'l affiliates
Largest U.S. Firm: DNP
Smallest U.S. Firm: DNP
International Affiliate: Horwath International
Fees Initial/Annual: $250/based on annual cash gross fees
Membership Requirements: Must be CPA practice; revenue of at least $100,000, not more than $3 million; acceptable peer review report; growth oriented; dynamic; outgoing, personable partners; more
Seeking Representation In: Las Vegas; Los Angeles; Sacramento; Little Rock; Colorado Springs; Jacksonville, Tallahassee; Boise; Detroit; Portland, Maine; more
Quality Control Program: Proprietary peer review, reports from AICPA peer review, generally requires sponsorship of a CPAmerica firm
Referrals Expected Between Members?: Yes
Does Association Track Referrals?: Yes
If Yes, Tracking Criteria: DNP
How Is Tracking Info Used?: DNP
Services Provided: A1 (annual), B, C, D1, E1, F1, G1, L1, M1, N1, O1, P1, Q1, R, S, T, U, V1, W
Education for Convergence of GAAP and IFAS?: Yes
Needs Assessment of Member Firms?: Yes
Plan to Meet Members' Potential Needs for Expertise, Assistance?: Yes
Network or Association? Association

CPAmerica International

Douglas H. Thompson, Jr., Chief Executive Officer
11801 Research Drive
Alachua, FL 32615
386-418-4001
Fax: 386-418-4002
E-Mail: dthompson@cpamerica.org
David A. Deeter, U.S. Chair
404-253-7500
Fax: 404-253-7501
Web: www.cpamerica.org

| 27/4 | 0 | 80 | DNP | DNP | 80 | 9/2 | 0 | 8 | DNP |

Reporting As: U.S. association with int'l affiliates
Largest U.S. Firm: DNP/Miami
Smallest U.S. Firm: DNP/Nashville
International Affiliate: Horwath International
Fees Initial/Annual: $7,000 ($1,000 w/application, remainder billed at $500/month for first year)/based on annual gross fees
Membership Requirements: Minimum $2.5 million revenue; acceptable peer review report; growth-oriented; dynamic; outgoing, personable partners; efficient; high-quality firm, well respected in market and good business and professional citizen
Seeking Representation In: Las Vegas; Los Angeles; Sacramento; Little Rock; Colorado Springs; Jacksonville, Tallahassee; Boise; Detroit; Portland, Maine; others
Quality Control Program: Proprietary peer review, onsite admission review
Referrals Expected Between Members?: Yes
Does Association Track Referrals?: No
Services Provided: A1 (many), B, C, D1, E1, F1, G1, L1, M1, N1, O1, P1, Q1, R, S, T, U, V1, W
Education for Convergence of GAAP and IFAS?: Yes
Needs Assessment of Member Firms?: Yes
Plan to Meet Members' Potential Needs for Expertise, Assistance?: Yes
Network or Association? Association

Association/Network Headquarters Contact Other (U.S. Or int'l) Contact	U.S. Association Staff (FT/PT)	Int'l Staff (FT)	U.S. Member Firms	Non-U.S. North American Firms	Non-North American Firms	U.S. CPA Firms	U.S. CPA Firms Joining*/Leaving*	Non-CPA Firms	Median Rev. ($M) U.S. Member Firms	Total Assoc. Net Rev. (N. America Only)	Details
CPASNET.COM Cornell Rudov, President P.O. Box 7648 Princeton, NJ 08543-7648 609-890-0800 Fax: 609-689-9720 E-Mail: crudov@cpasnet.com Jeff Coleman, U.S. Chair 410-561-4411 Fax: 410-561-4586 E-Mail: jeff.coleman@wabccpas.com Web: www.cpasnet.com	2/0	0	30	DNP	DNP	30	1/1	0	3	$500,000	**Reporting As:** U.S. association with int'l affiliates **Largest U.S. Firm:** Mercadien/Princeton, N.J. **Smallest U.S. Firm:** Pacios, Rausch & Co./Auburn, Maine **International Affiliate:** DNP **Fees Initial/Annual:** $850/$7,200 **Membership Requirements:** Territorial exclusivity; dedicated to marketing and growing practice; revenue of $1 million; peer review **Seeking Representation In:** Boston; Washington D.C.; Orlando; Columbus, Ohio; Indianapolis; Dallas; Phoenix; Los Angeles; San Francisco; Kansas City, Missouri **Quality Control Program:** Reports from AICPA peer review **Referrals Expected Between Members?:** No **Does Association Track Referrals?:** Yes **If Yes, Tracking Criteria:** Monthly questionnaire **How Is Tracking Info Used?:** Maintain database, attract members **Services Provided:** A1 (semiannual), B, C, D1, E1, G, H, I, J, K, L, M, N, O, P, Q, R, S, T, V, W **Niche Practices:** Auto dealers; real estate; construction; medical practice; legal; nonprofit; investment advisory services; outsourcing; technology; business valuations **Education for Convergence of GAAP and IFAS?:** Yes **Needs Assessment of Member Firms?** Yes **Plan to Meet Members' Potential Needs for Expertise, Assistance?** No **Network or Association?** Association
CPA-USA Network (formerly NACPAF) Kim Fantaci, Executive Director 136 South Keowee Street Dayton, OH 45402 937-222-1024 Fax 937-222-5794 E-Mail: email@cpa-usanetwork.org Chris Fogal, U.S. Chair Web: www.cpa-usanetwork.org	0/0 #	0	40	1	DNP	40	0/3	0	4.5	DNP	**Reporting As:** U.S. association with int'l affiliates **Largest U.S. Firm:** DNP/California **Smallest U.S. Firm:** DNP/Connecticut **International Affiliate:** Evancic Parrault Robertson **Fees Initial/Annual:** $850/$2,200 **Membership Requirements:** Geography, niches/specialization **Seeking Representation In:** Northwest, Southwest, Mid-Central U.S. **Quality Control Program:** Proprietary peer review **Referrals Expected Between Members?:** Yes **Does Association Track Referrals?:** No **Services Provided:** A (three/year), C, D, E, J1, S, T, U, X1 **Education for Convergence of GAAP and IFAS?:** Yes **Needs Assessment of Member Firms?** Yes **Plan to Meet Members' Potential Needs for Expertise, Assistance?** No **Network or Association?** Association
DFK International/USA Jay Hauck, Executive Director 2300 N Street, NW, Suite 200 Washington, DC 20037 202-452-1588 Fax 202-833-3636 E-mail: jhauck@dfkusa.com U.S. Chair: Bruce Madnick Web: www.dfkusa.com	3/0 #	3	25	14	120	25	1/2	0	9.0	$389.8 M	**Reporting As:** U.S. association with int'l affiliates **Largest U.S. Firm:** Friedman/New York **Smallest U.S. Firm:** DNP **International Affiliate:** DFK International **Fees Initial/Annual:** $500 application fee applicable to $5,000 initiation fee/$13,000–$25,000, based on formula, call for quote **Membership Requirements:** Must be willing to participate, share info, expertise; territorial exclusivity; must be among leading firms in market; independent; full-service firm (PCAOB registrants encouraged); growth-oriented, progressive leadership **Seeking Representation In:** Miami; Tampa; Detroit; Phoenix; Minneapolis; Cleveland; other cities with no DFK members **Quality Control Program:** Reports from AICPA peer review; other AICPA quality centers; PCAOB; DFK pre-admittance questionnaire and site visit to firm **Referrals Expected Between Members?:** Yes **Does Association Track Referrals?:** Yes **If Yes, Tracking Criteria:** Quarterly reports **How Is Tracking Info Used?:** Recordkeeping purposes only for domestic referrals; administrative fee (%) charged on int'l referrals **Services Provided:** A1 (several/year), B1 (varies), C, D1, E1, G1, S, T, W, X1 **Other Services:** Practice management survey, other surveys; managing partners conference; leadership programs for managers, new partners; audit/tax conference; annual partners conference/special interest groups in 12 areas **Niche Practices:** Members that have developed a niche will assist other members in developing the same niche **Education for Convergence of GAAP and IFAS?:** Yes **Needs Assessment of Member Firms?** Yes **Plan to Meet Members' Potential Needs for Expertise, Assistance?** Yes **Network or Association?** Association

¶520

Organization										
Enterprise Network Worldwide Patrick Pruett, Executive Director 624 Grassmere Park Drive, Suite 15 Nashville, TN 37211 615-377-3392 Fax 615-377-7092 E-Mail: Patrick@enterpriseworldwide.com Web: www.enterpriseworldwide.com	3/1	1	33	3	20	33	6/DNP	DNP	6	DNP
Firm Foundation Dean Sengstock, Executive Director 401 Main Street, Suite 1560 Peoria, IL 61602 866-548-2938 Fax: 309-673-9852 E-Mail: dean.sengstock@rsmi.com Web: www.firmfoundationcpa.com	38/4†††	DNP	26	DNP	DNP	26	13/0	0	2.3	DNP
HCAA (National CPA Health Care Advisors Association) Patrick Pruett, Executive Director 624 Grassmere Park Drive, Suite 15 Nashville, TN 37211 615-377-3392 Fax 615-377-7092 E-Mail: info@hcaa.com Brian Bastis, U.S. Chair bbastis@ryanandwetmore.com Web: www.hcaa.com	3/1	0	54	DNP	DNP	54	DNP	0	DNP	DNP

Enterprise Network Worldwide

Reporting As: Int'l association based in the U.S.
Largest U.S. Firm: DNP/Fort Worth, Texas
Smallest U.S. Firm: DNP/Tuscaloosa, Ala.
Fees Initial/Annual: $4,500/$6,000-$13,140
Membership Requirements: DNP
Seeking Representation In: DNP
Quality Control Program: Proprietary peer review; firm visit; member recommendations
Referrals Expected Between Members?: Yes
Does Association Track Referrals?: Yes
If Yes, Tracking Criteria: Spreadsheet
How Is Tracking Info Used? Internal purposes, future marketing
Services Provided: A (three/year) B1, C, D, E, G, I, J, K, L1, M, N1, O1, P1, Q, S, T, U, V1, W
Other Services: Member consultant networks, listservs
Niche Practices: Financial services; business valuation; forensics; healthcare; manufacturing; not-for-profits; real estate; construction; auto dealers; community banking
Education for Convergence of GAAP and IFAS?: Yes
Needs Assessment of Member Firms? Yes
Plan to Meet Members' Potential Needs for Expertise, Assistance? DNP
Network or Association? Association

Firm Foundation

Reporting As: U.S. association without int'l affiliates
Largest U.S. Firm: Vicenti, Lloyd & Stutzman/Glendora, Calif.
Smallest U.S. Firm: Kroening, Stangel, Swetlik & Zinkel/Manitowoc, Wis.
Fees Initial/Annual: None/fee scale based on annual revenues
Membership Requirements: Less than 10 FTEs; proof of professional liability insurance; copy of most recent peer review report; letter of comment; copy of most recent financial statement or tax return
Seeking Representation In: Entire U.S., including all states, regions, cities
Quality Control Program: Reports from AICPA peer review
Referrals Expected Between Members?: No
Does Association Track Referrals?: No
Services Provided: A1 (biannual), B, C, C1, E1, F1, G1, H1, I1, J1, M1, Q1, R, S1, T, U, V
Other Services: Technology consulting (inc. remote technology assessment); practice mgt. consulting (financial statistics benchmark assessment; strategic retreat facilitation); HR consulting (inc. employee engagement assessment
Education for Convergence of GAAP and IFAS?: Yes
Needs Assessment of Member Firms? No
Plan to Meet Members' Potential Needs for Expertise, Assistance? No
Network or Association? Association

HCAA (National CPA Health Care Advisors Association)

Reporting As: Niche-specific U.S. association
Largest U.S. Firm: DNP
Smallest U.S. Firm: DNP
Fees Initial/Annual: $1,500/$1,700
Membership Requirements: DNP
Seeking Representation In: DNP
Quality Control Program: DNP
Referrals Expected Between Members?: Don't know
Does Association Track Referrals?: No
Services Provided: A1 (biannual), B, D, E, K, M, S, T
Niche Practices: Healthcare
Education for Convergence of GAAP and IFAS?: DNP
Needs Assessment of Member Firms? DNP
Plan to Meet Members' Potential Needs for Expertise, Assistance? DNP
Network or Association? DNP

Association/Network Headquarters Contact Other (U.S. Or Int'l) Contact	U.S. Association Staff (FT/PT)	Int'l Staff (FT)	U.S. Member Firms	Non-U.S. North American Firms	Non-North American Firms	U.S. CPA Firms	U.S. CPA Firms Joining/ Leaving*	Non-CPA Firms	Median Rev. ($M), U.S. Member Firms	Total Assoc. Net Rev. (N. America Only)	Details
HLB International Peter Frost, Executive Director; 21 Ebury Street; London SW1W 0LD U.K.; 44-0-20-7881-1100; Fax: 44-0-20-7881-1109; E-Mail: mailbox@hlbi.com; David A. Stene, U.S. Chair; 952-944-6166; Fax: 952-944-8496; E-Mail: dstene@eidebailly.com; Web: www.hlbi.com	1/1	8	20	22	160	20	2/0	0	29	$1.91 B	**Reporting As:** Int'l network based abroad, but listing its information through a U.S. or "Americas" regional entity **Largest U.S. Firm:** Clifton Gunderson/Peoria, Ill. **Smallest U.S. Firm:** Simonton Kutac/Houston **Fees Initial/Annual:** None/based on revenue **Membership Requirements:** Growing firm; meet quality requirements; int'l business opportunities; attendance, involvement in conferences, meetings; prompt reporting **Seeking Representation In:** Detroit; Ohio; Las Vegas; Dallas **Quality Control Program:** Proprietary peer review; reports from AICPA peer review, AICPA quality centers, PCAOB **Referrals Expected Between Members?:** Yes **Does Association Track Referrals?:** Yes **If Yes, Tracking Criteria:** Annual reporting **How Is Tracking Info Used?:** To assess business development activities **Services Provided:** A1 (annual int'l, regional conferences, meetings), B, C, D, E, F, G, H, I, K, L, M, S, T, U, W, X1 **Niche Practices:** Int'l, U.S. tax, SALT; HR; IT; marketing; employee benefit plans; IFRS and extensive auditing resources; industry resources **Education for Convergence of GAAP and IFAS?** Yes **Needs Assessment of Member Firms?** Yes **Plan to Meet Members' Potential Needs for Expertise, Assistance?** Yes **Network or Association?** Network
Horwath International Frank B Arford, Chief Executive Officer; 420 Lexington Avenue, Suite 526; New York, NY 10170; 212-808-2000; Fax: 212-808-2020; E-Mail: farford@horwath.com; Web: www.horwath.com	10/0	4	7	3	109	5	DNP	23	20.1	$3.06 B	**Reporting As:** Int'l network based abroad, but listing its information through a U.S. or "Americas" regional entity **Largest U.S. Firm:** Crowe Horwath/Oakbrook, Ill. **Smallest U.S. Firm:** Horwath Hospitality & Leisure/San Francisco **Fees Initial/Annual:** Capital share/based on percentage of fee income and referrals **Membership Requirements:** Pre-member quality control review **Seeking Representation In:** N/A **Quality Control Program:** Proprietary peer review; reports from AICPA peer review, reports from PCAOB; firms' own QAR **Referrals Expected Between Members?:** Yes **Does Association Track Referrals?:** Yes **If Yes, Tracking Criteria:** Billing for services performed for clients referred to other member firms **How Is Tracking Info Used?:** To track growth **Services Provided:** A (annual, four add'l regional meetings), B, C, D, E, G, H, I, J, Q, T, U, W **Education for Convergence of GAAP and IFAS?:** Yes **Needs Assessment of Member Firms?** Yes **Plan to Meet Members' Potential Needs for Expertise, Assistance?** Yes **Network or Association?** Network
IAPA Susan Humphry, Chief Executive Officer; Old Chambers; 93-94 West Street; Farnham, Surrey GU9 7EB; 44-1252-720-810; Fax: 44-1252-720-830; E-Mail: s.humphry@iapa.net; Herb Alexander, U.S. Chair; 781-965-9100; E-Mail: info@aafcpa.com; Web: www.iapa.net	0/1	2	17	†5	178	17	1/2	0	11.7	$921 M	**Reporting As:** Int'l association based abroad **Largest U.S. Firm:** Berdon/New York **Smallest U.S. Firm:** DNP **Fees Initial/Annual:** £1,260 ($1,864)/£1,900 ($2,842) plus £325 ($486)/branch, £100 ($150)/partner (up to 20 partners) and 5% of fees earned from work referred within network; additional Americas Region fee $200 **Membership Requirements:** Capacity to serve int'l clients; good standing within national accountancy/regulatory bodies; financial viability; compliance with IAPA quality criteria **Seeking Representation In:** Chicago; Charlotte; Cleveland; Dallas; Detroit; Memphis; Minneapolis; San Diego; San Francisco; St. Louis **Quality Control Program:** Reports from AICPA peer review **Referrals Expected Between Members?:** Yes **Does Association Track Referrals?:** Yes **If Yes, Tracking Criteria:** Members submit completed referral forms annually **How Is Tracking Info Used?:** To track the success of the association **Services Provided:** A1 (three/year), B, E, G, L, Q, T, W **Education for Convergence of GAAP and IFAS?:** No **Needs Assessment of Member Firms?** Yes **Plan to Meet Members' Potential Needs for Expertise, Assistance?** No **Network or Association?** Association

¶520

Organization / Contact										

IGAF Worldwide
Kevin Mead, Executive Director
3235 Satellite Boulevard, Building 400,
Suite 300
Duluth, GA 30096
678-417-7730
Fax 678-999-3959
E-Mail: kmead@igafworldwide.org
Web: www.igafworldwide.org

6/0 | 0 | 39 | 5 | 102 | 39 | 9/2 | 0 | 10.2 | $1.33 B†

Reporting As: Int'l association based in the U.S.
Largest U.S. Firm: SMART Business Advisory and Consulting/Devon, Pa
Smallest U.S. Firm: Goluses & Co./Providence, R.I
Fees Initial/Annual: $5,000/based on revenue
Membership Requirements: Location; size; revenue; practice mix; industries served
Seeking Representation In: DNP
Quality Control Program: Proprietary peer review; reports from AICPA peer review, other AICPA quality centers, PCAOB
Referrals Expected Between Members?: Yes
Does Association Track Referrals?: Don't know
If Yes, Tracking Criteria: DNP
How Is Tracking Info Used?: DNP
Services Provided: A1 (annual; biennial; semi-annual; fee depends on conference), C, D, E, G, I, K, R, S, T, U, W, X1
Niche Practices: Audit/assurance; corporate finance (M&A, investment banking); energy/utilities; IT; marketing; real estate/construction; tax; transportation/warehousing; valuation; wholesale distribution
Education for Convergence of GAAP and IFAS?: DNP
Needs Assessment of Member Firms? DNP
Plan to Meet Members' Potential Needs for Expertise, Assistance? DNP
Network or Association? Association

INAA Group
Margaret Ross, Executive Director
c/o Jeffrey Crawford & Co.
25 Castle Terrace
Edinburgh, U.K.
EH1 2ER
44-131-228-6606
Fax: 44-131-228-4911
E-Mail: margaret@jeffreycrawford.co.uk
Web: www.inaa.org

0/0 | 0 | 7 | 3 | 44 | 7 | 2/0 | 0 | DNP | DNP

Reporting As: Int'l association based abroad
Largest U.S. Firm: DNP
Smallest U.S. Firm: DNP
Fees Initial/Annual: Euro 1,500 ($2,005)/Euro 2,900-5,700 ($3,884-$7,635)
Membership Requirements: Must provide full range of services or be able to provide referrals for work it cannot perform; have adequate professional indemnity insurance; territorial exclusivity; must not participate in any competing int'l group, network or association
Seeking Representation In: In U.S.: Houston; Denver; Miami; Orlando; Phoenix; San Francisco; Los Angeles; Washington D.C.; Canada; China; others
Quality Control Program: Proprietary peer review
Referrals Expected Between Members?: Yes
Does Association Track Referrals?: Yes
If Yes, Tracking Criteria: Quarterly billings raised by members in connected with referred work
How Is Tracking Info Used?: Regular reports to members
Services Provided: A1 (twice/year), B, G1, P1, Q, W
Other Services: Clients of member firms can use office facilities of other member firms when traveling
Education for Convergence of GAAP and IFAS?: Yes
Needs Assessment of Member Firms? No
Plan to Meet Members' Potential Needs for Expertise, Assistance? No
Network or Association? Association

INPACT Americas
Mara Ambrose, Executive Director
P.O. Box 495
Frederick, MD 21705-0495
301-694-8580
Fax 301-694-5804
E-Mail: mara@inpactam.org
Richard A. Mehall, U.S. Chair
309-662-4356
E-Mail: rmehall@guthoff.com
Web: www.inpactam.org

2/1 | 0 | 29 | 2 | 110 | 29 | 2/0 | 0 | 2.9 | $128 M†

Reporting As: U.S. association with int'l affiliates
Largest U.S. Firm: DNP
Smallest U.S. Firm: DNP
International Affiliate: INPACT International; INPACT Pacific
Fees Initial/Annual: $1,500/$6,600-8,100
Membership Requirements: Full-service firm; AICPA member; clean peer review; two or more partners; sufficient financial and personnel resources to participate fully
Seeking Representation In: Southeast; New England; Western states
Quality Control Program: Reports from AICPA peer review
Referrals Expected Between Members?: Yes, but not a membership emphasis
Does Association Track Referrals?: No
Services Provided: A1 (two partner conferences; others), B, C, E1, G, K, R1, S, T, V, W
Education for Convergence of GAAP and IFAS?: No
Needs Assessment of Member Firms? No
Plan to Meet Members' Potential Needs for Expertise, Assistance? Yes
Network or Association? Association

Association/Network Headquarters Contact Other (U.S. Or Int'l) Contact	U.S. Association Staff (FT/PT)	Int'l Staff (FT)	U.S. Member Firms	Non-U.S. North American Firms	Non-North American Firms	U.S. CPA Firms	U.S. CPA Firms Joining/ Leaving*	Non-CPA Firms	Median Rev. ($M) U.S. Member Firms	Total Assoc. Net Rev. (N. America Only)	Details
Integra International Richard Purcell, Executive Director 1364 Summit Drive Coquitlam, B.C. V3J 5L8 Canada 604-939-1872 Fax 604-817-1500 E-Mail: purcell@integra-international.net Martin Shulman, U.S. Chair 781-273-3950 Fax: 781-283-3470 mshulman@carasshulman.com Web: www.integra-international.net	1/0	1	25	4	63	25	2/0	0	3.6	$225.59 M	**Reporting As:** Int'l association based in U.S. **Largest U.S. Firm:** DNP/Los Angeles **Smallest U.S. Firm:** DNP/Denver **Fees Initial/Annual:** $1,000/$4,000 **Membership Requirements:** Minimum six professionals; must attend at least one conference/year; successful peer review; involvement in committee work; prompt, professional communication with other members **Seeking Representation In:** Louisiana; Florida; Oregon; North Carolina; South Carolina; Canada (Calgary, Ottawa, Winnipeg, Halifax); Japan; Taiwan; South Korea; Vietnam; China **Quality Control Program:** Proprietary peer review; reports from AICPA peer review **Referrals Expected Between Members?:** Yes **Does Association Track Referrals?:** Yes **If Yes, Tracking Info Used?:** Track number of referrals, not value **How Is Tracking Info Used?:** Marketing **Services Provided:** A1 (three/year), B, C, D, E, G, I, M, R, T, U, W **Education for Convergence of GAAP and IFAS?:** Yes **Needs Assessment of Member Firms?** No **Plan to Meet Members' Potential Needs for Expertise, Assistance?** Yes **Network or Association?** Association
JHI Ruth Abrahamson, International Executive Director 250 Consumers Road, Suite 301 Toronto, Ontario, Canada M2J 4V6 416-494-1440 ext. 231 Fax: 416-495-8723 E-Mail: international@jhi.com, americas@jhi.com Kenneth Kirkland, Chair, JHI Region of the Americas 781-356-2000 Fax:781-356-5450 E-Mail: kkirkland@kafgroup.com Web: www.jhi.com	0/0 #	6	26	9	90	25	1/2	1	34.9**†	$588.78 M**†	**Reporting As:** Int'l association based abroad, listing information through a U.S. or "Americas" regional entity **Largest U.S. Firm:** DNP **Smallest U.S. Firm:** DNP **Fees Initial/Annual:** $2,500/based on annual gross revenues (below $500,000: $1,725 regional plus $3,000 int'l; above $500,000: $4,450 regional plus $4,600 int'l) **Membership Requirements:** Must supply three references; undergo site assessment; send at least one rep to int'l and regional annual conferences **Seeking Representation In:** Dallas; San Antonio; Las Vegas; Seattle **Quality Control Program:** Reports from AICPA peer review **Referrals Expected Between Members?:** Yes **Does Association Track Referrals?:** Yes **If Yes, Tracking Criteria:** Members required to report referrals twice/year **How Is Tracking Info Used?:** DNP **Services Provided:** A1 (no add'l fee for annual conferences), B, D1 (varies), E1 (varies), G, H1, I, J, K, L, M, T, U, V **Education for Convergence of GAAP and IFAS?:** DNP **Needs Assessment of Member Firms?** Yes **Plan to Meet Members' Potential Needs for Expertise, Assistance?** DNP **Network or Association?** Association
Kreston International Jon Lisby, Executive Director Springfield Lyons Business Centre Springfield Lyons Approach Chelmsford, Essex CM2 5LB 44-1245-449-266 Fax: 44-1245-462-882 E-Mail: jon@kreston.com Web: www.kreston.com	0/0	5	8	DNP	DNP	8	0/0	DNP	129.5	$2.07 B	**Reporting As:** Int'l association based abroad **Largest U.S. Firm:** CBIZ/Cleveland **Smallest U.S. Firm:** Altus Economics/California **Fees Initial/Annual:** None/£395 ($591) per firm, £265 ($396) per partner **Membership Requirements:** Provider of major core products (audit, accounting, tax and consulting); 10 or more partners; int'l business expertise **Seeking Representation In:** All regions **Quality Control Program:** Proprietary peer review; reports from AICPA peer review, PCAOB **Referrals Expected Between Members?:** Yes **Does Association Track Referrals?:** Yes **If Yes, Tracking Criteria:** Biannual system; members report work undertaken for other members' clients **How Is Tracking Info Used?:** To monitor growth of referral business **Services Provided:** A1 (annual global, regional), B, C, D, E, F, G, I, J1, K, T, U, W, X1 **Education for Convergence of GAAP and IFAS?:** No **Needs Assessment of Member Firms?** No **Plan to Meet Members' Potential Needs for Expertise, Assistance?** No **Network or Association?** Association

¶520

Leading Edge Alliance
Karen Kehl-Rose, President
621 Cedar Street
St. Charles, IL 60174
630-513-9814
Fax 630-524-9074
E-Mail: kkr@the-LEA.com
R. Michael Cain, U.S. Chair
630-513-9814
Web: www.leadingedgealliance.com

| 2/6 | 2 | 46 | 5 | 104 | 46 | 5/1 | 0 | 27 | $2.06 B |

Reporting As: Int'l association based in the U.S.
Largest U.S. Firm: Marcum Kliegman/New York
Smallest U.S. Firm: Steinberg Advisors/Chicago
Fees Initial/Annual: $5,000/$17,500
Membership Requirements: Territorial exclusivity; $10 million revenue; member; PCPS/The AICPA Alliance for CPA Firms; participation in annual operations survey; practice mix
Seeking Representation In: Kansas City
Quality Control Program: Reports from AICPA peer review; other AICPA quality centers; PCAOB
Referrals Expected Between Members?: Yes
Does Association Track Referrals?: No
Services Provided: A (100+ annually); B; C; D1; E1; G; I; L1; M; N1; P1; Q1; R; S; T; U; W
Other Services: Special interest groups; surveys (firm financial operations; HR; IT; firm administration; other firm mgt. compensation); collaborative magazine for firm clients; free newsletter articles; staff training courses
Niche Practices: SALT; wealth mgt.; non-profit; M&A; int'l business; BV/litigation support; SEC; healthcare/medical practices; family business consulting; 404 work and IT assurance
Education for Convergence of GAAP and IFAS?: Yes
Needs Assessment of Member Firms? Yes
Plan to Meet Members' Potential Needs for Expertise, Assistance?: Yes
Network or Association? Association

MGI
Clive Mieville, Executive Director
Hudson House
8 Tavistock Street
London WC2E 7PF U.K.
44-1932-853-393
Fax 44-1932-854-323
U.S. Chair: Charles Postal
240-499-2040
Fax: 240-499-2075
E-Mail: cpostal@santospostal.com
Web: www.mgiworld.com

| 0/3 | 2 | 21 | 9 | 140 | 21 | 5/0 | 0 | 7 | $150 M |

Reporting As: Int'l association based abroad, listing information through a U.S. or "Americas" regional entity
Largest U.S. Firm: Braver PC/Newton, Mass.
Smallest U.S. Firm: Snead & Williams/Danville, Va.
Fees Initial/Annual: $1,500/0.18% of firm's turnover (min. $2,500, max. $13,500) plus $2,000 North America fee
Membership Requirements: Should not be a member of another int'l association of accounting firms; principals must be suitably qualified and permitted to practice as accountants and auditors; must be authorized and capable of carrying out audits of at least privately held companies in accordance with Int'l Auditing St'ds; provide advice on all domestic taxes and duties; provide bookkeeping and accountancy services in accordance with Int'l Accounting St'ds; must attend either an area or int'l MGI meeting at least every two years; more
Seeking Representation In: Cleveland; Chicago; San Diego; Phoenix; Denver; Kansas City; Syracuse; Milwaukee; Indianapolis; Detroit
Quality Control Program: Proprietary peer review; reports from AICPA peer review
Referrals Expected Between Members?: Referrals are frequent; however, the value of membership is based on outreach rather than referrals
Does Association Track Referrals?: No
Services Provided: A1 (annual general meeting; at least one area meeting/year for each of eight areas; fees vary per location, continent), B, C, D (some areas), E, F, G, H, I, J, K, L, M, N, Q, R, S (some areas), T, U, V1, W, X
Other Services: Corporate publications (MGI brochure in seven languages; members' guide; annual directory; poster; certificate; int'l meetings; marketing resource for individual and group support; regional marketing group support system; Doing Business In ... country guides; case studies; research; generic PowerPoint presentations; media relations advice/press pack; corporate identity guidelines; monthly news updates; e-newsletters
Education for Convergence of GAAP and IFAS?: Yes
Needs Assessment of Member Firms? Yes
Plan to Meet Members' Potential Needs for Expertise, Assistance?: Yes
Network or Association? Association

Moore Stephens North America
Steven E. Sacks, Executive Director
Route 80 West
Plaza II, Suite 200
Saddle Brook, NJ 07663
201-291-2660
Fax 201-368-1944
E-mail: ssacks@msnainc.org
William T. Young, U.S. Chair
239-628-6437
byoung@msnainc.org
Web: www.msnainc.org

| 2/DNP | DNP | 32 | 14 | 8 | 32 | 1/1 | DNP | 25.8 | $875 M |

Reporting As: Int'l association based abroad but listing its information through a U.S. or "Americas" region
Largest U.S. Firm: Wipfli/Green Bay, Wis.
Smallest U.S. Firm: Burnside & Rishebarger/San Antonio
Fees Initial/Annual: None/$20,000 to domestic operations plus a percentage of prior year's net revenues for int'l
Membership Requirements: DNP
Seeking Representation In: Midwest; Rockies; Southwest
Quality Control Program: Reports from AICPA peer review; other AICPA quality centers; PCAOB
Referrals Expected Between Members?: Yes
Does Association Track Referrals?: No
Services Provided: A1 (quarterly; semi-annually); B; C; D1; E1; F; G; H; I; K; M; O; R; S; T; U; V; W
Niche Practices: Valuation; litigation; forensic services; real estate; healthcare; employee benefit plans; construction; SALT; int'l tax; not-for-profit
Education for Convergence of GAAP and IFAS?: Yes
Needs Assessment of Member Firms? Yes
Plan to Meet Members' Potential Needs for Expertise, Assistance? DNP
Network or Association? Association

¶520

Association/Network Headquarters Contact / Other (U.S. Or Int'l) Contact	U.S. Association Staff (FT/PT)	Int'l Staff (FT)	U.S. Member Firms	Non-U.S. North American Firms	Non-North American Firms	U.S. CPA Firms	U.S. CPA Firms Joining/Leaving*	Non-CPA Firms	Median Rev. ($M), U.S. Member Firms	Total Assoc. Net Rev. (N. America Only)	Details
The Moss Adams Connection Scott Martin, Executive Director 601 W. Riverside, Suite 1800 Spokane, WA 99201 509-747-2600 Fax: 509-624-5129 E-Mail: scott.martin@mossadams.com Web: www.mossadams.com/mac/default.aspx	1/1	DNP	39	1	DNP	39	2/2	1	1.7	$83.1 M	**Reporting As:** U.S. association with int'l affiliates **Largest U.S. Firm:** Shea Labagh Dobberstein/San Francisco **Smallest U.S. Firm:** Sutter, Kunkie and Thompson/Moses Lake, Wash. **International Affiliate:** Praxity **Fees Initial/Annual:** None/One-third of 1% of gross fees, min. $3,600, max. $18,000 **Membership Requirements:** Generally, one member per geographic market; member in good standing with state, nat'l accounting boards/associations; satisfactory peer review (if available); industry group focus **Seeking Representation In:** California; Montana; Oregon; Wyoming; New Mexico; Colorado; Idaho; Arizona; Alaska **Quality Control Program:** Reports from AICPA peer review **Referrals Expected Between Members?:** Yes **Does Association Track Referrals?:** No **Services Provided:** A1 (annual), D1, G, I, K, R, S, U, V **Niche Practices:** Construction; manufacturing/distribution; financial institutions; auto dealers; business valuations; cost segregation; not-for-profit; R&D credits; healthcare **Education for Convergence of GAAP and IFAS?:** No **Needs Assessment of Member Firms?** Yes **Plan to Meet Members' Potential Needs for Expertise, Assistance?** Yes **Network or Association?** Association
MSA (CPA Manufacturing Services Association) Patrick Pruett, Executive Director 624 Grassmere Park Drive, Suite 15 Nashville, TN 37211 615-377-3392 Fax: 615-377-7092 E-Mail: info@manufacturingcpas.com Web: www.manufacturingcpas.com	3/1	DNP	22	DNP	DNP	22	DNP	DNP	DNP	DNP	**Reporting As:** Niche-specific U.S. association **Largest U.S. Firm:** DNP **Smallest U.S. Firm:** DNP **Fees Initial/Annual:** $1,500/$1,595 **Membership Requirements:** DNP **Seeking Representation In:** DNP **Quality Control Program:** DNP **Referrals Expected Between Members?:** Don't know **Does Association Track Referrals?:** No **Services Provided:** A1 (biannual), B, D, E, K, M, S, T **Other Services:** Listservs **Niche Practices:** Manufacturing **Education for Convergence of GAAP and IFAS?:** DNP **Needs Assessment of Member Firms?** DNP **Plan to Meet Members' Potential Needs for Expertise, Assistance?** DNP **Network or Association?** DNP
MSI Global Alliance James Mendelssohn, Chief Executive Officer 147-149 Temple Chambers 3-7 Temple Avenue London EC4Y 0DA, U.K. 44-20-7583-7000 Fax: 44-20-7583-7577 E-Mail: jmendelssohn@msiglobal.org Web: www.msiglobal.org	0/0	5	50	6	192	23	0/2	27	5.5	$1.1 B	**Reporting As:** Int'l association based abroad **Largest U.S. Firm:** Anderson ZurMuehlen & Co./Helena, Mont. **Smallest U.S. Firm:** McKerley & Noonan/Nashville **Fees Initial/Annual:** £800 ($1,196)/£2,550 – £5,850 ($3,813-$8,749) depending on number of partners **Membership Requirements:** Independent; medium-sized in marketplace; able to provide full range of commercial advisory services across broad range of industries; unaffiliated with any other association or network; focused on serving specific geographic market; able to commit to becoming active, long-term member **Seeking Representation In:** Atlanta; New Orleans; Las Vegas; Oregon; Minnesota; San Antonio; Indianapolis; Jacksonville; North Carolina; South Carolina **Quality Control Program:** Reports from AICPA peer review **Referrals Expected Between Members?:** Yes **Does Association Track Referrals?:** No **Services Provided:** A1 (one annual; three regional, eight local/year; fees vary), B, G, I, M, O, T, U, V, W **Other Services:** Co-branded marketing materials including 'branded signage; social networking through members-only Website; referral facilitation; int'l directory; proposal facilitation **Education for Convergence of GAAP and IFAS?:** No **Needs Assessment of Member Firms?** No **Plan to Meet Members' Potential Needs for Expertise, Assistance?** No **Network or Association?** Association

¶520

National Alliance of Auto Dealer Advisors
Cornell Rudov, President
P.O. Box 7648
Princeton, NJ 08543-7648
609-890-0800
Fax: 609-689-9720
E-Mail: crudov@cpasnet.com
Steven Rawlins, U.S. Chair
904-396-2202
Fax: 904-398-1315
E-Mail: sdr@mswopa.com
Web: www.autodealeradvisors.com

| | 2/0 | 0 | 11 | DNP | 11 | 1/0 | 0 | 8 | 60,000 |

Reporting As: Niche-specific U.S. association
Largest U.S. Firm: Wipfli/Minneapolis
Smallest U.S. Firm: W. Keith Argabright/Walnut Creek, Calif.
Fees Initial/Annual: DNP/$2,000
Membership Requirements: Operates successful auto dealer niche group; ability for at least one partner to travel to two meetings/year; strong interest in making auto dealer niche more successful; open to change and new ideas
Seeking Representation In: Seattle; Boston; Denver
Quality Control Program: Reports from AICPA peer review; significant auto dealer practice
Referrals Expected Between Members?: No
Does Association Track Referrals?: No
Services Provided: A1 (two/year), B, C, D1, E1, F, H, I, K, N1, O1, P, Q, S, T, U, V
Education for Convergence of GAAP and IFAS?: Yes
Needs Assessment of Member Firms? Yes
Plan to Meet Members' Potential Needs for Expertise, Assistance? Yes
Network or Association? Association

Nexia International
Nigel Hodges, Executive Director
4 Harley Street
London W1G 9PB U.K.
44-20-7487-4648
Fax: 44-20-7487-3484
E-Mail: nhodges@nexia.com
Larry Chastang, U.S. Chair
407-802-1250
Fax: 407-802-1250
E-Mail: lchastang@larsonallen.com
Web: www.nexia.com

| | 0/0 | 5 | 18 | 9 | 18 | 15/1 | DNP | 33.6 | $2.3 B |

Reporting As: Int'l network based abroad, but listing its information through a U.S. or "Americas' regional entity
Largest U.S. Firm: J.H. Cohn/Roseland, N.J.
Smallest U.S. Firm: Catrakilis & Co./Atlanta
Fees Initial/Annual: Equivalent six month fees/Varies (U.S. rev. < $45 M x 0.15%; $45-90 M x 0.1%; $90 M+ x 0.025%)
Membership Requirements: Meet quality control assessment; substantial regional/national presence; full-service firm; significant audit resource; committed to serving int'l clients
Seeking Representation In: Mountain West and Southwest
Quality Control Program: Proprietary peer review; reports from AICPA peer review, PCAOB
Referrals Expected Between Members?: Yes
Does Ass'n Track Referrals?: Yes
If Yes, Tracking Criteria: Members report to secretariat every six months
How Is Tracking Info Used? Review by board and billings of referral fees
Services Provided: A1, B, C, D, G, H, I, K, L, M, N, O, T, W, X
Education for Convergence of GAAP and IFAS?: Yes
Needs Assessment of Member Firms? Yes
Plan to Meet Members' Potential Needs for Expertise, Assistance? No
Network or Association? Network

NSA (Not-For-Profit Services Association)
Patrick Pruett, Executive Director
624 Grassmere Park Drive, Suite 15
Nashville, TN 37211
615-377-2392
Fax: 615-377-7092
E-Mail: info@nonprofitcpas.com
Web: www.nonprofitcpas.com

| | 3/1 | DNP | 20 | DNP | 20 | 1/0 | DNP | DNP | DNP |

Reporting As: Niche-specific U.S. association
Largest U.S. Firm: DNP
Smallest U.S. Firm: DNP
Fees Initial/Annual: $1,500/$1,200
Membership Requirements: DNP
Seeking Representation In: DNP
Quality Control Program: DNP
Referrals Expected Between Members?: Don't know
Does Association Track Referrals?: DNP
Services Provided: A1 (biannual), B, D, E, H1, K, M, S, T
Other Services: Listservs
Niche Practices: Not-for-profit
Education for Convergence of GAAP and IFAS?: DNP
Needs Assessment of Member Firms? DNP
Plan to Meet Members' Potential Needs for Expertise, Assistance? DNP
Network or Association? DNP

¶520

Association/Network Headquarters Contact Other (U.S. Or Int'l) Contact	U.S. Association Staff (FT/PT)	Int'l Staff (FT)	U.S. Member Firms	Non-U.S. North American Firms	Non-North American Firms	U.S. CPA Firms	U.S. CPA Firms Joining/Leaving*	Non-CPA Firms	Median Rev. ($M) U.S. Member Firms	Total Assoc. Net Rev. (N. America Only)	Details
PKF North American Network Terry Snyder, President 3700 Crestwood Parkway, Suite 350 Duluth, GA 30096 770-279-4560 Fax: 770-279-4566 E-mail: tsnyder@pkfnan.org Gary Johnson, U.S. Chair 702-304-0404 Fax: 702-304-0414 E-mail: gjohnson@jjwcpa.com Web: www.pkfnan.org	16/3	DNP	73	14	0	73	5/6	0	7.4	$6.18 M	**Reporting As:** U.S. association with int'l affiliates **Largest U.S. Firm:** Frazier & Deeter/Atlanta **Smallest U.S. Firm:** Lehmann, Ullmann & Barclay/Birmingham, Ala. **International Affiliate:** PKF International **Fees Initial/Annual:** $5,000/based on firm revenue **Membership Requirements:** Minumum $2.5 million in fees; located in a city where we need member; peer review **Seeking Representation In:** Dallas; Tampa; Sacramento; San Antonio; Kansas City, MO; Milwaukee; Columbus, OH; Indianapolis; Nashville; Raleigh, NC **Quality Control Program:** Reports from AICPA peer review **Referrals Expected Between Members?:** Yes **Does Association Track Referrals?:** No **Services Provided:** A1 (twice/year), B, C, D1, E1, G1, I, K, L1 M1, N1, O1, P1, Q1, R1, S, U1, W, X **Other Services:** First Research; ProfitsCents; Dr T's Plain Accounting Update; E&Y Online; financial consulting; family business consulting; performance; career excellence; HR strategic model; financial; technology survey; more **Niche Practices:** Business valuation/litigation support; business development/marketing; construction contractors; closely held family business; employee benefit plans; healthcare; hospitality; int'l business development; investment advisory services; not-for-profit; more **Education for Convergence of GAAP and IFAS?:** No **Needs Assessment of Member Firms?** Yes **Plan to Meet Members' Potential Needs for Expertise, Assistance?** Yes **Network or Association?** Association
Polaris International Julio Gabay, Executive Director 9200 South Dadeland Boulevard, Suite 510 Miami, FL 33156 305-670-0580 Fax: 305-670-3818 E-Mail: julio@accountants.org Larry King, U.S. Chair 972-702-8262 Fax: 972-702-0673 E-mail: king@ktagrouplp.com Web: www.polarisinternational.org	4/0	5	28	2	143	28	4/0	DNP	6.4	$543.15 M	**Reporting As:** Int'l association based in the U.S. **Largest U.S. Firm:** Rosen Seymour Shapss Martin & Co./New York **Smallest U.S. Firm:** Austin, Falls & Chandler/Denver **Fees Initial/Annual:** $2,000/$3,500-$15,000 **Membership Requirements:** Minimum two partners, 10 staff and $1 million U.S. revenue **Seeking Representation In:** Calgary; Montreal; New Orleans; Minneapolis; Pittsburgh; Los Angeles; Bridgeport; Indianapolis; Portland; Honolulu **Quality Control Program:** Reports from AICPA peer review **Referrals Expected Between Members?:** Yes **Does Association Track Referrals?:** Yes **If Yes, Tracking Criteria:** Firms report quarterly and annually **How Is Tracking Info Used?:** Shared among members, published in quarterly newsletters **Services Provided:** A1 (10/year), B, C, D1, E1, G, H, I, K, L, M, P, Q, R, S, U, W, X **Niche Practices:** SOX; SALT; M&A; int'l tax; SEC; administration; HR; family owned/managed businesses; employee benefits; business development **Education for Convergence of GAAP and IFAS?:** No **Needs Assessment of Member Firms?** No **Plan to Meet Members' Potential Needs for Expertise, Assistance?** Yes **Network or Association?** Association
Praxity Paul Hancock, Secretary General 5th Floor, Stephenson House 2 Cherry Orchard Road Croydon (S. London) U.K. CR0 6BA 44-208-774-4020 Fax: 44-208-774-4029 E-Mail: phancock@praxity.com Lisa Cines, North American Chair 301-231-6200 Fax: 301-230-7630 E-Mail: lcines@aronsoncompany.com Web: www.praxity.com	0/0	2	8	22	78	8	0/0	0	176	$3.2 B	**Reporting As:** Int'l association based abroad **Largest U.S. Firm:** BKD/Southfield, Mo. **Smallest U.S. Firm:** Feeley & Driscoll/Boston **Fees Initial/Annual:** 0.0125% of firm revenue/member firm: $10,000 plus % of net fee revenue; associate firm: $5,000 plus % of net fee revenue; correspondents: $5,000 **Membership Requirements:** Financial condition; int'l strategy; geographic relevance; size; excellent reputation **Seeking Representation In:** None **Quality Control Program:** Reports from AICPA peer review, AICPA quality centers, PCAOB **Referrals Expected Between Members?:** Yes **Does Association Track Referrals?:** Yes **If Yes, Tracking Criteria:** Request for firms to report billings from referred work **How Is Tracking Info Used?:** First year, yet to be decided **Services Provided:** A1 (throughout year), B, C, D, E, G, I, T, W **Education for Convergence of GAAP and IFAS?:** No **Needs Assessment of Member Firms?** Yes **Plan to Meet Members' Potential Needs for Expertise, Assistance?** Yes **Network or Association?** Association

¶520

Premier International Associates

Nick Florio, U.S. Chair
c/o Citrin Cooperman
529 Fifth Avenue
New York, NY 10017
212-697-1000
Fax: 212-697-1870
Web: www.premierinternational.org

Data: 0/0 | 0 | 6 | 3 | 19 | 3 | 0/0 | DNP | 14 | $217 M

Reporting As: Int'l association based in U.S.
Largest U.S. Firm: Citrin Cooperman & Co./New York
Smallest U.S. Firm: Entous & Entous/California
Fees Initial/Annual: None/$3,500
Membership Requirements: Territorial exclusivity, membership exclusivity, diversified services
Seeking Representation In: Florida; Boston; Chicago
Quality Control Program: Proprietary peer review; reports from AICPA peer review, PCAOB, equivalents
Referrals Expected Between Members?: Yes
Does Association Track Referrals?: Yes
If Yes, Tracking Criteria: Information provided by members
How Is Tracking Info Used? Information shared between members
Services Provided: A (semi-annual), G, T, W
Education for Convergence of GAAP and IFAS? Yes
Needs Assessment of Member Firms? Yes
Plan to Meet Members' Potential Needs for Expertise, Assistance? Yes
Network or Association? Association

RSM McGladrey Network

Debra K. Lockwood, Executive Director
401 Main St., Suite 1560
Peoria, IL 61602-1242
800-537-7178
Fax: 309-673-9852
E-Mail: deb.lockwood@rsmi.com
Web: www.rsmmcgladreynetwork.com

Data: 38/41†† | 0 | 95 | 0 | DNP | 95 | 3/4 | 0 | 11 | >$900 M

Reporting As: U.S. association with int'l affiliates
Largest U.S. Firm: Horne/Jackson, Miss.
Smallest U.S. Firm: Johnson & Sheldon/Amarillo, Texas
International Affiliate: RSM International
Fees Initial/Annual: None/fee scale based on annual revenue
Membership Requirements: $1 mill on in professional liability insurance; must provide most recent peer review report and letter of comment; must provide most recent financial statements and income tax return, client, banker, attorney references; specified geographic territory
Seeking Representation In: Contact association for open markets
Quality Control Program: Reports from AICPA peer review
Referrals Expected Between Members?: No
Does Association Track Referrals?: No
Services Provided: A1 (frequency, fee vary), B, C, D1, E1, F1, G, H, I, K, L1, M1, N1, O1, P1, R1 (varies), S, T, U
Other Services: Financial statistics (MAP) survey, retreat facilitation; M&A consulting; people, client satisfaction surveys, strategic planning, tax practice reviews
Niche Practices: Manufacturing, construction/real estate, financial institutions, healthcare, not-for-profit
Education for Convergence of GAAP and IFAS? Yes
Needs Assessment of Member Firms? No
Plan to Meet Members' Potential Needs for Expertise, Assistance? No
Network or Association? Association

Russell Bedford International

Geoffrey Goodyear, Chairman
Russell Bedford House
250 City Road
London EC1V 2QQ, U.K.
44-20-7410-0339
Fax: 44-20-7549-2337
E-Mail: info@russellbedford.com
Web: www.russellbedford.com

Data: 0/0 | 2 | 9 | 1 | 62 | 7 | 0/0 | 2 | 6 | $348 M

Reporting As: Int'l network based abroad
Largest U.S. Firm: NSBN/Beverly Hills, Calif.
Smallest U.S. Firm: DNP
Fees Initial/Annual: $1,000 ($1,496)/$2,475-$6,600 ($3,701-$9,871)
Membership Requirements: Exclusivity of representation, practice size, mix; interviews and inspection visit; participation in global quality control program
Seeking Representation In: Arizona, Colorado, Florida, North Carolina, Washington; Minnesota
Quality Control Program: Proprietary peer review; reports from AICPA peer review, other AICPA quality centers and PCAOB; interviews and inspection of offices
Referrals Expected Between Members?: Yes
Does Association Track Referrals?: Yes
If Yes, Tracking Criteria: Quarterly declaration by all members covering all new incoming and outgoing referral inquiries and income from earlier referrals
How Is Tracking Info Used? Monitoring purposes; charging of referral fees to recipients of referred business
Services Provided: A1 (annual global, Americas regional and European regional conferences), B, D1, E1, G1, H1 (fee varies), I1 (varies), J1 (varies), K, S, T, W, X1
Niche Practices: Private equity advisory; tax services; int'l tax; transnational audit; family business consulting; SEC practice
Education for Convergence of GAAP and IFAS? Yes
Needs Assessment of Member Firms? Yes
Plan to Meet Members' Potential Needs for Expertise, Assistance? Yes
Network or Association? Network

¶520

Association/Network Headquarters Contact Other (U.S. Or Int'l) Contact	U.S. Association Staff (FT/PT)	Int'l Staff (FT)	U.S. Member Firms	Non-U.S. North American Firms	Non-North American Firms	U.S. CPA Firms	U.S. CPA Firms Joining/ Leaving*	Non-CPA Firms	Median Rev. (SM) U.S. Member Firms	Total Assoc. Net Rev. (N. America Only)	Details
Western Association of Accounting Firms Alex Miller, U.S. Chair 160 Speer Street, Suite 1900 San Francisco, CA 94106 415-836-4000 Fax: 415-777-2062 E-Mail: millera@henming.com Web: www.waaf.org	0/0	0	11	DNP	DNP	11	0/0	DNP	10.2	None	**Reporting As:** U.S. association without int'l affiliates **Largest U.S. Firm:** DNP/Rancho Cucamonga, Calif. **Smallest U.S. Firm:** DNP/Bellevue, Wash. **Fees Initial/Annual:** None/out-of-pocket expenses to attend meetings and events **Membership Requirements:** Western United States; geographically specific; similar size to other members **Seeking Representation In:** San Diego; Idaho; Montana; New Mexico; Utah **Quality Control Program:** Proprietary peer review; reports from AICPA peer review; administrative review of firm operations **Referrals Expected Between Members?:** Yes **Does Association Track Referrals?:** No **Services Provided:** A (two/year), B, E **Education for Convergence of GAAP and IFAS?:** No **Needs Assessment of Member Firms?** No **Plan to Meet Members' Potential Needs for Expertise, Assistance?** No **Network or Association?** Association

Source: CCH, 2009 Annual Survey of CPA Firm Associations

¶ 525 CAN-SPAM

From e-lerts and e-newsletters to promotional offers, e-mail has become a standard part of many firms' marketing tactics. It's inexpensive and easy. Our mailboxes are full of these messages and, from our clients' point of view, there may be a lot wrong with these e-mails.

¶525

In 2003, Congress responded by enacting the Controlling the Assault of Non-Solicited Pornography and Marketing Act (CAN-SPAM). The law, which hasn't changed much since it was enacted, requires e-mail marketers to comply with certain rules. Most are these rules are straightforward and as the name of the act implies, intended to prevent spam. Firms that send these types of e-mails to their clients should:

- Include a relevant subject line.

- Allow recipients to opt-out or unsubscribe from the e-mail (generally through a link at the bottom of the e-mail).

- Include an address on the e-mail.

¶ 530 Competitive Intelligence: The Next Frontier?

Some thought leaders believe that competitive intelligence is the next corporate business practice to come to the professional services arena. According to Wikipedia, a broad definition of competitive intelligence, or CI, "is the action of gathering, analyzing, and applying information about products, domain constituents, customers, and competitors for the short-term and long-term planning needs of an organization." It is the ethical gathering of non-proprietary, open source data through secondary and primary collection techniques.

For CPA firms, this translates to monitoring what competitors are doing to compete in the marketplace. What publications are the partners in a competitor firm writing for? Where are they speaking? Are they quoted in the media? What are they reading? Does their firm's Web site have a client portal? Do they gather information about potential clients by offering white paper downloads on their Web site?

CI is related to both market research and knowledge management. Once you gather the information you need, you can use it to make your firm more competitive by integrating it into your marketing and business development strategy: are there new services you can offer or new markets to enter? CI may even lead to an innovation that makes your firm a market leader in a new service area.

¶ 535 The Chaos of Managing from a Distance

No discussion of the evolving geographic landscape would be complete without examining the roles of technology and specialization. Quite simply, the ability to physically serve a far-away client doesn't exist without technology. Technology is the sole reason why clients no longer regard geographic location as a barrier to engaging the firm they want to hire. And there's only one reason a client would *want* to hire a firm that's not located in its own backyard: specialized expertise. Today, you can have a national practice without having a network of locations. With technology, all you need is a deep niche.

That ability is a huge change that shakes up some of the traditional cardinal laws of practice management. Firms historically could see, feel, and touch their clients. That ability is now a nicety rather than a necessity. That's not to say that the human touch is no longer relevant, but through technology and expertise, firms can be more successful by having a few strategically placed regional outposts, such as a single West Coast office that serves multiple states.

Professional services firms today can practice practically anywhere based on exploitation of a niche. A Pittsburgh firm can't pick up a steel distributor client in Phoenix unless it has a deep niche and a technological backbone that's strong enough to ensure service through tools such as videoconferencing, Internet, email, and cell phones. The marriage of technology and specialization are territorial terminators: they have the power to eliminate the constraints of geography.

But the disintegration of geographic limitations also complicates practice management. Now firms must manage different types of employees than they're accustomed to managing, such as salespeople. They're dealing with tax issues that vary from state to state, city to city, and town to town. There are issues with time zone differences. Complications can arise from not having face time with clients or knowing them as well on a personal level. These complications also add to the demands on the firm's staff. Professional long-distance relationships require professionals at all levels to have better communications skills and to document discussions more diligently. These professionals may not see clients face to face, but firms can't let these clients fall into the trap of "out of sight, out of mind" or perceive that they're on the back-burner. Firms must rebuild their internal cultures to be proactive with clients who aren't sitting before their eyes. For example, firms must make an added effort to attend more conferences that are oriented toward their niches so that the firm's professional staff will be at places where clients and prospects also will be. Professionals must learn to schedule communication time with clients when they don't have much face time with them. They can't just walk into a client's business and see them like they once could, so alternatives to ensure maximum client service and loyalty must be created.

The complications that come with the dismantling of territorial boundaries are accompanied by a more complicated regulatory reality. New territorial frontiers come with different laws and rules that govern the practice of law and accounting beyond state lines. Firms that most successfully build practices without borders generally concentrate on specialties that are more applicable to all businesses rather than services that might be specific to certain regions or nations. Outsourcing makes use of the flattened geographic landscape, but it's most successful with compliance-oriented work and is less successful with high-value, subjective services like succession planning, tax planning, or consulting.

Consequently, high-value types of services are better positioned for national practices, and they probably will be for the foreseeable future. In 1987, there was no way to pick up restaurant client in San Diego if your firm was headquartered in Chicago, or a manufacturer in Mississippi if your firm was in Minneapolis. Now it's easy, and it gets easier all the time. The dissolution of geographic limitations creates a huge expansion of opportunity. For example, a Seattle law firm represented plaintiffs in a class action suit against an Atlanta-area water park stemming from an E. coli outbreak, because the law firm had built a reputation for expertise in class actions. Now geography just isn't as much of an issue. The mutation of geographic limitations provides opportunities to create national practices.

Mergers and acquisitions take new importance in this environment of chaos as geographic location increasingly takes on lesser importance. Nowadays, geographic strength isn't always enough for two firms to unite. Whether it's a true merger or an acquisition on the table, firms increasingly look for partners who will strengthen their existing specialties or help them create new expertise that they can build on and profit from in the long term. Larger firms continually have their ears to the ground for potential merger mates and acquisitions that will help them build or strengthen existing niches. Geography becomes a bigger issue when firms want to expand into a new territory. These days, a practice located outside an acquiring firm's geographic market can be *more* attractive rather than *less* attractive for potential buyers.

¶ 540   Invasion of the Aliens: Marketing and Business Development Experts

Marketing has come a long way. It is common for firms of all sizes to have some sort of marketing program in place, and the Association for Accounting Marketing (www.accountingmarketing.org), based in Mt Laurel, N.J., has nearly 1,000 members.

Many firms are also hiring business development professionals and training directors. Bringing these specialized practice development disciplines to the table elevates growth efforts to a new level of sophistication and effectiveness, but it also adds to the chaos.

Different skills are needed to manage people with these skills sets, and different metrics are required to measure the results of their work, which was long considered intangible and immeasurable. Within the marketing framework, there are so many specialties: print, branding, networking, promotions, publicity, and advertising, for example. These are skills that aren't the core talents of accountants, and it's rarely a job accountants are trained to do.

Marketing, business developers, and sales professionals are a different breed than accountants. Their expectations for success are different. Accountants can say, "I have 1,600 charge hours. I'm earning my keep." Marketing and business development people don't use those measurements as a yardstick for productivity. Historically, the marketing departments at accounting firms had a virtual revolving door. Continuity and retention was rare, and high turnover was expected. But retention rates improved as firms recognize that practice development professionals must be trained, motivated, and managed differently, and that they have different expectations of their employers.

At first, the marketers' role was tactical. The firm's marketer was charged with acquiring new clients. In the 1980s, most firm marketers oversaw massive direct mail campaigns and wrote firm brochures. Firms reasoned that if they didn't see reasonable growth and win a certain number of new clients from these efforts, then the marketers weren't doing their jobs correctly. There was no distinction between executing a program and closing business with prospects or winning new business. This misperception continued for a long time, but eventually the marketer's role began its evolution from tactician to strategist. Firms and their leaders began to understand that the marketer's role does not follow a direct path to the bottom line. Marketers may not have billable hours, but they have (and deserve) a line in the budget.

Figure 5.4 ——

Traits and Prerequisities of a Successful Business Developer

It's helpful for business developers to have a tendency to extroversion, of course, but too much is as troublesome as too little. Listening is a critical success factor for business developers, which means the ability to be patient is of great value. Self-confidence, without tending toward arrogance, also serves aspiring business developers well. Business development never stops. Because it is an ongoing process, the ability to persevere, without becoming a "prisoner of hope" (i.e., someone who doesn't realize they're lost and continues wasting time on follow-up measures) is a worthwhile trait for a business developer to have and nurture.

A good sales professional should have an excellent grasp of the essentials of your services—what they are, how they are delivered, and, prospect's needs and explaining why the firm is the right choice to meet those needs. However, because the sales professional is generally always teamed with a practitioner when meeting with prospects, a complete mastery of the technical intricacies of accounting is not required. In fact, focusing on FASB, SAS, GAAP, and GASS rather than the prospect's strategies, goals, worries and profits too early in the sales process can cause the sale to be lost.

In essence, the sales professional initiates the action, and then works in a complementary fashion with the accountant to convert the prospect into a client. A team approach to professional selling really works because it doesn't require all accountants to be Dale Carnegie or Zig Ziegler—they can focus on problem-solving rather than the next step in the sales process.

While sales professionals can play a key role in helping accounting firms achieve their business development objectives, they cannot do it alone. It's very important for all firm professionals, especially partners, to understand that their responsibility for cross-serving clients, as well as referral source and prospect development, will in no way be reduced when the firm hires a sales professional. Rather, the efforts of all will be optimized.

Keep in mind that hiring a sales professional may not cure a sales drought any more than buying a new golf club will cure a slice. Just as a quality firm's reputation will give the sales professional something of great value to bring to the market, the opposite is also true.

Hiring an individual whose character and sense of professional behavior aligns with the standards set for the firm as a whole can help assure that the person will be accepted by clients, prospects, and firm members.

Traits of a Successful Marketing Professional

Marketers must have many, if not all, of the traits noted above for business developers. In many ways, marketers are sales professionals too, but their target market is primarily internal—the firm's professionals. Marketers generally lead projects from a lateral position, so they need exceptional leadership skills, as well a strong sense of the best way to diplomatically get things done. They need to think like partners in order to see the big picture so they can hone the firm's marketing strategy and produce tangible results. Analytical thinking skills and being approachable round out the ideal traits of a marketer. Overall, the marketer needs to find innovative ways to get things done even when partners and other professionals seem unresponsive.

Like the sales professional, a marketing professional should also have an excellent grasp of the essentials of your services. Because a marketing professional is charged with establishing/building the firm's brand, he or she must clearly define what initiatives are in place to help establish and continually build the firm's image, gain credibility internally and externally, maintain good referral source relationships, and focus on initiatives that highlight the firm's expertise and image as a whole.

The marketer is almost always working with a formal, defined plan of action. Marketers are charged with more of the day-to-day initiatives surrounding creating and reinforcing the firm's brand, promoting services and products, and communicating the firm's message to outside sources. Specific activities could include:

- A dynamic, interactive, and innovative Web site,
- Educational opportunities encouraging strengthening relationships as well as developing new ones,
- Press releases and mailings to reinforce expertise in specialty areas (newsletters, e-news alerts, seminar and event promotions, etc.), and
- Determining which progressive initiatives would fit into the current marketing mix (e.g., blogs, podcasting, ad campaigns, online networks, etc.).

The traits of a marketing professional can help to establish what the sales professional role is and help in identifying and increasing new business.

Source: Excerpted from an article by Michelle Class, Marketing Director and Chris Perrino, Principal, Business Development Director, Barnes Dennig/Cinncinati in the May 2008 issue of CCH's CPA Practice Management Forum..

As the marketer's role grew, some firms began to realize that the traditional corporate model called for "marketing and sales," not just marketing. These firms added business developers to their teams. Business developers do have bottom line responsibility for bringing in new business. Consequently, they're generally paid a base salary plus commission.

Where firms have both positions, the two roles work together. The marketer strategizes and the business developer implements. For example, the marketing department may see that there is room for a franchise niche in the marketplace. The business developer's role would be to go into the market and set up meetings with potential clients.

The situation is ripe for chaos because partners usually have unrealistic expectations. Few take the time to think about how long it takes to initiate business development services versus the time it takes to actually see results. Partners often don't realize that it can take a year or two to get traction for new services. They are afraid of the idea of paying for non-billable staff and activities, such as those in the marketing and business development arena, for extended periods of time without seeing demonstrable results.

Marketing can't be measured by billable hours, but it can be measured. Firms now track the results of mailings, Web sites, seminars, proposals, and so on. Bothering to track results is useful only if there are consequences. If there is no interest in marketing programs directed toward a particular niche, it may be time to eliminate that niche. If a partner is not interested in attending seminars, that may indicate a lack of motivation. These types of data, which show up when marketing measures are put in place, are only as relevant as the steps that are taken to remedy them.

Understanding how to manage marketing and business development professionals is the primary differentiator between firms that effectively use these techniques and those that don't. Firms with successful, professional practice development teams have realistic expectations regarding the return on their investment (ROI) in marketing and business development activities, and they understand that ROI for these efforts can't always be documented in black and white.

That said, remuneration can be an issue. Across the board, firms struggle with how to compensate marketers for their contributions. Some firms offer straight salary, others use a salary plus bonus system. Whatever works best for your firm is fine.

Firms, regardless of their size, must improve their ability to attract and retain these professionals.

Figure 5.5 ——

Things You Can Measure

- The number of:
    - New client proposals won and lost in a given time period.
    - Cross-selling opportunities to existing clients in a given time period.
        - Number won.
        - Number lost.
    - New engagements in new niches in a given time period.
        - Existing clients.
        - New clients.
    - New engagements/inquiries resulting from a specific event/campaign and follow-up effort.
- Revenue increases or decreases in a given time period.
    - By client.
    - By service area.
    - By industry.
- Difference in profitability for clients who pay retainers vs. those who don't.
- Each billing partner's:
    - Realization rates.
    - Timely billing.
    - Write-offs by partner.
    - Follow-up and collection efforts.
- Track partner's non-billable time spent:
    - Marketing and business development efforts.
    - Mentoring others.
    - Community work.
- Marketing budget.
    - By project.
    - By industry.
    - By service area.
- What position your firm occupies in the marketplace and how that changes over time.
- Name recognition prior to and after a branding campaign.
- Number of proposals won that received assistance from the marketing department vs. number of winning proposals that did not receive assistance from the marketing department.
- Client satisfaction as measured by:
    - Online or snail mailed client satisfaction survey.
    - Personal interviews.
- Staff satisfaction as measured by:
    - Turnover rate.
    - Employee satisfaction survey.

Figure 5.6 ——

Drivers of Brand Credibility

1. Trust, as demonstrated through:
    a. High performance.
    b. Excellent communication.
2. Values.
3. Transparency.
4. Responsiveness.

.01 Managing the Marketing Function

The approach to managing the marketing function differs from firm to firm. There are many different models. For example, the Pittsford, N.Y.-based Bonadio Group, with six offices, has a COO who oversees the firm's Enterprise Group, which consists of marketing, information technology, human resources, facilities, and finance.

At other firms, a marketing committee oversees the function. Marketing committees should be limited to no more than a handful partners. Otherwise, the entire marketing function can be paralyzed by a lack of agreement between the committee members.

Still another model, arguably the most prevalent, has the firm's highest level marketer reporting directly to the managing partner. One of the benefits of this model is that it adds credibility to the marketing function. This can be especially helpful in firms that need to boost their marketing culture.

Figure 5.7 ——

Defining Responsibilities: Who Does What?

Marketing Team

- Work with partners to formulate a profile of the firm's ideal client in terms of service line, industry, and income.
- Create or purchase prospect lists.
- Research prospects.
- Scrub lists to be sure the right people are targeted.
- Develop marketing campaign.
    — Budget.
    — Plan program and content of each step.
    — Timing.
    — Depending on the campaign, it may be necessary to roll the program out in stages to the target list.
- Execute marketing programs.
- Maintain the database.
- Draft proposals and presentations.
- Prepare partners for presentations.

Partners, Managers, and Other Members of Sales Team

- Work with marketing to profile ideal client.
- Network.
- Set appointments with prospective clients.
- Follow up with prospective clients.
- Keep marketing in the loop about what is going on with each prospect.
- Close sales.

.02 Creating a Career Path

The time has come for firms to seriously address the fact that practice development professionals are dedicated career-oriented individuals who make a genuine contribution to the firm. A number of firms have recognized this reality by creating a partner track for these professionals. Depending on state law and firm desire, this may be an equity or nonequity partnership, and it may be called partner, principal, or something else. The important thing is that firms embrace the opportunities marketing and business development can create for their firms. High-value practice development professionals deserve to reach the upper echelons of firm leadership.

Firms that secured good business development pros early on made a smart move. The proliferation of these experts into professional services is becoming a standard of practice, and those that don't have one run the risk of having sub-par pipelines of new business and marketing efforts. Experience shows that when a firm has a professional marketer or business developer on staff, it has faster growth and attracts more sophisticated clients than firms that don't hire these people. Plenty of firms are successful without bringing these professionals on staff, but if used right, dedicated marketers can provide a distinct advantage.

Figure 5.8

Association for Accounting Marketing Survey Results

2005 total annual compensation, including base salary and bonuses. (U.S. dollars)

226 Responses

Under $30,000	4%
$30,000 to $44,999	13%
$45,000 to $59,999	24%
$60,000 to $74,999	13%
$75,000 to $89,999	11%
$90,000 to $109,999	8%
$110,000 to $129,999	6%
$130,000 to $149,999	3%
$150,000 to 199,999	5%
$200,000 or more	4%

Interestingly, most respondents said that the areas upon which their success is judged are project management/timeliness, brand awareness/loyalty, and budget-to-actual spending—things that don't really contribute directly to the top line and/or are hard to measure. Areas of practice growth and other metrics that relate to the bottom line were not generally considered as metrics of performance. As marketing and business development begin to expand their legitimate role within accounting firms, there will be an increased focus on metrics that are more tightly focused on financial performance of the firm. This approach will require marketers to work closely with firm leaders to identify the resources or tools required to capture the return on investment of marketing and business development efforts.

Source: 2006 Accounting Marketing/Sales Responsibility and Compensation Survey Results www.accountingmarketing.org

Figure 5.9

Sample Marketing Budget Items

- Advertising
- Brochures
- Business development activities
- Direct mail (including newsletters)
- Memberships (e.g., professional associations)
- Promotional items
- Seminars
- Sponsorships
- Subscriptions
- Trade shows
- Web site development and management

Note: Some items, such as advertising in charitable organization journals and attending charitable organization events, may fall into another budget line. Your firm may need to adjust the marketing budget accordingly.

¶ 545 Business Development Pipelines: An Anti-Chaos Tool

Pipelines don't only belong in oilfields. Pipeline reports are excellent barometers of what is going on in your firm's new business development efforts. Growth goals, marketing plans, the marketing budget, and every team member's role in the process should be established as part the firm's yearly strategic plan for business development.

The planning is the easy part: implementing the programs and tracking progress is the part most firms struggle with. Part of the issue is that the word "sales" still scares many CPAs who feel it just doesn't belong in the vocabulary of a professional services firm. This attitude is short-sighted in the 24/7/365 global economy we work in. Relationships are and probably always will be at the core of what we do. After all, we are privy to the most confidential financial information our clients can provide. CPAs are responsible for knowing what's right, what's wrong, and what needs to be done to make it better. We're great at doing this for our clients, but not quite as savvy when it comes to understanding what makes our own firms tick.

The other part of the issue is that we haven't yet developed tried-and-true methods of monitoring and measuring progress and accountability. We monitor our time, WIP, and accounts receivable pretty well. By tracking potential sales prospects for both new clients and cross-selling opportunities, pipeline reports can do the same thing for our marketing and business development efforts.

These reports don't have to be complicated. A simple table or Excel spreadsheet is all that is needed. That there is no learning curve is an added benefit. It can be difficult to estimate is the number of sales that are likely to close, but the outset, 10 percent is a good approximation. As time goes on, expectations can be adjusted up or down on the basis of substantive discussions with the client or prospect about the potential engagement.

The pipeline amount is calculated by multiplying the fee estimate by the probability of closing the deal. As a general rule, prospective engagements should be moved to inactive status at the two-year mark. (Companies that fall into this category should remain on the list for marketing communications, such as seminar invitations, and newsletters, but the likelihood of landing the engagement is largely diminished.)

The pipeline report is a tool for holding partners responsible for new business development, and it should be an agenda topic at every partner meeting, where partners should be required to report on:

- How their progress aligns with their individual marketing plan goals.
- Whether they've spoken to or met with their top clients about a needs assessment.
- Whether pipeline report items are stagnant or progressing.
- Their close rate.

It is surprising how much information can be gathered from this relatively simple tool. Sorting the columns and analyzing the results can tell an important story about how your firm works:

- Where the most successful leads come from.
  - Partner
  - Marketing initiative
  - Referral source
  - Other
- Who on the team is an effective closer.
- Reasons for and trends in wins.
  - Industries
  - Services
- Reasons for and trends in losses.
  - Industries
  - Services
- How many contacts it takes to make a sale.
- How long a typical sales cycle is for your firm.

Further analysis of this data can yield some essential facts that can impact on the firm's future:

1. *Which partners are not performing up to expectation?* Not everyone is a rainmaker, or even a mistmaker. Those are the technical and quality control partners who make the wheels of your firm's business move smoothly to service the accounting, audit, and tax needs of your clients. The partners you are looking for in this analysis are the ones who are, in effect, hiding out and collecting a paycheck. The firm can choose to offer coaching, impose financial sanctions (such as a fine or a deduction from bonus for not bringing in business for a defined period of time), opt for some other action, or ignore the situation. (Choosing the latter course of action could undermine the positive aspects of your firm's culture and add to the chaos of the firm dynamic.)

2. *Which partners and professionals have leadership qualities*? The pipeline report can help guide you in identifying the next generation of firm leadership. The people who are the most active in the business development process have potential for guiding the firm into the future.

3. *What marketing activities are working*? Tracking the source of the lead allows you to hone in on which referral sources really understand your firm and which marketing programs are performing best. This knowledge allows you to maximize your firm's marketing budget.

4. *What industry and service niches does the community look for in your firm*? Exactly where are your firm's strengths? A pipeline report can supply the answers by pointing out the niches and services that didn't respond to your marketing efforts.

As with most firm initiatives, there will be those who don't want to participate in the pipeline. But there also will be early adopters who believe the pipeline report will be a key element in defining the firm's future success. Most of the time, it takes about six months for the pipeline to become an integral part of the firm's efforts to define itself and lead the way for future direction.

Figure 5.10

Sample Business Development Pipeline Report

Target Co.	Source of Lead	Prospect (P) or Client (C)	Industry	Service	Fee Estimate	Date Lead Originated	Date Lead Closed	Partner in Charge	Team Members			1st contact date	Last contact date	Proposal date	# days in pipeline	Close probability (%)	Inactive
									Expert Practice Area Partner	Other	Closer						
Total pipeline ($$)																	
Total closed ($$)																	
% closed																	
% inactive																	

Figure 5.11

Sample Agenda for Monthly Pipeline Meeting

1. Review overall growth goals and results to date
    a. New clients
        i. Anticipated revenue to date and for rest of year
    b. New engagements/existing clients
    c. Lost clients
        i. Revenue to date
2. Compare to results for previous year
3. Review five-year comparison recap
4. Overview of pipeline activity
    a. Active leads
        i. Meetings/phone calls
        ii. New referrals
        iii. In process from marketing/business development programs

  b. Aged leads—leads with no activity for three months

   i. Leave on active list

   ii. Move off list, but continue passive marketing (e.g., newsletters)

5. Assess which programs are working

6. Review marketing/business development budgets

7. Discuss changes in marketplace and what needs to be done to address them

8. Discuss upcoming opportunities for networking, trade shows, etc.

9. Set goals for upcoming month

Figure 5.12

Typical pursuit process

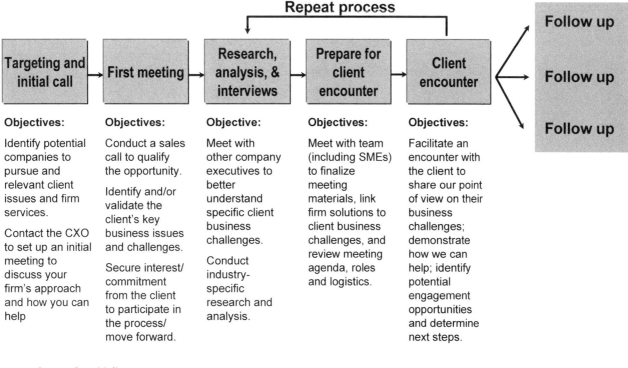

Source: Russ Molinar

Chapter 6
Growth + Specialization + Experience = Survival

¶ 601 It's All About Strategic Growth

One of the most predominant themes across the accounting profession continues to be growth. The reasons echo those of the other drivers in the profession: clients are looking for specialists, not general practitioners; the depth of specific industry knowledge that is required by the marketplace challenges the resources of smaller firms; staff shortages, especially at the senior level, make the pooling of resources an attractive option. We are seeing the concept of growth take several different paths, including the rise of boutique firms with specialized niches and organic growth and mergers and acquisitions.

We've also seen some innovative strategies, such as the alternative practice structure adopted by Bruce Schonbraun of Roseland, New Jersey's Cornerstone Accounting Group (formerly The Schonbraun McCann Group or SMG). SMG separated into two distinct and independent legal entities, one for attest functions and the other for consulting, that work together to meet clients' business needs. Other firms have formed separate entities as well, sometimes for ancillary services such as placement, family offices, and registered investment advisory services (RIAs). But Cornerstone took it to a new level: it sold its consulting practice to publicly traded FTI Consulting Group, a "global business advisory firm dedicated to helping organizations protect and enhance enterprise value in an increasingly complex legal, regulatory and economic environment"—a company that had no direct ties to the world of accounting. And that very succinctly tells us two important things: the direction the accounting profession is heading and the value outsiders place on our services.

To survive, firms will have to be very proactive in strategizing the direction they want to take and then implementing plans and programs that differentiate them from other firms.

¶ 605 Real ROI: Differentiation

"Differentiation is everything. My ability to differentiate our firm is our magic. It gives us our growth curve, our prominence, our morale, our higher salaries. I cannot overemphasize how important differentiation is. Without it, we won't grow. We won't get the best people. It's everything."

- Managing partner of one of the nation's fastest-growing accounting firms

The increasing blurring of differentiators between accounting firms is exacerbated because so many firms now have formal marketing plans and programs, tend to go to the same conferences, belong to the same associations, and learn from a lot of the same sources. It is difficult to maintain distinction when you and your competitors all rely on the same resources for information. We may be able to see the differences, but outsiders—clients and potential clients—don't. To them, all accounting firms look somewhat the same.

This lack of clear differentiation makes competing in and managing the chaos that envelopes firm management today much more difficult. Why should anyone choose your firm if everyone looks the same? If you can't compellingly demonstrate your firm's unique benefits, the marketplace can effectively toss a coin to decide which accounting firm to choose. The result is that services become commodities and fees plummet. We've already seen that, to a certain extent, in the preparation of individual tax returns. Every year, more and more individuals opt to either go to a fixed rate tax preparation service or file their own 1040s using an off-the-shelf computer product. For some smaller firms, this is the bread and butter of their practice. Without differentiating their firms, how can they convince their clients to stay, let alone pay a higher rate?

Even firms that do somewhat higher level work are affected by this phenomenon. Consider this common scenario:

A firm bids on a specific, routine piece of work—perhaps for a not-for-profit organization or a distributor. Some fairly sophisticated or large competitors that can do the work just as well also are bidding on the work. In the end, all the firms are showing the same strengths: client service, technical proficiency, great professionals, and timely delivery. To the trained eye, the firms bidding on the work really don't look alike, but to the prospect, the bidders *do* look alike, because no unique differentiators are coming to the forefront. What happens? The firm with the best relationship with the prospect or the best pricing wins the engagement.

¶ 610 The Benefits of a Strong Niche

Firms that are able to show their differentiation have an overwhelming advantage. Just being an expert in the traditional tax, accounting, and audit arenas is no longer enough to differentiate one firm from another. True distinctions now go to recognition in a particular industry or service. Cost segregation is a good example of a service that distinguished a number of firms. As far as industries, The Reznick Group of Bethesda, Md. has a nationally recognized housing specialty. Joseph Eve of Kalispell, Mont. has established a strong niche handling issues of financial importance to Native Americans, The Cornerstone Accounting Group, Roseland, N.J. specializes in real estate, and Rothstein Kass, Roseland, N.J. has a unique hedge fund niche.

The rifle-shot expertise these firms have developed allows them to highlight specific engagements and unique skills that gives them unparalleled qualifications competitors can't match. This high level type of differentiation attracts premium clients and creates premium service that commands premium prices.

Even individual practitioners can win significant competitive advantages by creating unique realms of high-value expertise. For instance, Tony Argiz of Morrison, Brown, Argiz & Farra, Miami, has few peers when it comes to expertise with auto dealerships.

These firms and individuals have developed a single-niche focus that they can call their own. It allows them to capture market share, easily sell their services, and command top dollar for the work they do. It's not only a brilliant strategy, but a successful one. Niches allow firms to differentiate themselves and provide a vehicle for illustrating the value they provide in return for premium prices.

Clients' affinity for professional services that target their niches and industries is a reflection of their increasing sophistication and business savvy. Top-notch clients want professional services providers who have a true grasp of their business issues. There was a time when clients didn't want a professional services provider who also serviced their competitors. They worried that confidentiality wouldn't be honored, their secrets would be leaked to competitors, and firms would play both sides of the fence in an attempt to keep everybody happy. Today's clients don't have those kinds of concerns. In fact, it's quite the opposite. Firms that don't have proven expertise in the client's industry probably won't be hired. And simply saying you have the expertise isn't enough. Has your firm been published in the area? Spoken at seminars? Provided benchmarking studies for the industry? Tactics such as these establish your firm as the go-to expert, and helps trigger success going forward.

Forgetting how much distinguishing your firm counts can be a costly oversight. To remain competitive, leaders must understand the relationship between showing how their firms differ from competitor firms and how that demonstration influences the client's perception of value for the services provided. The more valuable the client perceives a firm's services to be, the more the client is willing to pay for them and to stay loyal in the long term.

Figure 6.1

Referral Sources: What Not to Do

Keep in mind that when referral sources refer clients to your firm, they are doing so because they are relying on your reputation and trust that you will do the best possible work for the potential client they are referring. So, when a referral source asks how business is, *never* say anything like, "We're so busy we even have to work on Sundays."

Always leave the door open for new referrals—and possibly better work—by answering with a response that lets your center of influence know their belief is correct: "Business is good. We're busy, but we're still focused on growing our core niche areas."

Referral sources will be reticent to make referrals if they think you are too busy to handle more client work. And that may affect whether they will refer your firm well into the future.

Figure 6.2

Case Study: Tax Niches at SS&G Financial Services

Specialty tax services at SS&G Financial Services, a $50 million firm in Cleveland, are a prime example of how differentiation and specialization can pay off. For many years, the benefits to clients in specialty tax areas were generally reserved for large clients serviced by the largest CPA firms. In the past few years, these specialty tax services and niches began moving down the food chain, and now they're demanded by smaller clients as well. The tax specialty areas attracting the most attention are cost segregation studies, asset protection, research and development credits, personal property (in applicable states), sales and use, state and local, nexus issues, and interstate commerce. Attention to these specialty niches can provide significant revenue and even more significant value to client relationships.

SS&G Financial Services developed the capability to provide all of these services to its clients by re-training existing tax staff and by strategically hiring tax professionals who already possess these skills. The firm reviewed each client's tax situation with attention to these tax niche areas and has been able to reduce many clients' tax liability—both meaningfully and legally—by thoroughly understanding the intricacies of these tax issues and how they apply to specific clients. In some tax-only engagements, the firm has been able to provide these services on a contingency basis based upon the tax savings generated to the client. Many of the contingency engagements have generated significant success fees, in some cases totaling more than $100,000. The tax specialty niche has allowed the firm to perform significant value-added work for its clients.

There is a downside to trying to create a specified practice. Using a tax practice as an example, let's consider firms and practitioners who aren't capable of providing the requisite depth of or sufficient expertise to their clients. In such cases, the clients may wind up overpaying taxes because of the limited abilities of their tax practitioners. The complexities related to these specialized tax areas make it very difficult for tax practitioners to know everything, especially in highly specialized niche practice areas. Achieving and maintaining competence in these specialties requires a tax professional who is dedicated almost exclusively to these specific niche areas.

There are strategies that can help firms in this situation. They can, for example, consider strategies for acquiring the requisite expertise, or limit their practices to the areas where they already have the expertise required. Smaller practitioners could also consider forming alliances with larger firms to provide access to a full array of tax specialty services.

While investing in the necessary expertise to differentiate and specialize can be costly and time consuming, forgoing the investment has significant pitfalls as well. One is the risk of losing a client to another firm that can provide the comprehensive services the client requires. Another is the liability exposure when a tax practitioner is sued because he or she misses legitimate opportunities to significantly minimize his clients' tax burdens.

Tax specialties and niches are truly a double-edged sword that can either enhance your practice and your relationships with clients, or get your firm into various degrees of hot water by not providing the best possible service to clients.

¶ 615 New Sources of Business = Potential for Chaos

As firms struggle with the problem of differentiation, they are looking at where they can find new business. This can be another source of chaos. The old reliable fishing holes where professional services firms traditionally hooked new clients—referrals and reputation—aren't as effective as they once were. And new clients that come to the firm through these channels are quite likely to have a different dynamic.

There are some very basic reasons for this, each building on the last. First, the worker shortage faced by accounting firms is not unique. There is an across the board shortage of employees at all levels of knowledge and experience, but especially in Gen Y, where we would normally look for our next generation of leaders. Second, Baby Boomers are retiring from the entire spectra of business, not just accounting. Third, business succession is another issue that appears in privately owned business in every industry. Where is it written that a son will want to follow his mother into the family's real estate business or a daughter will want to take the reins at the family's retooling factory? The situation is forcing even second-and third-generation businesses to rethink their options.

Often, the result is that the company is merged into a rival company. Sound familiar? If it doesn't, it should. The result, in business as in the accounting world, is that the only the strongest and most forward-thinking will survive as independents. The others will either be merged into larger firms or forced to the fringes, where it is likely they will handle lower level engagements for lower fees.

The firms that survive will be handling clients who are looking for solutions to similar issues: a smaller work force that works more efficiently; lower turnover to reduce training costs; increased productivity; a pipeline of new business. Other, less directly bottom-line driven factors will also play a role, such as having a greener work environment.

2007-2008 Turnover Costs at Sample Firm:

2007-2008	Entry level tax accountant	Senior Accountant or Manager	Partner
Average annual compensation	51,000	72,000	250,000
2007 Turnover	4	6	1
2008 Turnover	5	5	0
Turnover Costs	$ 229,500	$ 1,188,000	$ 750,000
Grand Total			**2,167,500**

Source: Rebecca Ryan, Next Generation Consulting. A turnover calculator is available at *www.nextgenerationconsulting.com/KeepTalent.*

¶ 620 Creating a New Niche

Knowing the landscape is only part of the issue. It's how you decide to meet its challenges that is the other part. We've already decided that we need to be smarter about niches, but it seems that developing new niches is not necessarily a natural progression. Deciding whether to embark on setting up a new niche requires careful planning.

It is not enough to decide to start a niche just because your closest competitor offers it. Suppose, for instance, you think it is a good idea to start an estate planning/retirement planning practice area simply because demographic analyses show a huge wave of Baby Boomer retirements over the next number of yearsBut other factors come into play, including whether you have trained staff that can support the niche area.

In some respects, the Internet has leveled the playing field between us and our clients. Clients are increasingly sophisticated partly because there is so much free information on the Internet for them to read and absorb. That doesn't make them experts, but it does teach them enough for them to know a bit of jargon and ask smart questions. And that, in turn, gives them a certain amount of expertise about what they need from their professional services advisor. They will know pretty quickly if you meet their expectations.

.01 Some Determining Factors

The marketplace is daunting these days, and it is best not to be reactive and impulsive. That may have worked (emphasis on may have) even five or ten years ago, but these days things are moving far too quickly for firms to take such a risk. There are always opportunities; the key is using a strategic decision-making process to take advantage of them. It is still possible that you will make a mistake, but the risk of doing so will be greatly minimized.

As we often advise our clients, businesses fail due to one or more of the following reasons: no stated mission, inadequate planning, poor execution, failure to anticipate changes in the marketplace, using the wrong people in the wrong positions, too short a timeline, too little cash backing, or lack of strong support from top firm management.

- *Is there a unique need your firm is equipped to meet*? Evaluate your existing clients according to industry and service provided. What can you provide that is new and compelling? Is there something in the mix that stands out as either unique (e.g., new software you've developed that makes payroll easier), something you've done enough to qualify you as an expert (e.g., cost segregation studies), a service you can provide more cost efficiently than your competitors (e.g., a turnkey solution for tracking software), or particular knowledge you have that is on the leading edge of an inevitable change (e.g., international tax expertise that gives you true understanding of how IFRS works)?

- *Do you understand the potential niche well enough to walk the walk and talk the talk*? Can you use correctly use the language your audience will expect? Do you understand the nuances and the hot button issues? For example, if you are considering a niche in franchises, are you aware any new compliance requirements or whether retirement funds can be used to invest in franchises without tax consequences? If you are considering a niche in Asian businesses, do you have the right contacts across businesses in the United States to make it happen? Are you familiar with the tax and regulatory issues involved? Are you conversant with the language and culture of your target audience?

- *Have you tested the waters?* Do you know which other firms are already in the niche area and whether you are well-positioned to compete with them? Conducting a detailed competitive analysis before you commit to a new niche is the best way to manage the risk. It is always better to know what you are up against than to surmise that things will work out because you want them to.

- *No competition isn't always good news.* If your due diligence fails to turn up any competitors, that is not necessarily a good sign. Sometimes, it is better to build a better mouse trap than to be the first one in a particular market. We know of a client who invested $10 million to build a factory in China 15 years ago. Yes, the company's leaders were prescient, but they got there too soon to manage the maze of internal Chinese business and their venture failed. It is a good lesson. Not finding competitors may mean that other firms have been unsuccessful in penetrating the niche. That doesn't mean you won't be able to; it just means that extra care is needed.

See Figure 6.3 for a sample plan that, if followed, will help ensure the success of your niche practice area.

Figure 6.3

Developing a Niche Business Plan

1. Develop a mission or vision statement.
2. Evaluate the current situation.
   - a. Track 2-3 years of past revenue history to determine;
     - i. Total number of clients in the niche.
     - ii. Types of services performed for these clients.
     - iii. Average revenue per client.
     - iv. How long they have been with your firm.
     - v. Whether there has been an opportunity to expand the services you perform for them.
     - vi. Partners and staff who worked on these accounts.
   - b. Identify the target client: size, type of work, other parameters.
   - c. Name the person who will lead the team.
     - i. Does he have the right background and experience?

        ii. Does he have the passion and commitment needed to develop the niche?

        iii. Does he have a viable network of connections in the niche?

        iv. What will his responsibilities be?

        v. To whom will he report?

        vi. How will he be held accountable?

    d. Name the others who will be on the team.

        i. For each, what is his background and experience?

        ii. What will his responsibilities be?

        iii. What will the line of report be?

        iv. How will he be help accountable?

3. Conduct market research.

    a. What is the potential for increasing revenue share?

    b. Get statistics on the state of the niche.

    c. Establish which industry events the firm should attend.

    d. Conduct research through:

        i. Industry profiles.

        ii. Newspapers/business journal articles/industry media, both print and online.

        iii. Web sites of the top 5-10 companies in the niche.

        iv. Meetings with:

            1. Referral sources with ties to the industry.

            2. Leadership of clients in the industry.

4. Conduct a competitive analysis of the competition.

    a. Who are the leading firms in the niche?

    b. What services do they offer?

    c. If possible, find out how they price their services.

    d. Conduct research through:

        i. Reading articles on the Web and in print media.

        ii. Assessing who is advertising, particularly in industry media.

        iii. Going to trade shows to see who is exhibiting.

        iv. Talking to referral sources.

5. Set goals and criteria for accountability.

    a. Revenue goals for three years.

    b. Referral goals:

        i. Existing sources.

        ii. New sources.

    c. If additional certification is desired (e.g., PFP), set goals for team members.

6. Set a realistic budget that includes:

    a. Cost of marketing.

    b. Cost of education and training.

7. Prepare a detailed marketing plan, including measurement criteria, for all team members.

¶ 625 More Sophisticated Services

Clients are looking for higher level services that require better trained staff and updated technical expertise. The instantaneous communication we've become used to has filtered down to the business level: we, as accountants and business consultants, are expected to be aware of every development that affects our clients' business almost before it occurs. Keeping on top of it all is too big a job for most smaller firms, unless their business is concentrated on a specific niche area.

    This is a big change for firms who are used to having a general practice and getting new business primarily through referrals and reputation. Relationships still play an important role in referrals and winning engagements, but as clients struggle to remain competitive in their own businesses, their allegiance increasingly thins. Competitive bidding has become the norm, and firms need to be able to convince clients and potential clients they are up to the task of guiding them through economic highs and lows.

This new paradigm has another consequence: as client loyalty diminishes, price pressure descends on compliance work. Any work that a client needs but doesn't want and hates to pay for is price sensitive. High-value services that clients need *and* want command higher fees and greater client loyalty. Services that speak to a client's core sensitivities and provide direct, perceivable value fall into this category. They also tend to be areas that can help differentiate your firm from your competitors. Figure 6.4 contains an example of a broad service niche that can be offered in its entirety or in the increments that suit your firm's capabilities and expertise. And there are always firms that have the creativity, innovation and depth of staff that can take an existing service area to the next level.

Strategic business planning is a process that allows a client's management to address issues ahead of time rather than as they occur. The planning process addresses where a company has been, where it is now, where it's going, and how it plans to achieve its goals. Consequently, it ensures that a company is forward-thinking and focused on building its tangible and intangible assets so that it's positioned for future success. Accounting firms that offer business consulting can offer any or all of the following:

Figure 6.4 ——

Sample Service Areas That Can Help Differentiate Your Firm

- *Operational review of internal systems.* A firm can perform an operational review of all the client's internal systems of control to ensure that management is safeguarding its assets. It allows them to catch problems as they arise so they can be addressed on a timely basis. The process involves documenting in detail the current systems of internal control and compiling specific recommendations to improve systems and address material weaknesses. It entails looking at the existing human resources department, manufacturing processes, financial reporting, billing processes, upper management's involvement with running the company, disaster recovery plan, succession plan, information technology plan, and other key operational components. The results are presented to the company's leaders in the form of a written report.

- *Review of internal controls.* This service is normally performed in conjunction with operational reviews, but, if requested by the client, can be much more defined and limited to specific areas. Among the most common such engagements are job costing, review of chart of accounts, and financial reporting. These services effectively communicate the financial performance of the client, accounts payable process, billing, accounts receivable, payroll processing, and other key performance areas. Each system is documented, weaknesses are identified, and specific recommendations for improvement are compiled in writing to management.

- *Development of organizational chart.* The firm reviews the client's existing organizational chart and compares it to organizational charts of similarly sized companies in the same industry and within a relevant revenue size. The ultimate goal is to develop an organization that is streamlined, efficient, and maximizes the client's economies of scale without sacrificing service or overtaxing any department or individual. A properly structured organizational chart (1) defines the chain of command, (2) sets out the formal lines of communication, (3) clarifies the responsibilities of each level of staff, and (4) makes everyone accountable for fulfilling the requirements of their role. It also increases responsibility and accountability to the appropriate parties. One of the objectives that the firm strives to accomplish is eliminating as many direct links to the CEO as possible so that the company's top executive can focus on managing the business instead of putting out routine fires.

- *Internal financial models.* The firm can design internal control modules that allow the client's management team to effectively monitor their company's financial performance against its business plan. The financial models are designed to allow the client's management to review them quickly, recognize potential problems immediately, and explore solutions proactively. At the same time, the expert advisor who prepares the reports should be able to step back, recognize the issues, and alert management ahead of time. The service allows the client's management team to monitor gross profits on both a monthly and year-to-date basis. It also allows management to analyze key ratios such as working capital position, current and quick ratios, accounts receivable, accounts payable, operating cycle, inventory turns, direct labor as a percentage of sales, burden rate, and debt to equity. It can then figure out why the numbers have changed or compare them to a specific goal. For example, a client's goal may be to reduce accounts receivable from 90 days to 45 days within six months. This service helps it monitor monthly progress toward that goal and address any problems achieving it.

- *Feasibility studies.* The firm assists clients in analyzing a business situation before investing capital and human resources. These studies address such issues as break-even benchmarks, timetables for profitability, and long-term ROI. Feasibility studies can, in some cases, save clients big bucks and help them focus on how to make a venture successful in terms of capital and resources.

- *Executive coaching.* It's lonely at the top. If you're reading this book, you probably know the truth of that cliché all too well. Through this service, the firm can help the client's executives deal with all personnel issues, such as hiring, retention, developing, motivating, evaluating, promoting, and terminating. The benefits of this service can be intangible, because much of the value is provided to the client in terms of experience and education. It also has tangible benefits that incorporate the expertise of the firm and the advisor regarding specific techniques for structuring hiring processes, evaluation tools and processes, job descriptions, disciplinary processes, and legal processes and procedures. Executive coaching is also an effective way to help young people climbing the corporate ladder fast-track their professional growth and grasp the skills required to attain quicker access to the executive suite.

  Note: Executive coaching is different than life coaching, which helps clients, including top executives, with the process of determining and achieving personal goals.

- *Corporate retreats.* The firm can help clients properly plan for a strategic retreat. Retreats normally run for a set period of time, generally two days, and follow a strict agenda. Time is allotted for questions, discussion, social activities, and interaction. Retreats are an effective technique for pulling the management team together in an environment that's removed from day-to-day distractions so it can focus on their company's long- and short-term strategic plans. They also can be valuable team-building events.

- *Industry benchmarking.* The firm can help its clients participate in top-of-the-line business practices by benchmarking their financial performance against industry standards. Benchmarking also helps the client build a strong balance sheet so that it increases its flexibility and can absorb bumps in the road with minimal pain.

- *Mergers and acquisitions.* Whether a client is being acquired, merging, or adding another company to its holdings, the firm can assist in completing the deal promptly and properly. This service assists the client in due diligence, analyzes the financial aspects, structures the deal, assists with negotiations, prepares future financial projections and evaluations of operations and the existing corporate culture, and assists with or arranges financing. This service can help a client reach its desired growth goals or be a profitable vehicle to an exit strategy. Professional services firms are uniquely qualified to assist clients in this process by offering this service.

- *Business succession.* This is a high-value service for both large and small clients. Professional services firms can help small clients create a succession plan that ensures long-term viability and profitability upon the premature death or disability of the owner. These plans are designed to satisfy and protect creditors, stockholders, and other stakeholders in case of disaster. Business succession for larger clients includes strategically grooming and developing the next generation of management to run the company.

  Developing future leaders requires a significant investment of time—often five to 10 years, depending on the types of positions involved and the capabilities of the potential successors. If a client must conduct an executive search to fill key management positions from outside the company, the process can be very lengthy and has a 50-50 chance of being successful. Business succession planning can improve those odds. The service also helps the client work with tax professionals and structure a buyout that makes economic sense from a business valuation point of view.

- Other suggested high-value advisory services include:
  - Registered Investment Advisory Services (RIAs)
  - Employee benefit plan services
  - Outsourcing
  - Conflict resolution
  - Forensic accounting/litigation support
  - Business valuation
  - Eldercare services
  - Information technology
  - Human resources management
  - Executive recruiting
  - Turnaround and bankruptcy
  - R&D tax credits
  - Energy tax credits
  - Cost segregation studies
  - Family office practice
  - Strategic planning

Figure 6.5 ———————————————————————————————————————

Sample Categories for Benchmark Study

- Overview of purpose of study, including terms and definitions to be used throughout the study.
- Demographics and contact information.
- Administration and general information, including:
  — Number of staff in relevant job categories.
  — Allocation of workday for target purpose of study in each job category.
  — Line of report for each job category.
  — Written policies and procedures.
  — Communication policies and procedures.
  — Roles of marketing, business development.
  — Training policies and procedures.
- Budget, billing and funding, including:
  — Annual budget:
    - Who prepares.
    - Who approves.
    - What items are included:
      — Internal expenses
      — External expenses
      — Branding
      — Marketing
      — Advisory services (accounting, investment, attorneys)
  — Overall amount of budget.
  — Approximate percentage change (increase or decrease) from last year to this year.
- Technology:
  — Number of dedicated personnel.
  — Portion of budget allocated to technology advancement.
  — Security safeguards.
  — Training.
  — Recordkeeping.

¶ 630 Taking the Pulse

Do you remember the former New York City Mayor Ed Koch? He used to randomly stop people, shake their hands, and ask them "How am I doing?" Do you know how you are doing—in the eyes of your clients, that is? It is easy to bury your head in the sand and refuse to face the fact that not everything you do is up to your clients' expectations. It may be something very simple that is making them uncomfortable—perhaps the auditors who come to their office are dressed too formally (or too informally) but it may also be something deeper than that, something that may cause the client to leave your firm.

Just as we suggest you classify your clients to identify who the best ones are, we recommend that you check your ego, take a step back, and ask your clients to rate your firm. Think about it another way: have you ever gotten a tax client simply because the client thought the former accountant didn't maximize his allowable deductions? Do you think he told that person he was leaving? Do you think he told his friends? Chances are, if the client fits the statistical profile, he didn't tell the accountant, but he did tell nine other people. In this age of viral marketing, is that how you want your practice to be "marketed"?

It makes sense to be proactive about determining your firm's level of client satisfaction and committing to remedying any negative feedback you get. Keep in mind that if you don't respond to the concerns clients have voiced, their view of your firm is likely to become more negative.

Generally, surveying a cross-section of your clients on an annual or bi-annual basis is enough. The surveys may be conducted in person, on the telephone, online, or through snail mail. For telephone and in-person interviews, the interviewer should be familiar with the firm, including the services it provides and industries it services. Other than that, it is best if the interviewer has talking points, such as those suggested in Figure 6.7, rather than a "script." Sometimes the most useful information is obtained by an interviewer with excellent listening skills.

For some of your most valuable clients, it may make sense schedule personal meetings. In-person interviews always yield the most information because they provide an opportunity to ask and follow up on open-ended questions, read body language and cement a relationship. Often, it is best if the interview is conducted by the firm's marketing director or an outside consultant. As with other surveys that deal with sensitive issues, the goal is to get honest responses rather than those the respondent thinks you want to hear or will end the meeting most quickly.

Figure 6.6

Sample Performance Survey

AKRON

Overall

Quality of service 1 2 3 4 5 NA

What do you like the most about SS&G? _____

What can SS&G do to improve? _____

Please list other services you would like to see SS&G provide: _____

Other comments: _____

☐ Yes, you may use me as a reference

SS&G Financial Services, Inc. is focused on providing excellent client service. We strive to exceed our clients' expectations.

In order to maintain the high quality of our services, we gauge our clients' perception of our work.

To help us better serve you, please complete and return this survey. We value your opinion of our performance.

How are we doing?

Engagement Team

Capabilities 1 2 3 4 5 NA

Cooperation 1 2 3 4 5 NA

Timeliness 1 2 3 4 5 NA

Understands your goals 1 2 3 4 5 NA

Responsiveness 1 2 3 4 5 NA

Availability/Accessibility 1 2 3 4 5 NA

Keeps you informed 1 2 3 4 5 NA

Communication 1 2 3 4 5 NA

Comments:_____

Services Provided Depth of services 1 2 3 4 5 NA

Cost benefit 1 2 3 4 5 NA

Turnaround time 1 2 3 4 5 NA

Content/Accuracy 1 2 3 4 5 NA

Comments:_____

Thank you for your business.

We appreciate your time and input.

Name: _____ Company: _____

Phone: _____ E-mail: _____

What services does/did SS&G perform for you? _____

Engagement director: _____

RATING SCALE

On a scale from 1-5, please rate each item. Circle the number that matches your rating the closest.

1= Very Dissatisfied and 5 = Very Satisfied. Circle NA (not applicable) if it does not pertain.

Referrals

Is there someone that you would like to refer to SS&G?

Name: _____

Company: _____

Phone: _____

Resources Materials 1 2 3 4 5 NA

Web site 1 2 3 4 5 NA

Newsletter(s) 1 2 3 4 5 NA

Comments:_____

Worst <——————> Best Worst <——————> Best

Figure 6.7

Client Satisfaction Survey—Sample Telephone Interview

Client name: _____   Date: _____

Partner:_____   Other members of client team _____

Company: _____

Contact person/title: _____

Phone: _____

Interview conducted by: _____

Contact alerted by partner to expect call: _____

Duration of call: _____   Number of tries required to reach contact person: _____

Client Services Currently Provided

_____ Financial Statements	_____ Bus. tax return	_____ Bookkeeping
_____ Monthly	_____ Corp.	_____ Payroll
_____ Quarterly	_____ S-Corp.	_____ Sales tax
_____ Annually	_____ Partnership	_____ QB consultant
_____ Audit	_____ LLC	
	_____ Non-profit	

Consulting/business advisory (list) _____

Potential cross-selling opportunities _____

Talking points

- **Introduction**
    - Name, title
    - Purpose of call
    - Do you have a few minutes to answer a few questions now?
    - If not, is there a better time to call you back _____
- **On a scale of 1—5, with 5 being the highest, how would you rate us as your accountant or advisor?**
    - Are we responsive to your needs?
        - Reaching the right team members?
            - Partner in charge of your account
            - Other professional staff
        - Explaining our services?
        - Promptness in getting back to you?
        - Handling urgent situations?
        - Answering questions?
        - Providing information?

- — Timeliness of our work?
- — Working with your team:
  - Reaching the right people?
  - Enough lead time for responding to requests for information?
- — Quality of our work?
  - Financial advice
  - Business advice
  - Tax advice
  - Other (explain)
- We offer services in many areas. How likely are you to need any of the following services now or within the three months, six months, or year?
  - — Business valuation
  - — Forensic accounting/litigation support
  - — Estate planning
  - — Retirement planning
  - — Financing arrangements
  - — Cash management
  - — Budgetary controls
  - — Merger and acquisition advice
  - — Other _____
- We publish newsletters in the following areas: tax planning, construction, non-profits, manufacturing and mergers and acquisitions. Do you currently receive or would you like to receive our newsletters?
  - — Print or e-mail?
  - — What is your e-mail address?
- What are we doing right?
- Are there any unresolved or ongoing issues you would like to make us aware of?
- Do you have any suggestions for making this better?
- Would you recommend our firm to your friends and colleagues?
- Anything else you'd like to say:
- **Closing**: Thank you for taking the time to speak with me. Please call me if you have concerns or would like assistance with anything. My direct phone number is _____ and my e-mail address is _____.
- **Interviewer's comments:** _____

Figure 6.8 ———

Sample Letter: Client Satisfaction Survey

[DATE]

Dear Client:

We believe we have the finest firm of Certified Public Accountants in this area. However, unless you also believe this, we are not satisfied. In an effort to insure the quality of our services, we have engaged Jay Nisberg & Associates, an independent management consulting firm, to conduct a brief survey about your attitudes and feelings. It will take you only a few minutes to answer the questions listed on the attached form. Your candid replies will be greatly appreciated.

The results of this survey will be used to help us improve our firm. We are sincerely interested in doing that and need your input to make this effort successful. We have enclosed a prepaid envelope in which to return the completed survey to our independent consultants who will summarize the results and assist us in implementing any changes necessary to make our services more responsive to your needs.

It would be most helpful if you reply within one week. Thank you in advance for your cooperation.

Sincerely,

Managing Partner

¶ 635 The Legacy of SOX

.01 The Positives

SOX Section 404 certainly created a new realm of service offerings as well as a whole new revenue stream for those willing to explore the new landscape. The post-SOX environment became an all-you-can-eat buffet. The new services that sprang from the law made friends out of foes as traditional competitors began to pool their resources. The result is a lot of partnering on jobs and lots of cross-selling. Strategic alliances are popular and a necessity. They're a new way of doing business in the new economy and will increasingly become part of the professional services landscape. Firms can't be all things to all people, so they must partner up in different ways. Strategic alliances are an outgrowth of specialization and SOX.

.02 The Negatives

The avalanche of new work that SOX created and all of its related consequences—the limited availability of staff, the increased risk of litigation, new models for strategic alliances, and a new frontier of services to offer—forces firms to be more selective regarding the clients and the type of work that they'll accept. There was a time when any client was a good client. Not anymore. Even when economic challenges may make it seem that going back to this old way of thinking and accepting any clients in a knee-jerk reaction is the way to go, that is not the answer for firms that want to survive long into the future. Many of the same core issues remain, even though the way we think about them may have changed: staffing challenges (from not enough people to the right people), the increasing cost of resources (budgetary concerns are heightened), rising sensitivity to liability and risk (particularly important at a time when CPA firms are being sued for a lack of diligence in the Ponzi scheme scandals), and the increasing expectations of clients (no change here—only more of it). Firms need to maintain a high level of scrutiny in their client acceptance and retention practices and procedures.

You've heard it before, but it's worth repeating: Go through your client lists and grade them A, B, C, or D using a rating system such as the one in Figure 6.10. Then, dump those that rate a C or less by transitioning them to another firm, even if it's a major competitor. (There is a caveat here: it may be worth keeping some start-ups even if they fall into the C or D categories. The determination should be made on a case-by-case basis based on your analysis of their leadership team, industry of operation, funding sources, etc.)

Whittling your client list to those who merit only As and Bs is one of the most profitable moves you can make. This exercise is guaranteed to improve your profitability by removing your least profitable clients. Many experts believe that clients who merit grades "C" and lower cause up to 80 percent of your aggravation, so finding a way to replace them with more profitable business is key.

Here is another way to think about it: Most of your revenue comes from the top 20 percent of your clients. If you take the time to analyze those clients—industry, service provided, amount billed, extra engagements, referrals—you will find you have a relatively clear picture of your target clients.

Figure 6.10 ————————————————————————————

Guidelines for Classifying Clients

A-Level clients

- Operate in one of the firm's niche areas.
- Good growth potential.
- Strong financial position.
- Excellent recordkeeping.
- Very cooperative; work well with staff; supply requested information in a timely manner so work can be completed on time.
- Receptive to suggestions and additional services.
- Pay bills on time and without question.
- Annual fees fall into the top 20 percent of the firm's clients.
- Refer new business to the firm.
- Does not expose the firm to liability.

B-Level clients

- Operate in a niche in which the firm has some expertise.
- Moderate growth potential.
- Solid financial position.
- Good recordkeeping.

- Cooperative; work well with staff; generally supply requested information in a timely manner so work can be completed on time.
- Generally receptive to suggestions and additional services.
- Pays bills within 30 days; rarely questions bills
- Annual fees fall within the top 20 percent to 50 percent range of the firm's clients.
- Occasionally refers new business to the firm.
- Presents low risk of exposure to liability.

C-Level clients

- Don't necessarily operate in an area in which the firm has experience or expertise.
- Slow growth.
- Weak financial position.
- Fair recordkeeping
- Generally cooperative; need prompting and guidance to supply requested information; firm can sometimes get work done in a timely manner.
- Sometimes receptive to suggestions and additional services.
- Pay within 60 days; write-downs are sometimes required.
- Seldom refers new business to the firm.
- Presents moderate risk of liability exposure.

D-Level clients

- Operate in an area outside the firm's experience and expertise
- Stagnant growth
- Tenuous financial position
- Poor recordkeeping
- Generally uncooperative; doesn't supply requested information in a timely manner; firm can rarely get work done on time
- Not receptive to suggestion or additional services
- Pays bills after 90 days; frequent writedowns
- Annual fees in bottom 20 percent of firm's clients
- Never refers new business to the firm
- Presents high risk of exposure to liability

.03 Evaluating Prospective Clients

When prospective clients approach you, it makes sense to evaluate whether they meet the profile of your ideal client. There are many ways to conduct this analysis, but here is an easy way to determine whether it will be profitable to take the client on:

- Add up the staff time necessary for the account.
- Divide the total staff salaries on that account by the time you expect the engagement to take.
- Multiply the salary cost by the overhead ratio.
- Add that amount back to the salary cost to get your total cost for doing the business.
- Do you have staff available to do the work?
- If not, will you be able to hire someone to do it?
- Do you need a full-time person or a part-time person?

If the client meets your criteria for a good client—one that has the potential to be an A- or B- level client—you can hire that client. Otherwise, you can pass it along to another firm whose profile the client does meet (maybe even a competitor firm).

Figure 6.11 —————————————————————————————————————

Client Acceptance Criteria

	Acceptance Criteria	Acceptance: 1 = Strongly Agree, 4 = Strongly Disagree	Comments
UNDERSTAND CLIENT NEED			
1	We understand the context/background to the clients need		
2	We understand the client's business problem		
3	We understand the scope of required assistance		
4	We understand the client's desired result		
5	We understand the timetable for delivering results		
6	We understand the client's budgetary constraints		
7	We understand the client's preferences with respect to project approach		
8	We understand the client's ability to interact with and contribute to a project team		
9	We understand the client's requirements (format, timetable) for a proposal		
OPPORTUNITY FIT			
10	The opportunity fits with our service and industry focus		
11	We have identified a viable solution/proposition to meet the client's need		
12	Our proposed solution is straightforward (v. complex/untested)		
13	We believe we will be able to agree to a timetable with the client within which our solution can be delivered		
14	We believe we will be able to agree to a price/budget with the client within which our solution can be delivered		
15	We have relevant credentials and experience to sell the solution		
16	We have appropriate resources available to prepare and sell the proposal (including resources from third parties or subcontractors)		
17	We expect to have appropriate resources available to deliver the solution		
18	We believe it will be possible to achieve any necessary change management within the client		
19	It is a potentially profitable opportunity for our firm		
20	It has strategic value—credentials, competence development, or relationship development potential.		
21	There is likely to be follow-on or additional sales opportunities.		

	Acceptance Criteria	Acceptance: 1 = Strongly Agree, 4 = Strongly Disagree	Comments

CLIENT FIT

22	Market environment (political, environmental, economic): There are no market factors that could seriously impact our ability to complete the project (e.g., political unrest) or create uncertainty about inputs to the project (e.g., uncertain regulatory process).		
23	Client stability: The client is stable—well financed, experienced management.		
24	Client integrity: We know the background of management or key investors and have no concerns.		
25	Client access and commitment: The client is committing appropriate resources and will provide the access to information and people needed to perform the project effectively.		
26	Realistic client expectations: The client's expectations are realistic and/or can be effectively managed.		
27	This is an appropriate project for the client. It can deliver relevant business benefits.		
28	We understand the client's ability and intent to use/implement the results of the project.		
29	The status of the client relationship (our relation with the client, strategic partner or not, business history, current agreements, possibility to win the business) is good.		
30	There are no existing agreements (e.g., global agreements, frame agreements) impacting the scope, pricing, or delivery conditions for the project.		
31	Neither the firm nor any members of the project team (including third parties or subcontractors) have any potential conflicts of interest.		

SALES PROCESS

Client Intent

32	The client's rationale and sense of urgency to buy is good.		
33	The client understands the value to be realized in solving the problem.		
34	The client is committed to resolving the problem at the right levels of the organization.		
35	The client is willing to commit the necessary time, resources, and money.		

Competition

36	We know who the external competition is.		
37	We know the extent to which competitors are entrenched at client.		
38	The client is prepared/committed to using external help rather than internal resources.		
39	We are well positioned compared to our competition.		

Stakeholders

| 40 | We know who the key decision makers/influencers are. | | |

¶635.03

	Acceptance Criteria	Acceptance: 1 = Strongly Agree, 4 = Strongly Disagree	Comments
41	We have access to the key decision makers/influencers.		
42	We know the predisposition of the decision makers/influencers.		
Our Position			
43	We have an internal client coach or advocates with influence.		
44	Our firm is well perceived based on past work done with the client.		
45	The estimated cost of getting client buy-in, preparing a proposal, and negotiating the contract is acceptable		
46	The estimated time for getting client buy-in, preparing a proposal, and negotiating the contract is acceptable.		
Sales *Practicalities*			
47	We know the process & timetable for submitting a proposal and the client decision		
48	We have a strategy and activity plan for how to win the project.		
49	We have enough time to deliver an excellent proposal.		
50	We understand and accept any required or expected contractual terms including sub-contractor, pricing and warranty/liability terms		
	Total	0	
	Number of n/a's	0	
	Acceptance Rating	0.00	

Source: Muzeview, Inc.

.04 Background Checks of Potential Clients

The enactment of SOX caused many firms to take a step back and review their client acceptance procedures. The U.S. Patriot Act, which requires businesses to "know their clients," heightened firms' sensitivity in this area. As a result, the investigation of potential clients became accepted procedure for many firms. The relevant privacy laws and regulations must be followed when an individual is investigated. However, with the exception of state-regulated common law privacy laws, investigations for commercial purposes are generally unregulated as long as there is a legitimate business purpose.

Figure 6.12 ————————————————————————————————

Investigative Red Flags

1. *Frequent changes of professional service providers.* Could mean a firm is opinion shopping.
2. *Poor financial history.* Prior failed business or bankruptcy could indicate a person who takes unjustifiable risks.
3. *Work/business history.* Unstable address, employment, or professional history.
4. *Overly litigious as a plaintiff or defendant.* Signals a party who is not afraid to sue, presents a risk of non-payment, or who may not honor their agreements.
5. *High turnover in upper management.* Often indicates lack of internal stability.
6. *Short operating history.* Where were the principals before they were at the current firm?
7. *Foreign operations or plants.* Hoping you won't check whether there is a plant in Tunisia.
8. *Reluctance to provide references.* If they are reluctant to disclose information now, how will they be once they are a client?

9. *Pressure to get a deal done quickly.* Often a sign that they don't want you looking into their background.

10. *Regulatory actions.* Often indicates poor internal controls or a management team ignoring internal controls.

Source: Research Associates, Inc.

¶ 640 Mergers and Acquisitions: Always in Your Thoughts

Other than organic growth through specialization, firms grow through mergers with other firms. A merger is considered for a number of reasons, including increasing the firm's geographic footprint, adding a particular service area or expertise, as a tactic for making the firm larger, and as the ultimate succession plan.

The whole area of mergers and acquisitions is fraught with all sorts of difficulties. Nevertheless, some firms that haven't been able to resolve the cultural and specialization issues that have become fundamental to the profession will find themselves looking for either a growth or an exit strategy, and merging into another firm may be the strategy of choice. Statistics indicate that there will be a large number of mergers over the next few years, in part because of the sheer number of Baby Boomer partners who will want to retire and in part because the profile of a successful firm calls for a depth of knowledge and specialization few small firms, other than those with boutique practices, can offer. As a result, it is likely to become more difficult to find a buyer and the purchase price for a firm probably will be lower than the current return of between 1 to 1.5 percent of annual gross earnings. The firm's location, expertise, and rainmaking ability will impact the price, as will the terms of the buyout. Nevertheless, it is clear that one firm will emerge as the dominant firm, however the deal is pitched to the public.

It is a given that the acquiring firm will need to conduct a thorough due diligence examination. The current economic and ethical difficulties make it even more important for the acquiring firm to investigate the target firm's internal and external peer reviews, selected work papers, financial statements, and tax returns (preferably for larger clients and public companies, if any), pre- and post-merger, insurance coverage and exposure to litigation. In addition, items such as accounts receivable (particularly aging issues), software and technology used (an indicator of potential training and equipment costs), leases and contracts that are in force at the time of the merger, qualified retirement plan obligations, and any assumed liabilities need careful examination. The foregoing is not an exclusive list, but it highlights the most important issues to be considered.

.01 Positioning a Firm to Be Acquired

It is critical for firms to start positioning themselves sooner rather than later. The preparation process includes:

- Holding a partner meeting at which the partners decide to seek a merger and:
  - Establish a set of guidelines for which type of acquirer would be best (e.g., a regional firm, another small firm, etc.).
  - Define the role they would want in a new firm (e.g., number of seats on the executive committee, leadership of particular niches).
  - Set out the length of time partners would stay at the firm.
  - Determine what financial arrangements would be acceptable to the partners.
  - Discuss any other terms that could prevent the merger from occurring, such as the name or location of the firm or titles.
- Making the firm attractive to prospective acquirers by analyzing its client base and divesting the firm of its least profitable clients, as described above.
- Documenting what the firm offers a potential acquirer in terms of:
  - Industries and types of services.
  - Particular expertise or "star power."
  - Future prospects for growth.
  - Outstanding loans.
  - Existing pension and/or buyout obligations.
- Deciding which, if any, staff would be expendable and why.
- Determining how appropriate merger candidates will be identified and approached:
  - Firm committee.
  - Outside consultant.
- Setting a timeline for the search process to begin.
- Establishing a structured timeline (usually between 30-90 days) for how the process will proceed once a candidate is identified.

When acquiring firms do their due diligence investigations, the two primary measures they review are profitability and expertise. If you expect your firm to be acquired by a larger firm, your firm must fit on the same continuum as the largest, best-run firms.

.02 The Chaos of a Merger

Merger candidates also need to face some realities that can be hard to accept:

- *The managing partner won't be managing.* All of the partners in a merged firm need to understand that their roles will change, but the managing partner is the one whose role will be changing the most. From the role of firm leader—

someone who can initiate various strategies and plans—the managing partner's role will change to one of an equity partner with a limited leadership role.

All of this may seem manageable when it is a theoretical exercise; reality is very different. An ex-managing partner who will be in contact with his former reports on a daily basis needs to be mentally prepared for his or her new role. Speaking with others who have gone through a merger can be helpful. Having someone who can act as a mentor and a sounding board can help allay fears about a merger and act as a guide through difficult moments.

- *Other partners will have different roles too.* The new firm may or may not want the partner who was in charge of marketing to continue in that role. The administrative partner may no longer be involved with the firm's administrative function. All of these changes must be discussed during merger negotiations and documented in the merger agreement. Successful mergers don't leave room for these kinds of surprises.

- *The firm's name will change.* The name of the old firm will, in all probability, cease to exist. This can be extremely difficult for name partners, whose egos are inextricably bound to the firm. Firms that are not first generation firms at the time of the merger are already past this part of the transition, but for the founding fathers of a firm, this change is so traumatic that it is one of the most common reasons merger talks fail.

- *Some staff may be redundant.* Some staff may be redundant at the new firm and may lose their jobs. This topic, too, should be part of the merger talks. While this may be a good time for the firm to shed less productive employees, more valued staff may also be excessed. Decisions need to be made about severance packages, exit interviews, outplacement services, etc. HR must have a plan in place for the process.

- *Culture is important.* The culture of the larger firm may be radically different from the one at the old firm. This can cover all kinds of issues, from training on new software and systems to dress codes to reporting structures. Without proper training and assimilation, the merger can fail. This doesn't necessarily mean a demerger, but it does mean a less unified firm with less unified goals.

- *Compensation structure is a factor.* When firms merge, the partners in the acquired firm usually want a guarantee that their income will remain stable. If the merger is part of an exit strategy for some partners, retirement is likely to be planned for 12 to 24 months post-merger, and income generally is guaranteed for that period as long as business continues at its pre-merger level. (Translation: as long as client retention stays strong.)

- *Notifying internal and external clients.* The merged firm needs to have a communication process in place for announcing the merger.

  — *Employees need to be the first to know.* The grapevine will be working at full steam, so employees need to be told the facts as early as possible. Keep in mind that they'll be most interested in how they will be affected personally: will they be reporting to a new physical location; who will they be reporting to; are their jobs safe?

  — *Media and referral sources.* Referral sources and the media should get an announcement of the merger. The media may or may not be interested in interviews, but trade and local media will almost always run an announcement of the merger. The managing partner (or the marketing director) should be given the responsibility of speaking with the media upon request. Referral sources will want to know about the new entity and whether it means there will be more opportunity to exchange business leads.

  — *Clients.* Clients need to know about the merger. The firm's most important clients should be told in person by the partner in charge of their account; they should not find out through a third party. Clients, too, need to be reassured about whether the same team will still service their accounts, that their billing rates won't increase, and that the merger will result in even more efficient and effective management of their account.

The challenges posed by mergers are not easy. On average, the adjustment takes about two years. And, in the case of partners who are giving up a lot of autonomy, a positive attitude is a major factor in the success of the merger.

.03 Written Agreements Are Essential

Mergers require legal documents, including partnership agreements that spell out the duties and responsibilities of all parties to the agreement. Some items that should be negotiated include what happens to staff, clients, equipment, and the firm name if the merger falls apart.

The merger agreement also should have a date beyond which it can't be rescinded. Generally, that period of time is one to three years. If a partner or partners decide to leave the firm after the stipulated time period has elapsed, the terms of the partnership agreement take precedence over those of the merger agreement.

Figure 6.13 ——

Sample Letter Announcing a Merger

[Date]

Client name

Address

City, state

Dear [Name]:

We are pleased to announce that our firm is combining with _____. This combination will enable us not only to handle all of your individual and business tax and accounting requirements, but will also offer you access to new areas such as estate tax planning, financial planning, investment planning, retirement plan administration, management advisory services, business valuation, and litigation support.

Although we are very proud to offer our clients these additional benefits, rest assured that the traditional functions of our practice will remain. In these areas, you will receive the same quality service in the same manner that you have received in the past. I will remain actively involved with meeting your professional service needs. I will continue to be assisted by the same highly qualified staff in our current office.

The name of our firm will be _____. Future correspondence will reflect the name change, but I look forward to introducing you to my new associates before then.

If you have any questions regarding our dedicated team of professionals, please do not hesitate to call me.

Sincerely,

____, CPA

¶ 645 The Future Is Now

As we are writing this book, the United States is facing an extremely serious economic crisis. Some experts are calling it the worst crisis since the Great Depression of the 1930s. None of us has a crystal ball, but it is already apparent that one of the outcomes will be new legislation and new regulations. We can only assume that the level of oversight these new rules will require will be more far-reaching than SOX and are likely to affect clients in all of our major client service areas: accounting, audit, tax, and business consulting. In addition, the SEC may be reorganized or a new oversight board created.

Through all of the current—and coming—changes, whatever form they ultimately take, we need to be able to continue to service our existing clients *and* the new business that is likely to result. In addition to the strategic alliances we will need to help us help our clients, it is important for us to keep our cool and not make impulsive decisions that can hurt the firm going forward. Examples of this include:

- *Being reactive instead of proactive.* There will be opportunities to grow. It is the firm leader's job to see where those opportunities lie and to lay the groundwork for taking advantage of them. Think about the firms that were prescient enough to approach the Big Four after the enactment of SOX and ask for audit work. They are the ones that grew substantially since 2002.

- *Failing to service top clients more astutely.* It is a perfect time to cement relationships with your top clients. Visit them off the clock to discuss what they are going through. Help guide them to get through the hard times. Listen, listen, listen: there are bound to be some hints of new work in the conversation.

- *Cutting the marketing department.* Sure, your bottom line may look healthier in the short term, but who will remember you when the economy turns around?

- *Not hiring new staff.* This is a perfect time to bolster your experienced staff. Not so long ago you probably were afraid head hunters would poach your staff. Today; some well-trained and experienced CPAs are available and looking for work.

Chapter 7
Changing Role of Rainmakers

¶ 701 Rainmaking

It is a given that not everyone has the desire to be a rainmaker. Informal statistics show that only 5 percent to 10 percent of a firm's partners have the right blend of traits to take on this role. Traditionally, partners who were rainmakers also were firm leaders.

This pattern remained in place for a number of years, when the role of rainmaker began to evolve. The change came about because more and more firms began to adopt a marketing culture in which everyone in the firm plays a role. Rainmaking is still a highly valued skill, and it has an enormous impact on a professional's ability to affect his or her own compensation, but rainmaking is not the most valuable skill a leader can have. We aren't minimizing the value of rainmakers. Every firm needs, values, and rewards them, and rightly so. The difference is that they are no longer the only people bringing in new business. As the influence of accounting firm marketing has grown, so too has the marketing culture within firms. Everyone, from the receptionist to the managing partner has a stake in the firm's success and a part in bringing new clients to the firm.

Nevertheless, rainmaking remains a critical skill for anybody considered for partnership, and firms should teach and nurture staff at all levels in how to do it. Mentoring and shadowing are ideal techniques for developing rainmaking skills. Firms that make the mistake of not inviting young professionals along on sales calls and closing discussions are missing a real opportunity to show them first hand how it works.

Remember, when new hires get to your firm, they come with theoretical knowledge, but without practical experience. As time goes on, they learn how the work really is done. They get faster and more efficient and better able to spot when something isn't right. Some even become star technicians. It's the same thing with rainmaking; they won't all be able to bring in the same amount of new business, but watching a key rainmaker do his or her thing is an unparalleled experience. They will pick up some pointers, especially if you debrief them later. And it will send an important message: "We value you."

¶ 705 "Mistmakers" Count Too

Having rainmakers is great, but even they sometimes need help from others in the firm. Many firms are offering training and coaching in skills such as networking and listening to all partners and professionals so they can assist in the firm's marketing effort. A good marketing professional, whether an in-house person or a consultant, can help everyone bring in a little "mist" to support the rainmakers' efforts.

Figure 7.1

Some Rainmaking—and Mistmaking—Tips

Have a positive attitude. Business development takes perseverance and fortitude. Statistically, it takes seven "touches" from a marketing program to connect with a potential client. Also, for every new client that chooses your firm, you need to have 10 to 15 prospects in the pipeline, and cultivating that one win can take as long as two years.

Don't be intimidated by the cost. The cost of getting one new engagement can be high, in terms of both dollars spent and time invested. Yet if you keep doing things right, like reinforcing a positive firm culture that sparks viral name recognition, your efforts will pay off over time. To paraphrase a popular quote, marketing is not for sissies. You need to think strategically and for the long term.

Spend your marketing dollars wisely. Know which clients you want and use your resources to your best advantage: spend the bulk of your dollars marketing to your A- and B-list clients and to specific target markets.

Make sure everyone at your firm knows what you do. Even the most forward-thinking firms have vestiges of the old silo mentality. They may find they have lost an engagement with a new or existing client because no one mentioned that your firm has expertise in estate planning, for example. It goes back to firm culture: you are a team, and everyone on the team needs to know what all of the other players are capable of doing.

Make marketing everyone's responsibility. Everyone at the firm should be accountable for some level of marketing, and that should be listed as a goal on everyone's annual development plan. Consider a marketing-specific employee incentive plan to support this concept.

Getting a request for proposal (RFP) doesn't mean you're really in the hunt. Sometimes, the effort of responding isn't worth it. Before devoting resources to answering the RFP, determine whether the engagement is one that you want and can perform. There are clients who use RFPs to find the lowest bidder or the one that doesn't have a good due diligence process for vetting prospective clients.

If possible, meet with the prospect before responding. Use your best client-centric skills during the meeting: listen intently for cues about what the client really is looking for. Take potential team members with expertise in the industry or service along to the meeting so you can showcase the firm's expertise.

If you do respond, promise a little and deliver a lot. Those are good words to live by in any engagement. Think carefully about what the engagement entails. Then build in extra time to finish the task and a buffer to cover unexpected costs; you aren't familiar with how the client works.

Manage expectations. Always be open about exactly what the client can expect. For example, let the client know if you can't meet a promised deadline. And explain why. If you find the engagement didn't take as long as you thought, tell the client that too. You may lose a short-term profit, but you'll win a long-term ally.

Don't think of lost proposals—or lost clients—as failures. Instead, think of them as learning opportunities. Contact the client (or have the partner in charge of the account or your marketing director make the call) and ask frankly what did and did not go well along the way. You may learn something about your firm that you were unaware of.

Client satisfaction surveys shouldn't be scary. Client satisfaction surveys should be conducted on an annual or biannual basis. Select clients (generally from your A and B list) should get the survey. The results should be viewed as educational. Yes, there is the possibility that you'll hear something negative about the way your firm does or doesn't do something or the way a staff member acts while at a client's office. But those are things you need to know so you can work to correct them. It's much better to find out there is a problem at an early stage; otherwise, you might find out the same thing at an exit interview.

Communicate. Communicate. Communicate. Make it a point to take an A-list client or an important referral source to lunch once a month—nonbillable. Just talk about what is going on in the business world. You may discover that there is a need for a service your firm provides or can provide. And you can't put a dollar value on the good will this type of program creates.

¶ 710 Big Brother, Big Sister: Do Mentoring Programs Work?

Lots of firms have mentoring programs in which the rainmaker is supposed to train and nurture someone identified as either a rising star at the firm or a problem partner. The word "mentor" is defined as "a wise and trusted counselor or teacher." Frankly, that doesn't sound very much like an assigned position. Think about your own business life: who were your mentors? Were they partners at the firm where you first worked, or did they come from outside that environment? Chances are, your answer is the latter.

But today's firms are far more fluid than the firms many of today's leaders started at, and the young people we are hiring are looking for guidance from those same firm leaders. The difference is that in the old firm paradigm, the managing partner was viewed somewhat like a king ensconced in a corner office. The decisions that partner made were rarely challenged, unless it was by other partners behind closed doors. Today's managing partner is more accessible and held to a much higher level of accountability.

In the old paradigm, new employees pretty much did what they were told. Today, new hires frequently ask why things are done a particular way. The situation is ripe for mentors, but there are some things that can't—and shouldn't—be forced. Mentor/mentee relationships fall into that category.

No supervisor should mentor a direct report. This is as true for an incoming managing partner as it is for a new hire. Think about it: would you want your mentor to be the same person who is responsible for assessing whether you are progressing along your chosen career path and/or someone who controls your compensation and bonus? Would you want to expose your doubts and fears to that person? That makes for a very constrained relationship, not at all in line with the definition of mentor.

Mentoring programs can be valuable, and they can work, as long as they are carefully thought out. Some options include having mentees choose a mentor from outside their department or hiring business or life coaches from outside the firm to serve this function.

Figure 7.2

Case Study: It's All in How You Say It /Isdaner & Company, LLC Bala Cynwyd, Penn.

It's a matter of how you say it. At Isdaner, the goal is to groom business people, not just accountants. The fir, understands the delicate balancing act all of us perform as we strive to find that elusive perfect balance between our work lives and our personal lives, all the while trying to give our clients 100 percent service.

The firm's solution is multifaceted, but communication—both spoken and unspoken—is at the core of it all. The members (partners) are accessible and respectful of all employees. This means asking people to do things, not ordering them to do it, and thanking them for a job well done. When members refer to other employees, they refer to them by saying "they work with me" rather than saying "they work for me."

The firm encourages early interaction in the client relationship and involvement in the activities of the client's industry. Members trust and show confidence in the employees' ability to do the work assigned and don't micromanage. Employees are responsible for managing their workloads and setting priorities accordingly. Flexible work schedules are the norm. The flip side of this philosophy involves treating mistakes as learning experiences rather than catastrophes even when they feel like a disaster.

Allan Cohen, head of the firm's integrated services department, has weekly lunch meetings with his group and utilizes icebreakers to improve and deepen relationships with team members. He also uses these weekly meetings to share success stories and brainstorm client challenges.

Scott Isdaner, the managing member, epitomizes this message of trust and confidence in people. He knows how to bring people together and is skilled at giving negative feedback a positive spin. When he criticizes something an employee has done, he never makes it personal. Instead, he talks about how the situation occurred and can be done to prevent it from happening again. This skill makes others seek him out to resolve conflicts. In addition, he has found that humor is an excellent communications tool. Once, he even wore a dress for a part in a humorous murder mystery firm event. His ability to laugh at himself and be self-deprecating enhances his leadership ability and goes a long way toward creating a workplace that is warm and nurturing.

Isdaner's communication strategies have paid off in a big way: our firm has a 93 percent retention rate.

Figure 7.3

Six Behaviors of Leadership

According to management consultant Morrie Shechtman, Chairman of Fifth Wave Leadership, all good leaders share six basic personality traits:

1. *The glass is always half full.* Good leaders always believe another—possibly better—opportunity is just around the corner. That philosophy allows them to be focused and go with their gut decisions. In real life, this trait translates to the ability to turn down a lucrative engagement if the client doesn't meet the firm's new client criteria and deal with difficult situations such as confronting a partner who is causing a toxic atmosphere in the firm.

2. *All business is personal.* The work-life balance conundrum has caused a fundamental shift in the way businesses view employees. In a world where John needs to leave early to attend his daughter's soccer game and Mary has to leave early to pick up the kids from her ex-husband, the "secrets" of one's personal life are an open book at the office. Good leaders recognize this; they don't try to fight it. Good leaders also recognize when they have to intervene, and, when they do, it is in the role of an advisor rather than a fixer. This is relatively easy in a strictly personal scenario: if you believe someone is an alcoholic, tell them your suspicions and give them the phone number for Alcoholics Anonymous; don't try to be their counselor and confessor.

3. *Don't try to fix the world.* It's impossible. Good leaders understand this on a visceral level. This allows them to confront and handle conflict better than the rest of us. Their vision of the world shows a possible path to resolution and allows them to guide others along that path. Suppose, for example, a particular manager is so controlling that others don't want to work for him. A good leader will have the conversation, point out to the manager that this behavior is detrimental to the firm, and ask the manager to come up with an action plan for changing his behavior. Then, the leader will monitor his progress through feedback from the partners and staff. No, this isn't a Little Miss Sunshine scenario; it is a nuanced plan of action that allows the controlling manager to assess his behavior and find ways to fix it that work with his personality. If the leader simply told the manager to knock it off, nothing would change—except, perhaps, the manager's increased level of resentment.

4. *Confront and manage conflict.* This has been talked about a little in Item 3. But the truth is that you can't be an ostrich and a good leader. Leaders need to know what's going on in the firm, and for larger firms, that's not possible without feedback from performance evaluations (including upward evaluations), client satisfaction surveys, partner meetings, and meetings with various department heads. Good firm leaders may not want to know the details of every conflict, but they should be aware of the ones that affect the firm's

well being: Is there a toxic partner or other staff member? Is there the threat of a sex discrimination suit against the firm? Is the firm's largest client disputing a bill? Good managers are well aware that conflict is unpleasant, but they are willing to confront the issue and feel the pain, because they also recognize that well-managed conflicts can allow for growth and learning.

5. *Accept suggestion and criticism.* Leaders are people, not gods, and they won't always make the right choice. That's why good leaders surround themselves with people who are strong enough to challenge them. Being open to new ideas and ways of doing things empowers others—thus nurturing the next generation of leaders—and shifts the decision making process from a one-person mission to a team effort.

6. *Don't allow moodiness to poison the air.* We all have our moment, good and bad. But when a firm leader allows his or her mood to rule the mood of the firm on any given day, the firm's culture will be built on a very shaky foundation. Good leaders aren't ruled by their emotions.

Figure 7.4 ————————————————————————————

Survey Results: Personal Growth Plans/Performance Reviews

A survey of about 100 firms with annual revenue of between $5 million and over $100 million showed a trend toward having staff review partners and supervisors. Sixty percent of firms in this survey conduct regular partner reviews, although most still do not encourage staff participation in the review. Another trend is that 54 percent of firms use an electronic personal evaluation system.

Does everyone in the firm have a personal growth plan that is supported by their manager or supervisor?

Yes	36%
No	64%

How often do you review employee progress?

Annually	37%
Semi-annually	43%
Quarterly	12%
Other	8%

Does your firm conduct regular partner reviews?

Yes	54%
No	46%

If your firm conducts regular partner reviews, does staff participate in the review?

Yes	36%
No	64%

How often do you provide feedback to partners?

Annually	56%
Semi-annually	26%
Quarterly	18%

Source: Boomer Consulting, Inc. results of an instant survey taken at the 2008 Winning Is Everything Conference.

Figure 7.5 ————————————————————————————

Managing Partner: Sample Position Description 1

The managing partner is vested with the responsibility and authority for the overall management of the firm. The managing partner acts judiciously, on behalf of the firm, in all decisions and actions affecting the management of the practice.

Authority, responsibility, and working relationships with various groups are:

The Executive Committee:

- The managing partner automatically serves as a member of the committee.
- The managing partner informs the committee of all pending actions, decisions, or problems affecting the welfare of the firm and its members. This is done informally as frequently as feasible and formally at scheduled meetings of the executive committee.
- The managing partner is responsible for administering decisions of the committee, presenting concerns and recommendations to the committee, and working with the committee to develop and implement effective solutions and to reach optimum decisions.

- The compensation, constraints, and conditions of service are defined by the executive committee.
- The managing partner's performance is subject to review by the committee and the committee can recommend that he be replaced upon a vote of the partnership.

Partners-in-Charge:

- The managing partner administers firm policies and procedures in the local office through these partners.
- Problems, decisions, and situations of concern in a particular office are brought to the attention of the managing partner by the partner(s)-in-charge.
- The managing partner is responsible for effective control of local office operations and for providing adequate support to the partner(s)-in-charge in the performance of their duties.
- The managing partner meets with individual partner(s)-in-charge to review and appraise as frequently as required, but at least quarterly.
- The managing partner assists partner(s)-in-charge in organizing their office operations, developing departments and specialties, and maintaining performance standards. This is monitored through monthly reports and review sessions held with the partner(s)-in-charge.
- The managing partner recommends to the executive committee for action the removal and replacement of a partner-in-charge who is not performing satisfactorily or in those situations of resignation or withdrawal.

Technical Directors:

- The managing partner supports the work of technical directors and assists in establishing standards, developing quality control procedures, and training the professionals and partners. The managing partner is responsible for publishing and maintaining policies and procedures developed by the directors.
- The managing partner removes and replaces any director who is not performing effectively.

The Partnership:

- The managing partner is responsible to all partners to see that the firm's goals and philosophies are accomplished successfully and to the mutual benefit of all.
- The managing partner has the responsibility to prudently administer the business for the mutual advantage of all the partners.
- The managing partner annually conducts a review and evaluation of each partner.

The duties of the managing partner include, but are not necessarily be limited to:

Organization:

- Developing and maintaining an effective firm wide organizational structure consistent with firm goals and objectives.
- Defining criteria and actively pursuing acquisitions and the development of offices consistent with firm goals and objectives.
- Ensuring adequate departmentalized services and accounting specialties to best serve client needs.
- Monitoring firm wide, local office, individual partner, and staff goals programs.
- Implementing firm wide and local office business development programs, assisting in profitable expansion of existing clients, and development of new clients.

Finance:

- Exercising financial controls to achieve firm goals, including: financial reporting, billing rate determination, budget management, account billing, and receivables control.
- Assisting local offices in maintenance and control of expenditures, budgeting controls, billing, and collection procedures.
- Preparing consolidated financial statements and other financial information to help local offices control costs and perform profitably.
- Developing and maintaining a fiscal management information system including budget, operating costs, and other pertinent financial performance information, reported monthly.
- Providing adequate controls to assure that revenues earned will provide compensation for partners and staff above levels for similar positions available elsewhere.
- Achieving profit objectives for the firm.
- Providing and maintaining adequate insurance coverage for all appropriate areas of concern.
- Insuring adequate working capital by defining requirements, controlling partner withdrawals, maintaining borrowing lines, coordinating purchasing, and exercising sound fiscal management procedures.

Administration:

- Maintaining proper staffing levels to enable the firm to achieve its goals. This includes forecasting manpower requirements, recruiting, compensating, developing specialist skills, and evaluating and motivating performance.

- Ensuring adequate working conditions—space, equipment, supervision, and opportunity.

- Providing partner and staff training in technical as well as managerial skills.

- Control continuing professional education schedules for the firm in a way which will enable all professionals to achieve their goals.

- Administering the provisions of the firm staff manual covering all personnel and administrative policies and procedures. Monitoring and revising standards, policies, and procedures to insure continued effective operations.

- Developing and maintaining adequate compensation and benefits programs for partners and staff.

- Administering personnel programs for the mutual benefit of employees and the firm, including performance evaluations and reviews, compensation, benefits, hiring, training, promoting, and office location assignments.

- Determining long-range needs and goals for the firm and presenting them with plans and recommended actions to the partnership.

Partnership:

- Monitoring the partnership agreement: recommend changes, brief new partners, and ensure each partner's annual review. Administering the provisions of the partnership agreement for the mutual benefit of all partners.

- Keeping partners informed by scheduling and conducting annual and other special partnership meetings and otherwise keeping all partners apprised of current situations of concern.

- Providing a climate for mutual respect among partners by maximizing communications.

- The managing partner may assume, with the concurrence of the executive committee, any other duties, tasks, or responsibilities not herein specified, but which may become necessary to properly manage the practice for the benefit of the firm and its members.

- The managing partner must continuously be aware that he serves at the pleasure of the partnership and must conduct the management of the practice in accordance with sound business practices and in a prudent manner.

Figure 7.6

Managing Partner: Sample Position Description 2

The managing partner is responsible for the day-to-day overall practice operations. All decisions made by him shall be for the benefit of the partnership and the mutual well-being of its partners. The managing partner is charged with the responsibility and authority to:

1. Maintain the firm's quality control program and standards.

2. Administer the day-to-day operations of the business and its various offices.

3. Prepare and maintain the books, financial records, and management information of the practice.

4. Undertake those projects and activities necessary to maintain the practice in a sound business condition.

The executive committee is responsible for proposing candidates for the position and for proposing their removal.

The term of office of a managing partner is five years, and he is eligible for reelection for one additional five-year term. The managing partner's performance is subject to review and evaluation by the executive committee. He or she is elected or removed by a majority vote of the partnership.

The managing partner's authority and responsibilities include the following:

1. Act as chair of the executive committee, maintain communications between the executive committee and the partners, and carry out the decisions of the Executive Committee.

2. Keep partners informed by scheduling, calling, arranging and conducting annual and other special partnership meetings. Prior to each meeting he or she circulates an agenda requesting suggestions for additional items. Between meetings he or she keeps all partners apprised on current situations of concern.

3. Coordinate the development, implementation, and maintenance of the firm's philosophy, long-range plans, and organizational structure.

¶710

4. Oversee the determination of proper staffing levels to enable the firm to achieve its goals. This includes:
   - Forecasting manpower requirements.
   - Recruiting.
   - Assigning and implementing compensation levels.
   - Developing specialist skills.
   - Evaluating and motivating performance.

5. Ensure adequate working conditions.

6. Oversee partner and staff training in technical as well as managerial skills and control continuing professional education schedules for the firm in a way which will assist all personnel in achieving their goals.

7. Administer the provisions of the firm staff manual and partners' manual covering all personnel and administrative policies and procedures. Monitor and recommend revisions of standards policies and procedures to insure continued effective operations.

8. Administer programs for the mutual benefit of personnel and the firm including:
   - Performance evaluation and reviews.
   - Compensation.
   - Benefits.
   - Hiring.
   - Training.
   - Promotions.
   - Office location assignments.

9. Determine long-range needs and goals for the firm and present them along with plans and recommended actions to the executive committee.

10. Assume overall responsibility for the maintenance of the partnership agreement.

11. Administer the provisions of the partnership agreement.

12. Coordinate contracts between the firm and outside agencies (AICPA, State Education Department, etc.).

13. Recommend criteria and coordinate negotiations for the merger or acquisition of practices and development of new offices.

14. Maintain billing and collection policies.

15. Provide and maintain adequate insurance coverage including:
   - Professional liability.
   - Health care.
   - Other appropriate policies.

16. Monitor policies for evaluation, acceptance, and continuance of clients.

17. Initiate and approve business expenditures up to $7,500.

18. Oversee the coordination of staff scheduling and utilization.

19. Exercise financial controls to achieve the firm's goals, including:
   - Financial reporting.
   - Budget management.
   - Control of WIP and receivables.
   - Determination of reserves required for WIP and receivables on a quarterly basis.

20. Supervise the preparation of consolidated financial statements and other financial information to help each office control costs and perform profitably.

21. Establish and monitor firm standards of performance including write-offs, writedowns, chargeable hours, receivables collection, net realization, and other standards and statistics as may be defined.

22. Ensure adequate working capital, maintain borrowing lines, coordinate purchasing, and monitor fiscal management systems.

23. Develop and strive to achieve individual office goals in the areas of new business, productivity, and profitability.

24. Ensure that all personnel provide adequate and timely input to the firm's management information system.

25. Oversee all marketing activities and programs.

26. Actively monitor the new business activities of the firm as well as participate in those activities.

27. Set a proper example for the professional staff by participating in professional, civic, and community activities.

28. Administer firm wide policies, procedures, and practices.

29. Ensure adequate client contact and engagement control consistent with the firm's policies and procedures.

30. Assign to local office partners and staff, functions, tasks, and responsibilities commensurate with their abilities, interests, and knowledge.

31. Perform such other duties, as may be delegated by the executive committee, necessary to ensure effective operations of the firm.

The managing partner is authorized to perform such other acts, not specifically prohibited, to implement decisions and take action for the welfare of the partnership and its partners.

The managing partner is continually aware that he or she serves at the pleasure of the partnership and, therefore, must function in accordance with sound business practices, in a prudent manner, for the benefit of the firm.

Figure 7.7

Managing Partner: Sample Position Description 3

The managing partner is responsible for the day-to-day overall practice operations. All decisions made by the managing partner shall be for the benefit of the firm and the mutual well-being of its shareholders.

The managing partner is charged with the responsibility and authority to: (1) maintain the firm's quality control program and standards; (2) administer the day-to-day operations of the business and its various offices; (3) prepare and maintain the books, financial records, and management information of the practice; and (4) undertake those projects and activities necessary to maintain the practice in a sound business condition.

The managing partner's authority and responsibilities include the following:

1. Maintain communications between the executive committee and the partners and carry out the decisions of the executive committee.

2. Coordinate the development, implementation, and maintenance of the firm philosophy, long-range plans, and organizational structure.

3. Assume overall responsibility for the maintenance of the shareholders' agreement.

4. Administer the provisions of the shareholders' agreement.

5. Coordinate contracts between the firm and outside agencies.

6. Define criteria and coordinate negotiations for the merger or acquisition of practices and development of new offices.

7. Maintain billing and collection policies.

8. Monitor firm's capital requirements and arrange financing as required.

9. Provide and maintain adequate insurance coverage including: professional liability, health care, and other appropriate policies.

10. Monitor policies for evaluation, acceptance, and continuance of clients.

11. Coordinate the development and maintenance of firm brochures.

12. Approve all capital expenditures to $5,000 and approve increases in debt structure not exceeding $25,000.

13. Review and approve leasehold improvements, purchase, rent, or lease arrangements not exceeding $10,000.

The managing partner is authorized to perform such other acts, not specifically prohibited, to implement decisions and take action for the welfare of the firm and its shareholders.

The managing partner is continually aware that he or she serves at the pleasure of the shareholders and therefore must function in accordance with sound business practices, in a prudent manner, for the benefit of the firm.

The managing partner is also charged with the responsibility and authority for administering operations in a manner consistent with good business practices and in keeping with the policies, procedures, and guidelines established by the firm.

The managing partner works directly with and reports his activities to the shareholders while having direct access and recourse to the policy committee.

The managing partner's authority and responsibilities also include the following:

1. Develop and strive to achieve firm goals in the area of new business, productivity, and profitability.

2. Provide adequate and timely input to the firm's management information system.

3. Actively monitor the new business activities as well as participate in those activities.

4. Set a proper example for the professional staff by participating in professional, civic, and community activities.

5. Administer firm wide policies, procedures, and practices.

6. Prepare and administer the operating budget, including control of expenses and operating costs.

7. Ensure financial stability by exercising sound fiscal management control of billings, receivables, collection, shareholder and staff productivity, and operating costs.

8. Adhere to firm wide standards of performance including write-offs, write-downs, chargeable hours, receivables, collections, net realizations, and other standards and statistics as may be defined.

9. Ensure adequate client contact and engagement control consistent with firm policies and procedures.

10. Assign to partners and staff those functions, tasks, and responsibilities commensurate with their abilities, interests, and knowledge.

11. Coordinate staff scheduling and utilization.

Figure 7.8

General Services Director: Sample Position Description

General services directors are primarily involved in serving clients, and their activities are generally related to that function. The director is responsible for providing the best possible service to clients in accounting, audit, tax management services, and other areas.

Following are specific responsibilities related to general services directors:

1. Maintain good client relations.

2. The cost to the client should be comparable to the value given.

3. The effective diagnosis of clients' needs and the providing of all needed services for the client.

4. The effective use of specialists within the firm, when available, or in other instances from outside sources.

5. Responsibility for promptly billing and collecting for services rendered.

6. Adequate supervision and communication with the staff.

7. Effective delegation of responsibilities to staff personnel.

8. The shareholders are ultimately responsible for the quality of the job and must perform an adequate shareholders' review.

9. Demonstrate compliance with the policies of the firm.

10. Be a positive factor on contributing to firm morale.

11. Demonstrate a sense of total responsibility for the welfare and progress of the firm.

12. It is the responsibility of each general services director to find natural ways in which to build relations with potential new client sources and to bring new clients to the firm.

Figure 7.9

Technical Committee Chair: Sample Position Description

The technical committee chair has the overall responsibility to develop and administer the policies and procedures of the committee in the best interests of the firm. Such policies and procedures should be in accordance with all rules and regulations of professional standards pertaining to the committee's area of expertise.

The technical committee chair works directly with and reports to the managing partner while having direct access and recourse to the executive committee.

The technical committee chair's authority and responsibilities include the following:

1. The quality of the firm as it relates to the committee's area of expertise.

2. The development of the firm's philosophies and the determination of policies related to the practice of the firm.

3. Maintain an adequate and competent staff within the committee to discharge the responsibilities of the committee.

4. To exploit the possibilities for practice development through the committee's expertise of the firm known in the community.

5. The development of quality control through the establishment of adequate review procedures.

6. To serve the clients of the firm by providing necessary expertise and support for the managing partner.

7. To develop an agenda of training programs to increase the competence of the professional personnel, to coordinate the scheduling of such programs with other committees, and to plan implementation of the program to keep professional staff informed of current developments.

8. To sense the need for written firm policies related to the practice of the firm and to issue policy statements in writing as appropriate.

9. To develop the capabilities of the firm to provide additional needed services for clients.

¶ 715 Networking Magic

Networking can yield great results, but, alas, there is no magic. CPAs enter the profession for a variety of reasons, but often enough one of them is having a career that allows them to avoid socializing outside of their comfort zone. That's probably the main reason firms have such a low percentage of rainmakers.

There are ways around this, methods that can work well if the firm recognizes that there is no one-size-fits-all formula. Some people, even good networkers, never get over a feeling of stage fright before they enter a room filled with people they don't know.

The best way for the necessary skills to be taught is to mirror someone who is good at it. That is why it is important for rainmaker partners to take someone from the firm's next generation of leaders along to networking events. For the firm's leaders, networking is fun and the number of available networking opportunities is limitless. For those partners, it is critical to assess which meetings and events are likely to yield the best results.

.01 Memberships

Are you looking to enhance your presence in a particular niche? If so, identify the leading associations and media in the particular industry or service area. An Internet search can provide event calendars and media calendars that indicate opportunities to showcase your expertise. If you are seeking to create a general business presence in a specific geographic area, chambers of commerce and other civic organizations are a good place to start.

Another option is joining a formal networking group, where the members refer business to each other. Such groups operate at varying levels, some appropriate for small firms and others for larger firms. Often, these groups are fee-based, and those with a larger-firm focus often have a leadership training component. Depending on the commitment of the members, these types of networking activities sometimes sound more attractive than they turn out to be.

To get the maximum benefit from any organization you join, determine what your goal is in joining and commit to becoming an active member. Volunteer to be on a committee. Generally speaking, you will meet the most people, including decision makers, if you offer to serve on the membership, programming, or education committees. Over time, you will be able to measure whether the membership is valuable: Did the people you met become resources for your firm? Did your firm become a resource for someone else?

¶ 720 Successful Networking Requires Work

Earlier in this book, we talked about how important it was to classify clients and fire those who are not contributing to the firm's success. Well, the same is true of our referral networks: we need to look at them strategically so we can evaluate which are most valuable. In the case of referral sources, the squeaky wheel definitely shouldn't automatically get the attention.

Generally speaking, referrals come from four areas: our personal lives (e.g., friends and family), the organizations we belong to (e.g., religious congregations, service clubs), our professional lives (e.g., attorneys, bankers), and our clients (arguable the most important because referrals really are positive testimonials about the firm's quality). Referrals that come from any of these sources are easier to convert into new clients because they come with goodwill: they already know the firm from the person who referred them.

But these four groups can be broken down another way as well:

- *Those who refer frequently.* These sources are, effectively, mentors to the firm. They believe in the firm, and they make sure others know it: they advocate for your firm without being asked.

- *Occasional referrers.* These sources know your firm and understand its brand, qualities, and expertise. They respect your work and readily refer others to your firm, but they may also refer to other firms.

- *Very infrequent referrers.* These sources know your firm as "an accounting firm." They don't know your work very well, but they like you as an individual and trust that you do good work.

A very infrequent referrer may call you often and want to spend time with you, and that's great. But you need to assess where your time and effort will yield the most value: who should you take to dinner or ask to be in your golf foursome?

That doesn't mean turning away a referral source. It does mean weighing where you'll get the greatest return on your investment of time and resources. So how do you develop a strong referral network? By establishing goals and strategizing:

- Look for mutually beneficial channels. If you have a financial planning niche, networking with financial planners may not be the best option because you'll be after the same clients. But it may be a good choice if you're looking to hire an experienced financial planner.

- Assess whether you're adding value to your referral sources. Are you making referrals to them, or is the relationship a one-way street? If you have only 10 new estate planning clients per year, how many estate planning attorneys or financial planners can your referral network support?

- Become comfortable asking for referrals. Most of us are reticent to do this, but it really isn't difficult. For instance, when someone thanks you at the end of an engagement, you can say something like, "Thank you. I'm delighted you're happy with the job we did. Do you know anyone else who can benefit from our services?"

Figure 7.10 ———————————————————————————————————————

Networking Tips

- *Do your due diligence.* Before attending a function, determine who else is likely to be at the function? Will there be decision-makers? Will anyone be there you particularly want to meet? What is the dress code? (If you are unsure, it is best to err on the side of formality.)

- *Prepare an infomercial.* When someone asks what you do, make it interesting. Don't just say, "I'm a CPA." Instead, say something like "I help businesses become more successful by reviewing the company's financials looking for ways to help them operate more efficiently." Rehearse your statement so it sounds natural.

- *Promote conversation by asking open-ended questions.* There are many responses to the sample infomercial, for example: "Really. What do you look for?" "What kinds of efficiencies have you found?"

- *Have some small talk topics ready to go.* Industry topics, current events, and books and movies are a few examples.

- *Listen. Listen. Listen.* If you think there is a connection—compatible industries, good chemistry—listen to what the person is saying. Look for opportunities to follow up.

- *Don't get boxed into a long conversation that will keep you from meeting other people.* Plan an exit line for such eventualities.

- *Repeat the person's name in the conversation.* Everyone likes to think they are memorable, and hearing one's name is a good way to do that.

- *Networking events aren't marathons.* You don't get a prize for collecting the most cards. You might get one for meeting one or two people who become valued members of your network.

- *Become a resource for others.* Give generously of your time or expertise.

- *Post-meeting strategies.* When you leave the meeting, jot down identifying notes on the back of any business cards you've collected. It will help you remember who told you they were planning to sell their business and whose wife was just appointed to a powerful board in one of your firm's niche areas. Then, use the information when you send follow-up notes or make follow-up phone calls.

———————————————————————————————————————

.01 Social Networking

There's a new(ish) wrinkle on the networking landscape: social networking. If you remember the Rolodex and the power of the contacts in it, you'll understand the concepts behind social media. You may never understand why people post their pictures or disclose personal details, but you'll get the basic concept: the strength of who-knows-who-knows-who. It's a real life version of six degrees of separation.

There are many different tools, some of them geared toward professionals and others not. MySpace, for example, is well known, but most of the people who use it are still in school. The social networks that are most popular for professionals include:

- LinkedIn, which is specifically designed to uncover the shared relationships people aren't aware of. For instance, through LinkedIn you may discover that you belonged to the same fraternity as the president of a company in your firm's target market. You don't know him personally, but your audit manager does. The introduction goes from cold and maybe to warm and for-sure.

- Facebook, originally designed to be similar to MySpace, is emerging as a more business-oriented site.

- Ryze.com, a free social networking website is designed to link business professionals, particularly new entrepreneurs.

- Twitter.com is another free social networking and micro-blogging service. Twitter users send "tweets" (text-based posts, up to 140 characters long) to the Twitter Web site, *via* the Twitter Web site, instant messaging, or a third-party application such as Twitterrific or Facebook.

All of the social networking sites work in a similar way. You go to the site, sign up for free, and create a profile. The profile can be as minimal or as detailed as you wish; it all depends on how you plan to use it. Once you are signed up, you can use it to ask questions of the people in your network (e.g., "does anyone know of a CPA firm in Kentucky with a specialty in dental practice) or ask for an introduction to someone you'd like to meet but who you would never just bump into (e.g., the fraternity brother described above).

Most social networks have internal groups that you can belong to: accounting firm marketers, or Big Four alumni, or an alumni group from your firm for instance. You can also look for people to connect to and ask them to join your network. On LinkedIn, there is also a place for endorsements: "Joe Partner is the most responsive and knowledgeable CPA I've ever worked with. His cost segmentation study revealed ways we could save $100,000 per year."

There are, of course, risks associated with participating in online social networks. We've all heard the stories of college students who lost job opportunities because they imprudently posted risqué photos on their MySpace or Facebook page. It is sound advice to keep your profile simple. Don't post anything that could potentially embarrass you or your firm. Web pages have a half-life roughly equivalent to the time it takes for a plastic bag to dissolve in a landfill.

As with other types of networks, it is the quality of your contacts—not the quantity—that makes it work. Don't be seduced by the ease with which you can connect with people. As a general rule, it is safest to connect only with people you know, want to know, or whose reputation meets the standards your firm sets for accepting new clients.

.02 Other Online Tools

There are many other online tools, and more crop up all the time. Some of the tools to be aware of include:

- *YouTube.* A Web video sharing site that lets anyone store short videos for private or public viewing. Videos are streamed to users on the YouTube site (www.youtube.com) or via blogs and other websites. Many CPA firms have posted recruiting videos on YouTube.

- *Del.icio.us.* A community bookmarking website in which users can save Web pages they find and share them with other users.

- *Flickr.* Online photo management and sharing application.

- *Digg.* A Web site that accepts links and brief descriptions to news articles, videos and podcasts from members, all of which are voted on by other members.

- *Dogpile.* Puts the power of all the leading search engines together in one search box to deliver the best combined results.

.03 Online Reputation Management: RSS Feeds

The Internet has many pros, but there are also cons. Many of the cons concern the fact that you can't control what's posted on the Internet. Did a disgruntled employee leave your firm? Did you fire someone? Do you want to know what people are saying about an existing client you think is in financial difficulty? A potential client who is engaging your firm to perform a forensic audit?

Apart from a simple Google search, online tools are available to assist in your search. Most of these tools require you to have an RSS (Really Simple Syndication) feed. According to www.searchwindevelopment.com, an RSS feed is:

RSS is an XML-based vocabulary for distributing Web content in opt-in feeds. Feeds allow the user to have new content delivered to a computer or mobile device as soon as it is published. An RSS aggregator or RSS reader allows the user to see summaries of all their feeds in one place. Instead of visiting multiple Web pages to check for new content, the user can look at the summaries and choose which sites to visit for the full versions.

RSS feeds you can subscribe to for this purpose include: Google.com/alerts (based on queries or topics); Technorati.com and backtype.com (which monitor blogs); boardtracker.com (for discussion boards); twitter.com (name mentions); and friendfeed.com (social media).

.04 The Generational Piece

Some firm leaders are disconcerted by social networking and have a difficult time realizing how much a part of life it is for young employees who grew up in a world of public confession a la Oprah, the visuals of music videos, and the sound bites of TV news. Using ear buds for an i-pod is no big deal, and Blackberries beep all day. The sensibilities are different, and so are the methods of communication.

It is key that leaders avoid a knee jerk reaction ("Turn that off now. This is a workplace.") and recognize that these tools are here to stay. Firms need to embrace the positive aspects of new and emerging technologies, such as the many anecdotal stories about how quickly questions are answered simply by instant messaging a friend.

.05 Protecting Your Firm

It also is important to protect your firm by having policies in place for what and how firm equipment is used. As you draft your firm's policy, keep in mind that your most important goal is protecting the integrity of your firm. Some basic items that might be included in the policy include:

- Any software downloaded or installed on the firm's computers must comply with all applicable licensing agreements and copyrights.
- When downloading software, you must comply with the firm's procedures.
- The computer may not be networked to any networks not specifically authorized by the firm.
- All confidential material must be sent using the firm's secure network.
- Material that would be considered inappropriate, offensive, or disrespectful to others may not be accessed or stored.

¶ 725 Public Relations

The definition of public relations (PR) is "accurate, consistent and timely communications that convey the right message to the right audience." PR can include public speaking, writing, media commentary, and community participation.

Many CPAs cringe when they hear that PR is added to their job responsibilities. The truth is that in many cases PR either comes naturally—as it generally does for rainmakers—or it can be taught. Some aspects can be outsourced: for example, ghostwriters and copywriters can be hired; media coaches can help with presentation skills.

A scattershot approach is unlikely to be successful, but creating and implementing a public relations strategy can be an effective tool for establishing your firm's expertise and shoring up your reputation. There are three critical steps to formulating an effective plan:

1. Identify your goals and objectives (e.g., increasing your market share by becoming known as the best source for tax strategies for physician practices).
2. Determine the fact(s) that differentiates you from your competitors (e.g., lowest price, most knowledgeable on a particular topic).
3. Establish the three to five most important facts about your firm that will form the basis of your message.

Once these core concepts are developed, the strategies and tactics to implement the plan need to be developed:

- Pay attention to the publications, Web sites and other media in the area (e.g., are they paid or free subscriptions, are they put out by an industry association, are the articles they include in depth studies or fluff); identify the most visible reporters as well as the sources they use most often (e.g., are any of your competitors on the list?).
- Building relationships with reporters in your niche areas can pay great dividends. They often are interested in stories about new and different topics or a fresh approach to a popular one. Even if your suggestion isn't used, you have established yourself as a source.
- Local media can be a good source of free publicity. They often publish announcements of new hires, promotions, and awards you have received or given to others. But never, ever tell a reporter you see them as an avenue of free publicity.
- Learn which reporters handle the information you want to get out. Online and print resources are available that have this information.
- Always return a reporter's phone call immediately.
- Send a laminated postcard with your information to these reporters with an introductory note. Include your cell number: reporter's deadlines are not always during the traditional work day, and there is an old adage "he who answers the call gets quoted."
- Show that the firm's PR strategy is working by compiling a book of clippings.
- If you are lucky enough to meet with a reporter, limit your pitch to one good idea. Ask how you can help him or her understand specific things, such as the new legislation, the industry, or service you provide.
- Write letters to the editor that express your opinion on a controversial issue.
- When reporters do call, have a team designated to respond. Every firm has people who can think on their feet and those that need to reflect on what they say without speaking. In our 24/7/365 news cycle, only those in the first group should be on the routing list.
- When TV or radio are in your media mix, it makes sense to invest in a coach who can give valuable feedback on aspects of an appearance that you may not consider, such as body language (where to look, how to sit, how your hands should be held), where to look (is the camera on?), and what to wear.

It would be remiss to fail to mention that PR doesn't exist in a vacuum: to get the most ROI, it needs to be part of an overall marketing and branding strategy. Consider the experience of Blum Shapiro/West Hartford, CT. The firm developed a close relationship with the Connecticut Business & Industry Association (CBIA), which represents more than 10,000 businesses in

Connecticut, and many prominent business leaders. Several years ago, the firm sought sponsorship of CBIA's annual survey of Connecticut businesses. This sponsorship has become a critical tool in the firm's effort to keep Blum Shapiro visible in the business community all year long. The survey is used by state leaders to help shape state policy, and the Blum Shapiro CBIA Business Survey is featured in nearly 100 media articles a year.

Figure 7.11

Sample Media Card

I would be pleased to provide you with any editorial quotes in my areas of expertise: firm management, strategic planning, building a niche, mergers and acquisitions.

Gary S. Shamis, CPA, M.Acc.

Areas of Expertise:

* Firm management
* Strategic planning
* Building a niche
* Mergers and acquisitions

Named 2008 E&Y Entrepreneur of the Year (Northeast Ohio) in the financial services area; named as one of Accounting Today's most influential people nine times; author of dozens of practice management articles; national and international speaker on practice management issues.

CONTACT INFORMATION

Ph: (440) 248-8787

Toll free: (800) 869-1834

Fax: (440) 246-0841

Email: gshamis@ssandg.com

Gary S. Shamis, CPA, M.Acc.
Managing Director
SS & G
32125 Solon Road
Cleveland, Ohio 44139

www.ssandg.com

.01 Crisis Communications

Crisis communications begins with preparedness. The speed at which news travels makes it necessary for firms to be ready to react to crises. Andersen's demise is a prime example why this is so important, particularly for firms with SEC clients.

.02 Outsourcing the PR Function May Be an Option

Depending on the scope of the firm's PR initiative—branding, niche recognition, crisis—many firms find they have better success when they outsource the PR function. That may mean hiring someone to ghostwrite articles for the firm or someone to nurture and oversee relationships with the media or clip media references. One part of the PR function cannot be outsourced: there needs to be a point-person in-house for crisis communications, even if it's just to give talking points to the PR person.

Cost is a consideration, and there are three ways PR experts can charge for their time: project rate, retainer, and hourly. Anyone on retainer should be required to submit an accounting for their time each month. The number of hours will vary, but in most cases this it works out well for the firm. Hourly billing and project rates can cost less overall, but it is sometimes difficult to get the buy-in you need for infrequent projects.

¶ 730 Advertising Can Pay Off

Imagine you've got the hottest ticket in town. You arrive at the theater, pick up a playbill, and find those great seats. Suddenly, there is a friendly reminder: "Is your cell phone off?" The request doesn't come from the stage. It's on a bookmark, tucked inside the playbill, and it features your company logo:

As a courtesy to your fellow theatergoers and the actors on stage, please make sure to turn off your cell phone . . . before the performance begins. After the show, turn ON your cell phone and give us a call.

West Hartford, CT-based Blum Shapiro uses playbill advertising in the nation's oldest musical theatre, the Goodspeed Opera House in Connecticut. The firm has gained visibility through this unique marketing effort.

Roseland, NJ-based J.H. Cohn uses drive-time radio to reinforce its name and its brand. RSM McGladrey advertised on MSNBC during the presidential election.

Firms across the country are implementing innovative advertising campaigns; budget and firm culture are the best guides for what is appropriate for your firm.

¶ 735 Community Involvement

Involvement in community activities yields positive results in two ways: it reinforces your firm's brand (i.e., its mission and values), and it fosters a feeling of teamwork among the staff. Giving back to the community is a positive value that is particularly important to the younger staffers who are the firm's future. Most causes, other than religious or political, are universally embraced. Firms with a nonprofit niche may want to avoid activities that can be viewed as partisan, but much of that can be deflected by either alternating the recipients on an annual basis, creating a unique program such as a scholarship program at a local school, or creating a policy stipulating that only non-client entities will benefit from the firm's efforts.

Some firms tie community involvement to their employee incentive plans, while the program is completely voluntary for others. Where the program is strictly voluntary, firms show their support by allowing a certain amount of paid time off, usually one or two days per year.

Chapter 8
Get What You're Worth

¶ 801 Value Proposition

As new paradigms for practice development and service offerings emerge, don't fall into the common trap of underpricing your services. If you develop unique niches, hone hard-to-find expertise, differentiate your practice, and provide top-of-the-line service, you'll be able to command premium prices. Don't squander that opportunity! Getting paid what you bill—and what you deserve—for services you provide should not be negotiable. But there are some ways of making sure you do:

- *Sell positively.* Remember, and remind the client, that you are selling something of value. Don't apologize for how much a value-added service will cost. Know the difference between features and benefits, and be prepared to illustrate the benefits of the services you provide to your clients and the long-term win for the client.

  If technical work is involved, you can increase the perception of value by bringing in the experts who'll work on the engagement. Let them discuss the intricacies of the work, the skills required to perform it, and the rewards the client will enjoy. Never diminish the perceived value by slashing the price to get the engagement.

- *Remember that changes in the client's situation aren't your responsibility.* Neither are changes in law or in regulatory affairs. These circumstances may change the nature of the engagement, but your firm shouldn't absorb the cost. If the nature of the work changes, the nature of the pricing may have to change too. Methods to change requests—UNICAP, cash to accrual, change in ownership, and related complications—are circumstances beyond the scope of the original engagement and should be reflected in fees charged to the client.

- *Good communication is critical to maintaining good client relationships.* When such situations arise, however, be sure to communicate with the client to mitigate the gap in price expectation. Discuss any additional time required. Just because an engagement is priced at a fixed fee doesn't mean that any additional services provided didn't add value or that your firm should give them away.

¶ 805 Calculating Profit: Profitability and Productivity Ratios

Accounting firms can't charge the same fee to every client or for the same type of engagement. It goes back to rating clients: some are just very high maintenance. When deciding what to bill clients, remember that clients don't look at the same things as you do. This is the model you need to go by when pricing engagements:

Professionals Evaluate	Clients Evaluate
Cost	Benefits
Effort	Results
Investment	Return
Activities	Outcomes

.01 Utilization Rates

Utilization rates allow you to measure the productivity of individuals within your firm. For example, in a typical firm of 25 or more, the total available hours for an experienced staff member should be about 1600-1800 chargeable hours annually, including overtime. Nonchargeable time adds about 200 hours. It includes paid time off, CPE and other training, administrative work, and marketing. Computerization has reduced the number of billable hours.

.02 Realization Rates

The realization rate is the ratio of actual billed and collected dollars divided by standard dollars. For example, if you bill a client $2,000 and the WIP (work-in-progress) is $2,500, then your realization rate is 80 percent (assuming the client pays the entire bill). Firms with a low realization rate—generally considered below 85 percent—should evaluate the reasons. It may be that:

- The firm's budgeting and engagement planning are inadequate.

- A partner is performing work that can be delegated to someone who bills at a lower rate.

- The fee was calculated incorrectly and was too low.

Keep in mind that the realization rate for new clients is likely to start low and get higher over time. That's due to the learning curve—once you become familiar with the client and how it works, the rate will go up.

.03 Margin Rates

Some firms are now emulating corporations: they are measuring their gross and net margin (or profit) rates rather than their realization rates to calculate their profitability. Your gross margin rate will give you a snapshot of how you compare to other firms, for example, whether your salary or benefits cost is higher than your competition's or your hourly rates are too low. In effect, gross margin indicates how efficiently your firm is using staff and supplies.

Your net profit rate provides a picture of how efficiently your firm is run and presents opportunities to make changes. You may discover, for example, that paying for the partners' golf outings is not a productive marketing cost or that by using a client as your advertising agency, you are paying 10 percent more than you need to. By trimming some of these costs, you can increase the firm's profitability.

¶ 810 Billing Rate Formulas

Higher fees and lower write-down percentages are preferable to low fees. Various methods are used to arrive at billing rates for partners and others working on various assignments. The rates are based on some combination of the person's education, experience, and level of experience, as well as a comparison of the rates charged by comparable firms in the same geographic area. The firm's fee structure should be reexamined at least annually.

.01 Traditional Billing

Typically, firms arrive at their billing rates by dividing a staff person's annual salary by his or her annual available hours multiplied by a standard number (usually around 3.5 percent to 4 percent) to cover overhead and expenses.

While known as the traditional formula, there are problems with the calculation: nonbillable time is built in, there is no allowance for overtime, the cost of the firm's benefits package isn't considered, the standard multiplier doesn't take high overhead costs into account, and the firm's specific experience isn't factored in.

.02 Total Employment Cost Formula

It is more accurate to arrive at billing rates using the employee's total employment cost (i.e., salary plus non-wage benefits) as the basis of the formula, dividing that amount by the total number of billable hours, and multiplying that result by a standard number that reflects the firm's overhead and profit.

An employee's total employment cost (also called total compensation cost) includes:

- Annual salary.
- Estimated annual overtime expense.
- Health and life insurance premiums.
- CPE costs.
- Other training costs.
- Vacation and personal/sick time accrual.
- Holiday pay.
- Professional liability insurance expense.
- Projected costs for profit-sharing and/or retirement plan contributions.
- Memberships, dues, and subscription costs.

.03 Seasonally Adjusted Formula

Most CPA firms have fluctuations in their workloads. During busy season, it is not unusual for CPAs to work more than 200 hours per month. When the workload is lighter, the number of billable hours drops commensurately. Some firms recognize this by adjusting their rates seasonally. If your firms chooses to use this method, these are the steps that should be taken:

1. Calculate the weighted average of the hours worked each quarter by everyone at the firm who has billable hours.
2. Calculate the premium (or discount) ratio per quarter.
3. Apply that ratio to each person's billing rate.

Some firms that use this billing method aggressively market services that their clients need but don't necessarily want to pay regular billing rates for. For instance, they may offer estate planning services at a lower rate. The obvious downside to this is that the client may think the seasonal rate is the firm's new rate. If you use this technique, you must clearly communicate the terms to the client.

.04 Fixed, Flat, Quoted, or Bid Fees

Generally, this method can work very well for defined services such as tax returns: filling out a Form 1040EZ costs one amount; filling out a Form 1040 with a Schedule C costs another. The firm doesn't put any extra value on whether the return is filled out by a partner or a senior.

.05 Contingent Fees

By definition, a contingent fee is any fee arrangement that depends on the finding or result of a given service. For a while, contingent fees worked well for many firms. However, Reg. § 10.27 changed the parameters of when such fees are acceptable and precluded their use in all but a few limited scenarios:

Regulation § 10.27 Fees

(a) In general. A practitioner may not charge an unconscionable fee in connection with any matter before the Internal Revenue Service.

(b) Contingent fees —

(1) Except as provided in paragraphs (b)(2), (3), and (4) of this section, a practitioner may not charge a contingent fee for services rendered in connection with any matter before the Internal Revenue Service.

(2) A practitioner may charge a contingent fee for services rendered in connection with the Service's examination of, or challenge to —

> (i) An original tax return; or

> (ii) An amended return or claim for refund or credit where the amended return or claim for refund or credit was filed within 120 days of the taxpayer receiving a written notice of the examination of, or a written challenge to the original tax return.

(3) A practitioner may charge a contingent fee for services rendered in connection with a claim for credit or refund filed solely in connection with the determination of statutory interest or penalties assessed by the Internal Revenue Service.

(4) A practitioner may charge a contingent fee for services rendered in connection with any judicial proceeding arising under the Internal Revenue Code.

(c) Definitions. For purposes of this section —

(1) *Contingent fee* is any fee that is based, in whole or in part, on whether or not a position taken on a tax return or other filing avoids challenge by the Internal Revenue Service or is sustained either by the Internal Revenue Service or in litigation. A contingent fee includes a fee that is based on a percentage of the refund reported on a return, that is based on a percentage of the taxes saved, or that otherwise depends on the specific result attained. A contingent fee also includes any fee arrangement in which the practitioner will reimburse the client for all or a portion of the client's fee in the event that a position taken on a tax return or other filing is challenged by the Internal Revenue Service or is not sustained, whether pursuant to an indemnity agreement, a guarantee, rescission rights, or any other arrangement with a similar effect.

For specific questions about contingent fees, consult your state society, the AICPA, or an attorney.

.06 Blended Hourly Rate

Once the budget for a particular engagement is projected, the partners involved decide who will do what work on the assignment. For example, a partner who bills at $175/hour may be projected to do 15 percent, a manager billing at $100/hour may do 45 percent, and a staff accountant billed at $65/hour may be responsible for 40 percent of the work. The formula for determining the blended rate would be:

$$(175 \times 15\%) \times (\$100 \times 45\%) \times (\$65 \times 40\%) = \$97.25$$

The firm would round up the amount and calculate the bill for the engagement at $100 per hour.

Blended hourly rates can work well, particularly with established clients. That's because it is easier to estimate the amount of time that will be required by each level of staff. You pretty much know how profitable the engagement will be.

If you choose to use a blended hourly rate with a new client, you may be leaving yourself open to underestimating the true cost of the engagement, and perhaps losing the profit you expected. For example, if you find yourself doing much of the work you thought the manager would be doing, you would effectively be working for $100/hour rather than your standard billing rate of $175/hour.

.07 Discounted Fees or Volume Discount

This method can work well for certain assignments. For instance, you may be able to offer a discounted fee for tax return preparation to all the employees of your biggest clients. In addition to bringing in additional revenue, this can be a good way to strengthen your client relationships.

.08 Value Billing

There is an ongoing debate about the benefits of value billing. Value billing is an alternative to hourly billing. At its most basic level, value billing can be defined as billing that is based on the value of the services rendered to the client relative to the client's gain. Using value billing, a reasonable hourly rate is multiplied by a reasonable estimate of the number of hours it will take to complete the assignment. Other factors, including your knowledge of the client, the client's perception of your expertise, and the client's billing and collection history, enter into determining the price as well. Value based fees usually are quoted as a range, with language such as the following added to the engagement letter:

"We have issued a few change orders for clients whose work started to go over the fixed price."

Figure 8.1 ———————————————————————————————————————

Sample Value Billing Portion of Engagement Letter

Our fees generally are based on the time required at our regular rates for the services and personnel assigned. Other appropriate factors also are considered, including the difficulty of the assignment, the degree of skill required, the time limitation imposed on us by others, the experience and ability of the personnel assigned, and the value of the services to the client. Our regular fees are set out at the end of this letter. Any out-of-pocket costs pursuant to this engagement letter will be billed separately.

Assuming access to adequate records and documents, internal controls, and the availability of your personnel to provide clerical and other assistance, we estimate that our fee will be between $X and $Y for performing the following services:

  [List of services.]

We will attempt to minimize our fees without sacrificing the quality of our work. If we encounter any difficulty or unusual circumstances not contemplated when this estimate was prepared, we will discuss them with you and arrive at a new estimate before we incur any additional costs.

We are available for performing other services that your company may require, such as estate planning services, at our regular hourly rates.

Figure 8.2 ———————————————————————————————————————

Sample Language for Range of Fees

We estimate that our fees for these services will not exceed $45,500 for the audit. The fee estimate is based on anticipated cooperation from your personnel and the assumption that unexpected circumstances will not be encountered during the audit. If significant additional time is necessary, we will discuss it with you and arrive at a new fee estimate before we incur the additional costs. Our invoices for these fees will be rendered each month as work progresses and are payable on presentation.

¶ 815 Don't Underestimate the Power of the Engagement Letter

The importance of communication cannot be stressed enough. The client needs to be aware of the "rules" of the engagement. That is one reason why it is so important to send engagement letters to both new and existing clients. The letter should be specific about the services your firm will undertake and the preparatory work expected of the client. The fees and services stated in the engagement letter should reflect the careful planning you put into the budgeting process. As a general rule, the letter should include language that allows modification of the terms of the engagement if extra work is needed, for example if your firm needs to do additional preparatory work because the client failed to have the proper records ready and in order.

Remember, a signed engagement letter signals a contractual relationship and all of the legal responsibilities and ramifications that come along with that status. It is evidence of your firm's agreement with the client in the event of litigation.

Several sample letters are included in the Practice Tools section for your convenience. However, there are certain clauses that do not appear in these letters that you may wish to include. One of them is a clause stipulating that mediation is the first course of action in the event of a dispute. Given the litigiousness of our society, it might be a good idea to include the following language as a standard part of all of your engagement letters:

In the event that we become obligated to pay any judgment or similar award, agree to pay any amount in settlement, and/or incur any costs as a result of any inaccurate or incomplete information that you provide to us during the course of this engagement, you agree to indemnify us, defend us, and hold us harmless as against such obligations, agreements, and/or costs.

You agree that any dispute that may arise regarding the meaning, performance or enforcement of this engagement will, prior to resorting to litigation, be submitted to mediation, and that they will engage in the mediation process in good faith once a written request to mediate has been given by any party to the engagement. Any mediation initiated as a result of this engagement shall be administered within the county of [County and State], by [Name of Mediation Organization], according to its mediation rules, and any ensuing litigation shall be conducted within said county, according to [State] law. The results of any such mediation shall be binding only upon agreement of each party to be bound. The costs of any mediation proceeding shall be shared equally by the participating parties.

Any litigation arising out of this engagement, except actions by us to enforce payment of our professional invoices, must be filed within one year from the completion of the engagement, notwithstanding any statutory provision to the contrary. In the event of litigation brought against us, any judgment you obtain shall be limited in amount, and shall not exceed the amount of the fee charged by us, and paid by you, for the services set forth in this engagement letter.

This engagement letter is contractual in nature, and includes all of the relevant terms that will govern the engagement for which it has been prepared. The terms of this letter supersede any prior oral or written representations or commitments by or between the parties. Any material changes or additions to the terms set forth in this letter will only become effective if evidenced by a written amendment to this letter, signed by all of the parties.[1]

Another clause you should consider including is a records retention clause:

It is our policy to retain engagement documentation for a period of seven years, after which time we will commence the process of destroying the contents of our engagement files. To the extent we accumulate any of your original records during the engagement, those documents will be returned to you promptly upon completion of the engagement, and you will provide us with a receipt for the return of such records. The balance of our engagement file, other than the reviewed financial statement, which we will provide to you at the conclusion of the engagement, is our property, and we will provide copies of such documents at our discretion and if compensated for any time and costs associated with the effort.[2]

Figure 8.3

Sample Engagement Letter—Audit

Dear _____:

We are pleased to serve as independent auditors/accountants of [*Entity*]. This letter is intended to outline our understanding of the nature and scope of the [*audit*]procedures to be performed, as well as confirm the objectives and terms of our engagement.

We will audit the balance sheet of [*Entity*]as of [*date*] and the related statements of income, retained earnings, and cash flows for the [*year/years*]then ended. Our audit will be in accordance with generally accepted audit standards and will include such tests of the accounting data and procedures as we consider necessary.

The objective of our audit is to express an opinion on the fairness of these financial statements in conformity with generally accepted accounting principles.

We expect our report to read as follows:

We have audited the accompanying balance sheets of [Entity]as of [date] and the related statements of income, retained earnings, and cash flows for the year(s) then ended. These financial statements are the responsibility of the company's management. Our responsibility is to express an opinion on these financial statements based on our audit(s).

We conducted our audit(s) in conformance with generally accepted auditing standards. Those standards require that we plan and perform the audit to obtain reasonable assurance about whether the financial statements are free of material misstatement. An audit includes examining, on a test basis, evidence supporting the amounts and disclosures in the financial statements. An audit also includes assessing the accounting principles used and significant estimates made by management, as well as evaluating the overall financial statement presentation. We believe that our audits provide a reasonable basis for our opinion.

In our opinion, the financial statements referred to above present fairly, in all material respects, the financial position of [Entity] as of [date]and the results of its operations and its cash flows for the year(s) then ended in conformity with generally accepted accounting principles.

We will notify you promptly if facts and circumstances dictate that we issue a qualified report or that we disclaim an opinion.

In you intend to reproduce or publish all or part of our auditor's report in connection with the financial statements, we require you to submit master or printer's proofs for us to review.

Our engagement cannot be relied on to disclose errors, irregularities, or illegal acts, including fraud or defalcations, that might exist. However, our firm's philosophy is to provide our clients with quality services and to have a positive,

---

[1] **Source**: Naplia Professional Liability Insurance.   [2] **Source**: Naplia Professional Liability Insurance.

continuing relationship with our clients. This positive approach means that we carefully analyze your records and will inform you of any such matters that come to our attention.

Our fees are based on hourly billing rates and the amount of time spent on your engagement. Billing rates are based on the experience and technical expertise required to perform the engagement. The billing rates for this engagement will be as follows:

[List billing rates. These should be higher than your standard rates.]

Interim billings will be submitted as work progresses and expenses are incurred. Invoices are issued monthly and are payable upon receipt. Continuation of services is contingent on timely payments. A finance charge of *[percent]*% per month (*[percent]*% annually) will be assessed on all accounts over 30 days old.

If the terms are acceptable to you and the services outlined are in accordance with your understanding, please sign below and return this letter to us. A copy is enclosed for your files.

We look forward to our association with you and your staff and appreciate the opportunity to serve *[Entity]*. Please call if you have questions about any aspect of our engagement.

Sincerely,

[Partner]

[Firm]

APPROVED: _____
                                       [Entity]

By: _____   Date: _____
               [Authorized Representative]

Figure 8.4

Sample Engagement Letter—Year-End Review

Dear [Name]:

We will review the balance sheets of *[Entity]* as of *[date]* and the related statements of income, retained earnings, and cash flows for the *[year/ears]* then ended, in accordance with standards established by the American Institute of Certified Public Accountants (AICPA). We will not perform an audit of such financial statements, the objective of which is the expression of an opinion regarding the financial statements taken as a whole and, accordingly, we will not express such an opinion on them. Our report on the financial statements is presently expected to read as follows:

We have reviewed the accompanying balance sheet of [Entity] as of [date] and the related statements of income, retained earnings, and cash flows for the year(s) then ended, in accordance with standards established by the AICPA. All information included in these financial statements is the representation of the management of [Entity].

A review consists principally of inquiries of company personnel and analytical procedures applied to financial data. It is substantially narrower in scope than an audit in accordance with generally accepted auditing standards, the objective of which is the expression of an opinion regarding the financial statements taken as a whole. Accordingly, we do not express such an opinion.

Based on our review, we are not aware of any material modifications that should be made to the accompanying financial statements for them to conform with generally accepted accounting principles.

Our findings cannot be relied on to disclose errors, irregularities, or illegal acts, including fraud or defalcations, that may exist. However, we will inform you of any material errors that come to our attention and any fraud or other illegal acts that come to our attention, unless they are clearly inconsequential.

If we are unable to complete our review of your financial statements because of restrictions or limitations imposed by you or other company personnel, we will not issue a report on such statements as a result of this engagement.

Our fees for this engagement will be $*[amount]*, based on fees charged to other clients based on similar work.

Interim billings will be submitted as work progresses and expenses are incurred. Invoices are issued monthly and are payable upon receipt. Continuation of services is contingent on timely payments. A finance charge of *[percent]*% per month (*[percent]*% annually) will be assessed on all accounts over 30 days old.

If the terms are acceptable to you and the services outlined are in accordance with your understanding, please sign below and return this letter to us. A copy is enclosed for your files.

We look forward to our association with you and your staff and appreciate the opportunity to serve *[Entity]*. Please call if you have questions about any aspect of our engagement.

Sincerely,

[*Partner*]

[*Firm*]

APPROVED: _____

[*Entity*]

By: _____   Date: _____

[*Authorized Representative*]

Figure 8.5

Sample Engagement Letter—Compilation

Dear [Name]:

We will compile, from information you provide, the [*monthly/quarterly/annual*] balance sheets and the related statements of income and retained earnings of [*Entity*] for the [*year/years*]ending [*date*]. We will not audit or review such statements. Our reports on your [*monthly/quarterly/annual*] financial statements, which will omit substantially all disclosures required by generally accepted accounting principles and statement of cash flows, are expected to read as follows:

We have compiled the accompanying balance sheet as of [date] and the related statement of income and retained earnings and cash flows for the period then ended, in accordance with the standards established by the American Institute of Certified Public Accountants (AICPA).

A compilation is limited to presenting in the form of accounting statements information that is the representation of management. We have not audited or reviewed the accompanying financial statements and, accordingly, do not express an opinion or any other form of assurance on them.

Management has elected to omit substantially all of the disclosures required by generally accepted accounting principles. If the omitted disclosures were included in the financial statements, they might influence the user's conclusions about the company's financial position, results of operations, and cash flows. Accordingly, these financial statements are not designed for those who are not informed about such matters.

If for any reason we are unable to complete the compilation of your financial statements we will not issue a report on such statements as a result of this engagement.

The distribution of our report is restricted to the internal use of the management of your company, and, accordingly, will not be distributed to outside parties to obtain credit or for any other purpose without our prior express written consent.

Our engagement cannot be relied upon to disclose errors, fraud, or other illegal acts, including fraud or defalcations, that may exist. However, we will inform you of any material errors that come to our attention, unless they are clearly inconsequential. In addition, we have no responsibility to identify and communicate significant deficiencies or material weaknesses in your internal controls as part of this engagement.

Our fees for these services will be [*at our regular rates/$amount*]. Out-of-pocket expenses incurred in connection with the performance of our services will be billed separately.

Interim billings will be submitted as work progresses and expenses are incurred. Invoices are issued monthly and are payable upon receipt. Continuation of services is contingent on timely payments. A finance charge of [*percent*]% per month ([*percent*]% annually) will be assessed on all accounts over 30 days old.

If the terms are acceptable to you and the services outlined are in accordance with your understanding, please sign below and return this letter to us. A copy is enclosed for your files.

We look forward to our association with you and your staff and appreciate the opportunity to serve [*Entity*]. Please call if you have questions about any aspect of our engagement.

Sincerely,

[*Partner*]

[*Firm*]

APPROVED: _____

[*Entity*]

By: _____   Date: _____

[*Authorized Representative*]

Figure 8.6

Sample Engagement Letter—Public Company Tax Engagement

Dear [Name]:

This letter is to confirm the arrangements for our income tax engagement and to clarify the nature and limitations of our services. In accordance with the Sarbanes Oxley Act, this letter is intended to verify authorization for tax services by the Company's Audit Committee.

We will prepare your [year] federal income tax return, and income tax returns for the states of _____, (collectively, the "returns") with supporting schedules, and perform related research as considered necessary. This engagement pertains only to the [year] tax year, and our responsibilities do not include preparation of any other tax returns that may be due to any taxing authority. Our engagement will be complete upon the delivery of the completed returns to you. Thereafter, you will be solely responsible to file the returns with the appropriate taxing authorities.

If, during our work, we discover information that affects your prior-year tax returns, we will make you aware of the facts. However, we cannot be responsible for identifying all items that may affect prior-year returns. If you become aware of such information during the year, please contact us to discuss the best resolution of the issue.

Your returns may be selected for review by one or more than one taxing authority. Any proposed adjustments by the examining agent are subject to certain rights of appeal. In the event of such government tax examination, we will be available upon your written request to represent you during the examination and/or during any appeal. Any such representation will be the subject of, and governed by, a separate engagement letter.

Certain communications involving tax advice may be privileged and not subject to disclosure to the IRS. By disclosing the contents of those communications to anyone, or by turning over information about those communications to the government, you (or other employees) may be waiving this privilege. To protect this right to privileged communication, please consult with us or the corporation's attorney prior to disclosing any information about our tax advice.

Our engagement cannot be relied upon to disclose errors, fraud, or other illegal acts that may exist. However, we will inform you of any material errors that come to our attention and any fraud that comes to our attention. We will also inform you of any other illegal acts that come to our attention, unless clearly inconsequential. Our responsibility as tax preparer is limited to the period covered by our audit and does not extend to any later periods of which we are not engaged as auditors.

Our services are not designed to provide assurance on internal controls or to identify reportable conditions, that is, significant deficiencies or material weaknesses in the design or operation of internal control. Accordingly, we have no responsibility to identify and communicate significant deficiencies or material weaknesses in your internal controls as part of this engagement. However, during the procedures, if we become aware of such reportable conditions, we will communicate them to you.

In order for us to complete this engagement, and to do so efficiently, we require unrestricted access to the following documents and individuals within your company: _____. Specifically, we must receive sufficient information from which to prepare your returns within a reasonable period of time prior to the applicable filing deadline, specifically, on or before _____. Any failure to provide such cooperation, and to do so on a timely basis, will impede our services, and may require us to pursue an extension of the due date of your returns, suspend our services, or withdraw from the engagement.

The law provides various penalties and interest that may be imposed when taxpayers understate their tax liability. You acknowledge that any such understated tax, and any imposed interest and penalties, are your responsibility, and that we have no responsibility in that regard. If you would like information on the amount or circumstances of these penalties, please contact me.

We may encounter instances where the tax law is unclear, or where there may be conflicts between the taxing authorities' interpretations of the law and other supportable positions. In those instances, we will outline for you each of the reasonable alternative courses of action, including the risks and consequences of each such alternative. In the end, we will adopt, on your behalf, the alternative which you select after having considered the information provided by us.

Our fee includes only incidental research. Such research will often provide us with only a "reasonable basis" for the position taken on the return. In that event, it may be necessary, in order to avoid possible penalties, to also include with the return a disclosure statement on IRS Form 8275. We will inform you of any such situations before we finalize the return.

Our fees for this engagement are not contingent on the results of our services. Rather, our fees for this engagement, including preparation of your returns and any representation of your interests during an examination by a taxing authority and/or any subsequent appeal, will be based on our standard hourly rates, as set forth on the attached rate sheet. In addition, you agree to reimburse us for any of our out-of-pocket costs incurred in connection with the performance of our services.

In the event that we encounter unusual circumstances that would require us to expand the scope of the engagement, and/or if we anticipate our fees exceeding the aforementioned range, we will adjust our estimate, and obtain your prior approval before continuing with the engagement.

If the terms are acceptable to you and the services outlined are in accordance with your understanding, please sign below and return this letter to us. A copy is enclosed for your files.

We look forward to our association with you and your staff and appreciate the opportunity to serve [*Entity*]. Please call if you have questions about any aspect of our engagement.

Sincerely,

[*Partner*]

[*Firm*]

APPROVED: _____
                                                     [*Entity*]

By: _____   Date: _____
             [*Authorized Representative*]

Figure 8.7 ————————————————————————————

Sample Engagement Letter—Litigation Support Engagement

Dear [Name]:

You have asked me to review certain documents relating to a lawsuit involving your client. Should the information I derive from such a review prove useful to your client's position, you have also asked that I provide expert testimony on your client's behalf. Any written reports or documents that I might prepare are to be used only for the purpose of this litigation and may not be published or used for any other purpose without my written consent.

My firm will bill you at my standard hourly rate of $[*amount*] for all time spent. Further, under my direct supervision and control, other members of my firm may work on this engagement, and we will bill you for their time spent at their standard hourly rates, which range from $[*amount*]to $[*amount*].

We will require a retainer of $[*amount*] before we begin this engagement. The retainer will be applied against our final invoice, and any unused portion will be returned to you upon our collection of all outstanding fees and costs related to this engagement. In addition, you agree to reimburse us for any of our out-of-pocket costs incurred in connection with the performance of our services.

In the event fees and costs are not paid by [*date*], we reserve the right to terminate our services to you and your client.

We look forward in assisting you with this matter and hope our services will be beneficial. If you approve of the engagement terms described above, please sign below and return this letter to me. A copy is enclosed for your files.

Sincerely,

[*Partner*]

[*Firm*]

APPROVED: _____
                                                     [*Entity*]

By: _____   Date: _____
             [*Authorized Representative*]

Figure 8.8 ————————————————————————————

Sample Engagement Change Order for Additional Accounting and Consulting Services

From time to time during the course of our relationship, additional accounting and consulting services may be requested or required. We are committed to insuring that our clients receive the highest level of service and, therefore, attempt to identify and solve problems before they compound. The additional services to be rendered will be discussed and billed separately through this change order agreement. Once agreed to by both parties and executed, this change order becomes an addendum to and extension of the scope of services, terms, and fees agreed to in the original letter of engagement dated _____.

¶815

Change Order Number: _____

Date of Change Order: _____

Previous Engagement Fee: _____

Fee for Change Order No. 1:   _____

Total To Date Engagement Fee: _____

Description of Additional Services and Expanded Scope of Engagement:

 Additional Service Area 1 -

 Additional Service Area 2 -

 Additional Service Area 3 -

The services described above are in accordance with our requirements and acceptable to us.

_____   _____

[Firm]

_____   _____

[Date]   [Date]

Figure 8.9 ————————————————————————————————

Sample Client Termination Letter

Dear [Name]:

I am writing to give you formal notice that as of the date of this letter, the Firm will cease to render any professional services to your company. I regret that disengagement has become necessary, but our decision is based upon ongoing conflicts within the company's management, including our inability to obtain cooperation from the company's management team on critical engagement issues.

We are not aware of any impending tax or financial reporting deadlines that the company must meet. However, we urge you to promptly retain successor tax professionals in order to ensure that you don't miss any future deadlines.

I wish to call your attention to the company's outstanding account with this Firm for past services rendered in the amount of $2,500.00, which is currently past due. Termination of future services does not discharge your obligation to make full payment of that past due balance. A copy of the outstanding invoice is enclosed.

We will forward any original documents in our possession to you promptly under separate cover. If you wish us to provide a successor accounting or tax professional with information concerning your company, please provide me with a letter informing me of the precise information you wish us to produce. Upon receipt of your written request, we will, at a minimum, follow the standards of our profession in cooperating with successor professionals.

Please contact me with any questions you may have.

Sincerely,

[Engagement Partner]

Chapter 9
Nobody Likes Billing and Collections, But It Pays the Bills

¶ 901 A Necessity of Business

Billing and collections are uncomfortable issues for many accountants. The discomfort probably stems from the days firms considered themselves practices rather than businesses and treated their clients accordingly. But billing and collections are high priority issues. Accounting firms can't be profitable if they don't follow the advice they give to clients.

Good billing and collection practices can increase your firm's revenue by 10 percent or more. Who wouldn't be happy with that, especially during a time of economic turmoil?

¶ 905 Create a Written Billing and Collections Policy

Not surprisingly, creating a written policy is essential because it provides a guideline for what is expected. The policy should hold billing partners accountable, and there should be consequences for not billing in a timely manner and for failing to follow up with delinquent clients. Your billing and collections policy should include the following:

- Define "billable time" and "chargeable time" (don't automatically assume everyone is on the same page, particularly new hires)
- Billing rates:
  — What profitability ratio will be used?
  — What billing rate (or combination of rates) will be used?
  — Who will authorize their use?
- How will support services be billed?
- Who oversees write-downs?
  — When and why?
  — Who authorizes write-downs that exceed the limits?
- Will retainers be required? When?
- Will you have a staggered billing policy?
  — For example, half of estimated fee for tax preparation when the return is brought in with the balance due upon delivery of the completed return.
  — For example, building in performance incentives for timeliness, preparedness, etc.
- Will there be WIP limits?
- Is a system in place to lock out clients who are in arrears and prevent more work being done on the account?
- When will an invoice be flagged as past due?
- Will interest be charged on past-due balances?
- Who will authorize exceptions?
- How often will statements be sent?
- How many statements will be sent before collection efforts commence?
- When will the firm suspend services to delinquent clients, and who authorizes exceptions?
- Under what circumstances will partial payments be accepted and who authorizes them?
- How will information on each partner's billing and collections activities be reported and disseminated to others in the firm?
  — Monthly partner meetings:
    - One-on-one?
    - At a partner meeting?

— On the firm's intranet?

- What are the consequences to a partner who does not bill timely or follow-up with delinquent clients according to the firm's written procedures?
  - How will the consequences be enforced?
- Who will do the collections:
  - Partner?
  - Administrative staff?
  - Outside collections agency?
- What is the collection process:
  - Number of letters before proceeding to phone call?
  - Number of phone calls?
- Methods of payment
  - Will credit cards be accepted?
  - Will online payments be accepted?
- Documentation procedures and processes.
- How will billing disputes be handled?
- Will legal action be taken, and, if so, when?

.01 Will Litigation Be an Option?

One of the core decisions you need to make when formulating your billing and collections policy is whether you are going to litigate. Some firms have a blanket policy that prevents suing the client. Firms that take this view would rather write-off an occasional bad debt than risk damage to their reputation.

Another consideration is the litigiousness of our society. It is far from unheard of for a client who is being sued for nonpayment of fees to turn around and counter-sue for malpractice. Unfounded expensive cross-complaints has made at least one malpractice insurer rewrite its errors and omissions (E & O) policy. Check with your carrier to be sure it will defend you if the client files a cross-complaint for malpractice. Again, the firm's level of risk and exposure should be the guiding factor in this decision.

.02 Using Collection Agencies and Attorneys

There are certain guidelines that should be followed if your firm chooses to outsource the collection function:

- Make sure the agency specializes in commercial accounts and is experienced in handling collection matters of the type you seek to resolve.
- Make sure the agency is bonded and insured in the state in which you conduct business and that its insurance has never been cancelled. (Cancellation of insurance can be a red flag for poor service or risky collection methods.)
- Review the fee schedule. Although collection agencies generally work on a contingent fee basis, which may obligate your firm to pay 30-50 percent of the fee collected on individual accounts and 15-25 percent of business accounts, it is possible to retain collection agencies on an hourly basis, which can cost significantly less.
- Check references.
- Ask to see samples of correspondence and telephone scripts that will be used on your firm's accounts.
- Check for membership in the Commercial Law League of America (CLLA) and the American Collectors Association (ACA). Such organizations require their members to adhere to certain standards.
- Do a due diligence check at the Better Business Bureau to see whether any complaints have been filed against the agency.
- Request a "hold harmless" agreement to protect your firm from liability for claims by clients against the agency or the attorney for harassment.
- Retain the right to withdraw an account at any time, and reserve the right to veto an agency decision to bring suit.
- Understand the process and policies the collectors will use, such as the following:
  - How and how often debtors will be contacted.
  - How often the firm will receive progress reports.
  - How and when collected amounts will be remitted to the firm.
- Before signing the collection agency contract, carefully review it to ensure that it spells out the obligations of both parties and that you both agree on all provisions.

¶ 910 The Billing Process: Software Provides Many Options

By allowing firms to analyze each person's available time and billable time, time and billing software has revolutionized the billing process at CPA firms. However, the available packages vary by both price and features. When evaluating the options, it is a good idea to consider:

- Whether the software is compatible with your current hardware.
- The vendor's reputation for supporting the product.
- Ease of use.
- Ability to customize reports.
- Whether it is possible to add additional features in the future.

It allows firms to measure each individual's productivity as well as how their nonbillable time is spent. Recorded time can be evaluated according to client, type of service, and billing partner. Time and billing software also provides better control over WIP and accounts receivable. Most software packages can be customized for different purposes, so you can have anything from a non-customized report to a highly-customized report. The software can be programmed to do things like flag accounts that exceed any credit limits imposed on the client and provide detailed WIP reports that include:

- Every client's demographic information.
- A list of everyone assigned to the account, their hourly billing rates, and the type of work they performed.
- Rate codes.
- Fee formats.
- Cost formats.
- Billing adjustments.

A summary recap at the end of the report would reflect current fees, current costs, and total work-in-process. The statement itself can be formatted to accommodate the client's preference, from a single dollar amount to a detailed report of the work performed.

The software can also be used to generate internal reports related to productivity. This information can be used for firm budgeting purposes (such as estimating future cash flows or staffing needs) or for setting individual productivity goals.

¶ 915 Business Dashboards and Flash Reports: An Early Warning System

Business dashboards are intended to do for your business what your car's dashboard does for your car: provide an at-a-glance picture of the firm's status. Some elements that could be included are accounts receivable, aging reports and WIP. Flash reports are the drivers of the dashboard. Each flash report monitors a different key business area, such as new business or realization rate. In top firms, these reports open when firm leaders turn on their computers. They allow leaders to monitor how the firm is doing in real time. The information usually is presented in visual format, such as spreadsheets, charts, and graphs, rather than words, so it is easy to track important changes.

Business dashboard software is available, but, depending on your firm's needs, it may be enough to create Excel spreadsheets for this purpose. The dashboard can be set up to update on a daily, weekly, or monthly basis, depending on your firm's requirements.

The important thing is that dashboards are updated regularly so they can immediately alert you about things that need attention. For instance, if they show a higher sales volume in a particular service area, you may need to think about hiring another staff person or taking someone off another engagement to ease the workflow. Conversely, if you have lost a piece of business from a client, you can move quickly to meet with that client to find out what the problem is.

Business dashboards aren't standard yet. Still, where they are available and properly used, they can be very effective. Because they allow needed information to flow through to the firm's decision makers to be analyzed and acted upon quickly, they enhance the firm's nimbleness.

¶ 920 Collections Best Practices—Following the Rules

Unfortunately, we've all found ourselves in the position of having to chase a client for payment. It is an unpleasant place to be, for both parties, but sometimes it needs to be done.

The best guidance in this area stems from the same source as many other aspects of our business: client relationship. Consequently, there is no hard and fast rule for determining when payment should be pursued—it's about the relationship. If your client normally pays within two weeks of receiving an invoice and three weeks have gone by, you may want to call and see what's going on. Particularly if you want to keep the client, it is important to find out what is causing the delay. It may be something you can help the client work out, such as working with slow-paying clients or problems with a line of credit. You need to come up with a strategy that works for both of you and allows you to maintain a good relationship, even if that means deferring payment for a set period of time or offering a one-time discount on the fee.

Your response might be different if you are dealing with a marginal client or one you were thinking about firing anyway. The goal in all collection negotiations is to minimize or eliminate the firm's risk exposure.

.01 Holding Partners Accountable

Partner accountability is the number one deterrent for delinquency. The partner's role has changed through the years as his or her responsibilities have broadened from sheer technical expertise and knowledge to include advising clients on how to help their businesses succeed. Not only should partners be on top of what is going on with their clients—a task made much easier by monitoring billing and collection software—but they should be in a position to know which of their clients is at serious financial risk. The ebbs and flows of the economy are an indicator of which clients should be monitored most closely; for example, clients in the real estate and construction sectors are most vulnerable during a housing downturn. Partners with clients in those areas should initiate contact with their clients and assess the level of their exposure to a down market. This may manifest in anything from a smaller volume of work for your firm to defaulting on your firm's bills.

Some firms hold partners financially responsible for reducing accounts receivable balances by charging the partners' capital accounts if their receivables exceed set maximums. In many firms, partners are allowed average receivables balances of 75 days of annual billings. Here's how it works: divide 365 by 75 to arrive at a turnover rate of about 4.9 percent. Accordingly, a partner who has about $490,000 in annual billings would have an annual receivables balance of $100,000. If that partner's receivables balance rose to $150,000, he or she would be charged interest of 10 percent on the excess. In this case, the penalty would be $5,000 (10 percent of $50,000).

Another effective method is requiring partners to assume personal liability for fees incurred while continuing to service clients who fail to pay. For example, there may be a 90-day payback requirement on all clients. Beyond that point, the partner's draw is charged for any additional service fees incurred until the debt has been satisfied. The partner's draw is replenished after the full amount is paid.

Partners with a high realization rate should be rewarded. Consider offering an annual bonus to partners who maintain an average receivables balance below the firm's standard (usually 45 days).

.02 Legalities

Once the client acknowledges the debt, ask for partial payment as a sign of good faith. Such payment provides formal acknowledgment of the debt in the event litigation becomes necessary.

State and federal law governs certain aspects of the collections process. The Federal Trade Commission Act and the Fair Debt Collection Act as well as many state laws prohibit the following activities:

- Pretending to be someone else to collect a debt.
- Using a fake identity on a letterhead or when making phone contact with the debtor.
- Implying you are an attorney, represent a collection agency or that you are employed by a governmental agency if you are not.
- Sending out collection notices that appear to represent official court documents.
- Threatening to turn the debt over to "your legal department" if your firm doesn't have one.
- Making threats to turn the debt over to a collection agency or attorney or to file a suit against the client without actually intending to do it.
- Imposing excessive finance charges beyond what the firm usually charges other late payers.

It is also illegal to harass a debtor, ruin their reputation, or invade their privacy. You may check the following records, which can be found at the county courthouse, to help confirm or refute information the client has given you concerning their status:

- Grantor/Grantee Index, which reveals any judgments or liens against the client.
- Plaintiff's Index, which reveals any suits filed against other businesses.
- Defendant's Index, which discloses any suits filed against the client.
- Municipal Court Index, which reports whether the client has ever been evicted or passed any bad checks.
- Criminal Index, which tells whether criminal charges have ever been filed against the client.

.03 Letters You Can Use

To ensure that you are compliant with all of the laws and regulations in this area, it is a best practice to discuss them with your attorney. In addition, anyone at your firm must be trained to comply with your firm's billing and collections practices and procedures.

All communication regarding collections, whether written or verbal, should be addressed to the person who has the authority to pay.

Figure 9.1 ————————————————————————————

Response to Complaint Regarding Fees

Dear [*Name*]:

This letter is in response to your telephone conversation with [*Name*]concerning your bill. Although both the procedures used and the time charged were confirmed by a partner prior to billing, we reviewed them against your request to determine if an error was made. Our review indicates that the work we performed was necessary, completed efficiently, and authorized by [*Name*] in your office.

We regret that you disagree with this bill. However, we compared our procedures with those we apply to engagements for other businesses like yours. The comparison shows that our work on your account required virtually the minimum amount of time for such an engagement. That was due in large part to your promptness and thoroughness in supplying the information we needed.

We value our association with you and strive to treat all of our clients with fairness. Our fees are based on the time involved to complete the work, and our billing rates are comparable to those of other accounting firms in the area with the expertise and resources necessary to service your needs.

If you wish to discuss the matter in greater detail, please call me to arrange a meeting.

Sincerely,

[*Partner*]

[*Firm*]

Figure 9.2 ————————————————————————————

Reminder Letter

Dear [*Name*]:

After reviewing your account, I noticed that there is a $[*amount*] balance due for services performed for you by our firm in [*month, year*].

Perhaps you have misplaced or overlooked our invoice. It is also possible that we neglected to inform you that our invoices are due upon presentation. I have enclosed a copy of the invoice(s) that remains outstanding as of this date.

If there is any problem in regard to the quality of our services, we want to know how we have not measured up to your expectations. If it is simply a matter of overlooking the invoice, we would appreciate payment as soon as possible.

Thank you for your consideration.

Sincerely,

[*Partner*]

[*Firm*]

Figure 9.3 ————————————————————————————

Request for Payment Plan

Balance due: $[*amount*]

Dear [*Name*]:

I must ask you to review the amount of your indebtedness to us. You are a valued client, but unfortunately we cannot continue to serve you if your invoices remain unpaid.

On several occasions we have called to remind you of these obligations, and each time you replied that the amount would be paid in full. However, we have not received any payment to date. Please call me immediately to discuss payment arrangements.

I hope we can resolve this quickly and with as little inconvenience to you as possible. Please contact me as soon as possible or send a check by [*date*].

Sincerely,

[*Partner*]

[*Firm*]

Figure 9.4

Account 30 Days Past Due

Dear [*Name*]:

Since it has not been returned to my office, I must assume that you received my letter of [date] concerning an unpaid balance on your account of $[amount]. Your lack of response would indicate either indifference to, or disagreement with, the amount due. In either event, it would be mutually beneficial to discuss this matter.

Please call me before [date] so that we can resolve this issue. Thank you for your prompt response.

Sincerely,

[*Partner*]

[*Firm*]

Figure 9.5

Reminder of Broken Commitment

Balance due: $[*amount*]

Dear [*Name*]:

Your unpaid invoice with us is now seriously past due. [Name], of your office, promised to mail a check to us on [date], but we have received no payment as of today. Although we reminded you of your prior commitment, the balance remains unpaid.

I'm sure you would like to resolve this matter and any disruption in services provided to you. Please mail your check today.

Sincerely,

[*Partner*]

[*Firm*]

Figure 9.6

Notification of Services in Jeopardy

Balance due: $[*amount*]

Dear [*Name*]:

We have received no payment on the above amount, which is long past due.

According to our collections policy which you read and acknowledged on [*date*], we reserve the right to discontinue services on an account that becomes two months delinquent. We would like to continue our working relationship with you, but we cannot expend time and effort without being paid. Therefore, we must insist on immediate payment.

Please send your check today so that services to you will continue uninterrupted.

Sincerely,

[*Partner*]

[*Firm*]

Figure 9.7

Final Notice/Collection Agency

Dear [*Name*]:

On [*date*], [*Name*] promised payment of $[*amount*] per week on the account. Instead, we received only $[*amount*] per month for [*number*]months [*list months*]. We were willing to receive $[*amount*] each month. However, we have not received a payment since [*date*].

On the [*date*] billing statement, we wrote that this account would be turned over to an agency for collection unless we received payment by [*date*]. We wanted to give you every opportunity to settle this account before pursuing this option. However, since you will neither return our phone calls nor make mutually agreed upon payments, we can only assume that you have no intention of honoring our agreement. Therefore, you leave us no choice but to follow our firm's collection policy.

This letter is an official notice that unless we receive full payment of $[amount] by [*date*], your account will be referenced to [*Collection agency*] for collection on that date. Our agreement with [*Collection agency*] states that we agree to carry to court any account referred to it for collection if the agency deems it necessary.

According to the engagement letter you signed on [*date*], you remain responsible for any attorney fees or court costs required to collect past due fees. Please consider taking a step toward preserving your credit rating now and avoiding possible additional charges by paying this account today.

Sincerely,

[*Partner*]

[*Firm*]

Figure 9.8

Effective Telephone Collection Techniques

Making collection calls is never an experience one looks forward to. By following the suggestions listed here, you may be able to avoid some of the unpleasantness and frustration that can occur.

- Be polite and professional. Remain calm and factual, but firm.

- Be a good listener. Give the client a chance to explain why payment is late. A friendly, understanding attitude can be very effective.

- Try to relate to the client's situation with statements like these:

    — "We need your help to resolve this problem."

    — "We'd like to work with you to handle this situation."

    — "Let's find a way to work this out together."

- Have any information you might need—engagement letters, updated billing files, and collection records—handy so you can refer to them as needed.

- Before discussing the bill, remind the client about all the work you've done and the positive results you generated. Try getting the client to agree with you on an issue like the scope of services performed. Then, you can move on to more complicated issues like the time and level of expertise required.

- Never apologize. Your firm performed a service, and you should be paid. Maintain control of collection discussions by clearly stating the client's obligation to pay.

- Never imply that your firm needs the money. This type of appeal is seldom effective and can create a negative impression of your firm.

- Ask for a promissory note. The note many bc cither a single note or a series of notes. By signing the note, the client is agreeing to the amount owed and cannot contest the charge at a later date.

- You may tell the client that it is the firm's policy to suspend services if the account remains unpaid after a certain date. If you do this, you must be prepared to lose the client and write off the outstanding amount.

- Threats of legal action should only be made if the firm intends to follow through. Otherwise, your firm could be sued successfully for harassment.

Chapter 10
The New Competition

¶ 1001 How Do You Define "Competitor"?

Only a decade or two ago, firms could define their competition pretty easily. Back then, your competitor looked pretty much like you, practiced in your local market, and did a lot of the same type of work. Some competitors were bigger. Others were smaller. They may have been in practice longer than you, or not as long. But, for the most part, it was pretty easy to understand who your competitors were.

The nature of competition has morphed radically since then, and that evolution adds considerably to the chaos of managing a professional services firm in the 21st century. Pivotal factors in the mutating face of competition include technology, SOX, and the emergence of a global economy.

Technology was the earliest and most profound instigator of these changes; SOX triggered more catalysts for the changes in firm management and the intrinsic nature of inter-firm competition than any other factor; and the global economy is the 800-pound elephant in the room because it changed the way business is conducted.

¶ 1005 Technology as a Competitor

Technology is at the heart of "the new competition." It's wrought such earth-shaking change so quickly that we still haven't fully grasped its impact or maximized its potential. And the changes just keep coming.

In 1968, the average professional services firm spent zero percent of its gross revenue on technology. Today, firms typically spend seven to eight percent of gross revenue on technology, and that number is climbing. In the 1970s, technology amounted to an adding machine, carbon paper, and a typewriter. The copy machine and Lanier word processor were considered high-tech. Basic tools of the trade were erasers, legal pads, and columned paper. In the 1980s, many of us were tied to mainframes and were couriering information to them. Tax software? No such thing. It's an under-acknowledged fact that the No. 1 source of changing competition for professional services firms was the development of smart software programs.

Some of the most basic and proprietary functions performed by the accounting profession—general ledger, payroll, depreciation spreadsheets, financial statements, and tax returns—which generated billions of dollars in revenue each year were replaced in the 1990s with smart software programs that could do better work and deliver it faster for a fraction of the cost. The actual books, ledgers, and journals used to practice the profession for almost a century gave way to virtual documents and changed forever the skills required to perform the jobs and tasks associated with them.

TurboTax is a case in point. When TurboTax was first introduced, it was targeted to CPAs. Accountants could buy the program to complete 1040s—individual tax returns—for their clients. It became the tax return software of choice, and the CPAs who used it perfected the service, strategies, procedures, and methodologies associated with it. Then, TurboTax executives analyzed the numbers game. They realized that there are 40,000 accounting firms in the United States, and that many of them would buy TurboTax. But, they reckoned, there are millions of hardworking Americans who file 1040s. Wouldn't the company make more money by lowering the software's price and aiming for higher volume by targeting laypeople who want to do their own tax returns rather than paying a CPA to prepare them? Yes, they concluded. TurboTax became a product for the mass market and a huge competitor for accounting firms. QuickBooks, a bookkeeping software program, followed a similar path. As a result, competition offerings changed.

In hindsight, the accounting profession reacted gracefully to these changes. As technology began to dominate the lower-end work traditionally performed by CPAs, accountants conceded the territory and upped the value of their own service offerings. Software could perform basic tax returns and general ledger functions on a mass scale more quickly and efficiently than humans could, so accounting firms surrendered the low end of their services and replaced it with more profitable offerings. As it turns out, the more profitable work was also more valuable in the hearts and minds of clients. The new competition from technology forced CPAs to reshape their skills to provide services that offered the client higher value. Clients began looking at CPAs for advice and consulting rather than solely for compliance functions. Accountants, as a group, made a good trade. They went with quality over quantity. In the end, computer software did for accounting firms what the cotton gin did for cotton farmers—it pulled the lower-value nugget out of the entire pod with startling efficiency, leaving the high-value fruit intact, and in the process, revolutionized the entire profession.

Some fought technology, but in general, firms that ignored technology's impact on the profitability of low-end work went out of business. As they fought for their right to do 1040s, they began competing with software and not with other accounting firms. For the first 75 or 80 years of the profession, accounting firms' major competitors were other accounting firms. Many practitioners didn't realize that suddenly they were also competing with technology. And even those who did often made expensive mistakes by not passing costs of their technological investments on to clients. They weren't comfortable raising prices for a job that once took them 10 hours when technology could now do it in one hour. They didn't account for the costs of the new efficiencies and didn't pass those costs on to the clients who reaped the resulting benefits. But they learned, and that oversight was a bump in the road that was generally corrected before the consequences of that mistake became devastating. Technology emerged to the forefront and has been indispensable ever since.

Technology is one of the new competitors, but it's also a relatively new standard of practice. It has evolved into a neutralizer. Laptops, cell phones, PDAs, electronic document management, WiFi, smart phones, and a host of other technologies have become so prevalent that they're no longer differentiators in helping a firm attract either new clients or new talent. They're standards that firms must pay for and manage simply to remain competitive. While they give little or no discernable competitive advantage—other than the short-term, temporary benefit experienced by early adopters—they're unavoidable costs required to prevent a firm from falling below baseline.

Firms can, in general, make better use of their technology, however. Some experts estimate that most CPA firms use 20 percent or less of the available capacity of their software programs. Understanding and using the remaining 80 percent can increase efficiency and boost profits.

Technology changed professional services appreciably and will continue to. Outsourcing is the next great frontier for technology at professional services firms. Key issues will be how information is communicated and protected during its transfer as places like India increasingly provide cheaper and equally qualified labor. In many cases, outsourcing allows a firm to deliver better turnaround and lowers the cost of doing it. Over time, we'll see an increasing number of firms using technology in association with outsourcing and facing related security issues. But eventually, every firm will need outsourcing capabilities as a competitive neutralizer as the advantages presented by outsourcing are leveled, just as every firm needs Web access, e-mail, and laptops.

There's a predictable chain of events as new technologies emerge. At first, everybody starts by asking if they have to have it. Can they stay competitive if they don't? Then, it becomes another cost of doing business, simply because *not* having it creates a competitive disadvantage. The result is improved efficiency—along with increased chaos for management.

Figure 10.1 ————————————————————————————

AICPA's 10 Top Technology Initiatives for CPA's—2009

1. *Information security management.* Proper Information Management protects the integrity, confidentiality and availability of information in the custody of an organization and reduces the risk of information being compromised. It is an integrated, systematic approach that coordinates people, polocies, standards, processes, and controls used to safeguard critical systems and information from internal and external security threats.

2. *Privacy management.* The right to privacy is a commonly assumed fact, and failure to protect sensitive information can cause serious damage to an organization's reputation and subject it to legal penalties. Privacy Management involves the strategies and safeguards used to protect the privacy of an organization's records that include resources, restricted assets, personnel, client and customer personally identifiable information. Safeguards are enforced so that this information cannot be released to or accessed by unauthorized subjects. The initiative includes complying with local, national and international laws.

3. *Secure Data File Storage, Transmission and Exchange (Formerly known as Securing and Controlling Information Distribution).* Stored data can be altered to commit fraud, intercepted by an unscrupulous person en route and altered, and laptops storing vast amounts of confidential information can be lost or stolen. Strategies that can mitigate these risks include encrypted storage disks and laptop hard drives, message digests used to identify altered data, digital certificates, secure channels using Secure Sockets Layering (SSL) or Transport Layer Security (TLS) for purchase transactions, and Virtual Private Networks (VPNs) which allow for more permanent secure data channels.

4. *Business Process Improvement, Work Flow and Process Exception Alerts.* Business Process Improvement initiatives assist with controlling and documenting processes across the organization, most commonly in accounting or content management (paperless) applications. Transaction processing and audit trails are being replaced with automated processes, work flow, exception alerts, and electronic authorizations.

5. *Mobile and Remote Computing.* Enabling people to work from anywhere and at any time is the goal of Mobile and Remote Computing. Technologies used in Mobile and remote computing include Terminal Services, Citrix, Virtual Desktop Interface, Cellular broadband and WiMAX, and remote control applications. A paperless office environment is essential to support mobile users who want to access and collaborate on digital documents from remote locations.

6. *Training and Competency* Knowledgeable and competent employees who address issues with confidence are a key differentiator among competitors. As technology develops and is in a constant state of change, training methods must also change. On-site training has given way to computer-based training (CBT), pod casts, web casts, distance learning, etc.

7. *Identity and access management.* Identity and Access Management involves the implementation of physical, technical, and administrative controls that limit access to company resources to authorized persons. A challenge exists with achieving easy access by authorized users while making resources inaccessible to unauthorized users.

8. *Improved Application and Data Integration.* Effective decision support and business intelligence systems rely on information systems which "talk to each other" seamlessly and where information is readily available in a form that expedites business decision making. Disparate systems continue to exist within organizations and duplicate databases reside within these multiple systems.

9. *Document, Forms, Content and Knowledge Management.* Documents, Forms, Content and Knowledge Management (the "paperless" office) is the process of electronically capturing, indexing, storing, protecting, searching, retrieving, managing, and controlling information using scanning, forms recognition, optical character recognition (OCR), centralized data repositories, and the management brings structure and control to information, allowing organizations to harness the intellectual capital contained in the underlying data.

10. *Electronic Data Retention Strategy.* Electronic Data Retention Strategy involves technologies that enable appropriate archiving and retrieval of key information over a given (statutory) period of time. Strategies include policies and processes to ensure destruction of information from storage and archival media in a timely and consistent manner, as well as the impact of eDiscovery rules and regulations regarding retained data.

Source: AICPA 2009

¶ 1010 XBRL: The Universal Language of Financial Reporting

Around the world, XBRL is fast becoming the standard for creating financial reports from the vast data pools of business information available today. The evolution of XBRL began when, in 1999, the AICPA gathered a group of CPAs with a background in accounting transactions, accounting reporting, and technology and asked them to consider how financial reporting could be enhanced through the expanded use of technology. This group formed the committee that created the language and definitions that would first be named XFRML (eXtensible Financial Reporting Management Language) and then broadened to be XBRL (eXtensible Business Reporting Language).

To improve understanding of XBRL, there is a whole new dictionary of terms that need to be understood. The glossary of term is worth reviewing (see Figure 10.2).

Fundamentally, XBRL derives its syntax format from programming languages XML and HTML. These are query languages that are used to attach tags to each individual data element. A simple example can be observed from financial statement reports like a balance sheet. This statement could contain a few or a lot of data elements—assets like cash, inventory, and receivables; liabilities like accounts payable and loans payable; retained earnings like owner's equity; and retained earnings. Each XBRL "element" is a factual account. While one accounting system may call the money held in a bank account "Cash in Bank," another system may call it "Checking and Savings Accounts" or "Cash and Equivalents." The bottom line is that each of these descriptions identifies cash available within the company.

Converting the company's balance sheet data to an XBRL format with XBRL tags creates an "instance document." Taking instance documents from two or more companies can support direct comparisons of accounts such as "Cash" without concern for the original number coding or definitions of each account.

The SEC and other financial regulators and agencies, such as the Federal Deposit Insurance Corp. (FDIC) and the European Central Bank Supervisors have enacted XBRL initiatives. In addition, the IFRS, which is likely to converge with U.S. GAAP in the near future and has already been adopted by over 100 countries for listed companies, uses XBRL.

According to Denver-based Richard Oppenheim, one of the leaders in the area:

"There are significant new value based opportunities for CPAs in public practice surrounding the growth of digital data analysis. Services include, but are not limited to, audit support tools, financial planning and analyses, business operations consulting and so on. Business executives need the advice and counsel of their CPA to help sort through the expanded volumes generated in today's data oriented environment.

As a business expands, there is the need to determine how to respond to regulators in multiple jurisdictions. This includes city, county, state, and federal regulators of all sizes. In addition, any consideration for expanding to an international marketplace will include the concerns for different accounting standards and reporting rules. Doing business internationally does have a cost to understand how to deliver information in a report form that is acceptable within each country.

To further complicate the problem, data elements are described with multiple definitions, even in the accounting world. For example, the term "inventory" can have many subsets that further define the company's inventory data. It can be finished goods, work in process, raw materials or some other component. The method of costing could be FIFO, LIFO, MARKET, or some other designation. Moreover, any single element of information can be redefined and modified by one or more jurisdictional regulations.

To overcome mass confusion issues, XBRL uses a unique word vocabulary for describing exactly individual elements of data. It is this ability to provide a universal glossary that enables the various accounting and recordkeeping systems to be compared and contrasted for any business analysis."

Most accounting software programs have already integrated XBRL coding and syntax. In addition, many software applications are designed to be used specifically to convert data into XBRL and provide resources for XBRL formatted reports, including:

CreativeSolutions	www.creativesolutions.com
Microsoft FRx	www.frxsoftware.com
Rivet Software	www.rivetsoftware.com
SnappyReports	www.snappyreports.com
UBMatrix	www.ubmatrix.com

Figure 10.2 ——

XBRL - A Glossary of Terms

The terminology used in XBRL often overlaps with other terms.

XBRL Terms Definitions

Item	Definition
·**context**	The information that allows a fact or set of facts to be understood in relation to other information. Context needs to be identified inside an ·instance document and typically includes time, organizational entity, reporting segment, and scenario—whether the fact is budget, actual, interim, or final.
·**DTS**	The discoverable ·taxonomy set consists of files that are related, typically as interlocked modules. Both taxonomies and instance documents can refer or import other taxonomies so as to re-use concepts that have been defined elsewhere. A DTS is a mechanism in ·XBRL that facilitates this re-use.
·**DWG**	The ·XII Domain Working Group. This is a (members only) standing committee that is charged with (1) facilitating the creation and adoption of taxonomy best practice and (2) gathering business requirements for ·XII. It does this through a range of guidance materials as well as a number of communication and outreach initiatives. Not to be confused with jurisdictional domain committees, which are often (but not always) set up in a ·jurisdiction to manage the creation of a local GAAP ·taxonomy.
·**element**	The base definition in a ·taxonomy of a single category of facts.
·**extension**	A ·taxonomy that is developed by an organization to add corporate-unique concepts or to modify default taxonomy relationship structures. An extension is often used merely to add a concept to those available in a GAAP set of disclosures to take account of the particular circumstances of an organization. This is generally to allow market differentiation of a particular market participant. However, extensions are also used to modify a base ·taxonomy for the purposes of a particular reporting organization. For instance, a company may choose to use a different label for a standard GAAP ·taxonomy, or to alter the way that a sub-total is calculated, to take account of a company-specific circumstance. Most companies involved in reporting to securities regulators will choose to use extensions.
·**FRIS**	Financial Reporting Instance Standards are a set of guidelines for the preparation of high quality, highly interoperable ·XBRL ·instance documents. The majority of FRIS guidelines can be implemented by way of software that creates instance documents, so it is properly regarded as a supporting set of materials. FRIS conformance can be tested by way of a specialist set of conformance suite tests.

XBRL Terms Definitions

Item	Definition
·FRTA	Financial Reporting ·Taxonomy Architecture. A long title for the ·taxonomy *best practices* document created largely by the ·DWG. FRTA aims to ensure that taxonomies that are built around the world use ·XBRL in some specific ways. This is in order to improve the interoperability of those taxonomies and to simplify the software development process for tools that need to process financial taxonomies. FRTA only relates to Financial Reporting taxonomies. These best practices are strongly encouraged by way of the ·Taxonomy Recognition Process (TRP). To reach the recognition level of "Approved," it is necessary for a ·taxonomy to be FRTA conformant. FRTA conformance can be tested by way of a specialist software conformance suite, as well as a range of manual checks.
·IASB	The International Accounting Standards Board. See also ·IASCF.
·IASCF	The International Accounting Standards Committee Foundation. The governing body of the IASB. The IASCF has sponsored a range of IFRS related ·XBRL activity by both volunteers and staff, including the creation of the IFRS ·taxonomy.
·IFRS	International Financial Reporting Standards; see *http://www.iasb.org.uk* for more information.
·instance document	Instance documents are also called ·XBRL Data Documents and are sometimes shortened to IDs (this is to be discouraged as "ID" has a special meaning in the ·specification). Instance documents contain one or more sets of ·context information that allows the consistent identification of: · The organization(s) that is reporting information · The date(s) for which information is being reported; and the · Details of any segments (such as the different divisions that are reporting inside a single organization) and details of any scenarios (such as "budget" figures, "forecast" figures, and "actual" figures) that are being used. Instance documents must also contain one or more unit identifiers that define the units of measure in use: typically currencies but can also be physical or derived measures such as BrakeHorsePower, Meters, and Shares. Finally, and most importantly, instance documents contain a "set of facts" that comprise a set of tags that are used by a ·taxonomy, the data that relate to those tag concepts, and the identifiers that place the information in context.
·ISC	The International Steering Committee of ·XII. The governing body, in effect a board of directors, with membership elected by ·jurisdictions (for Jurisdictional seats) and the ·ISC itself for "at large" representatives.
·jurisdiction	Self-governed, generally country-specific not-for-profit organization, recognized as the peak ·XBRL authority in that area by ·XII by way of vote of the ·ISC. Jurisdictions (for a list see *http://www.xbrl.org/jurisdictions.aspx*) must agree to the XII *branding and intellectual property policies*. Jurisdictions bring together a diverse range of organizations, from report preparers through to software vendors, intermediaries, accountants, accounting organizations and official bodies, such as regulators and accounting standards setters. Since some of these organizations compete with each other, it is necessary for a suitable neutrally regarded facilitator to simplify the operation of the jurisdiction. Jurisdictions can be not-for-profit companies, unincorporated bodies, or simply subordinate committees or working groups of the facilitator. Jurisdictions act to promote and facilitate adoption in their area, including by developing relevant country or industry taxonomies. At the time of writing, the ·IASCF was unique in not representing a country. This situation comes about by way of its supra-national characteristics.
·LRR	The Link Role Registry, a publicly accessible database that allows advanced users of XBRL to define new types of relationships between reporting terms.
·period	The date or time to which a fact in an ·instance document relates. It can be a point in time (e.g., December 31, 2002) which is referred to as an "instant" but is also known as a "stock" figure amongst some reporting communities (especially statistics). Alternatively a period can be referred to as a "duration" which is a reporting period that extends over a known time (e.g., the 12-month period ending December 31, 2002). Statisticians refer to this second type of period as a "flow."
·semantics	The meaning of an expression. The semantics of the various parts of ·XBRL itself are defined in the ·specification, but this is unlikely to be of interest to most end-users. Users of ·XBRL can create their own semantics in at least two ways. The creation of taxonomies by defining reporting terms and the way that they relate to each other is the most common way that ·XBRL allows the creation of comprehensive meanings. However, where it is possible to extend the ·XBRL itself (for instance by creating a new type of relationship in the ·LRR) it is necessary to define the meaning of that relationship.
·specification	The technical set of rules that governs the *syntax* and fundamental *semantics* of all ·XBRL materials, both the definitions that create ·XBRL dictionaries or *taxonomies* and the data, or *instance* documents. This is the main intellectual property of ·XII.
·spec	Shorthand for the ·specification.
·SWG	The ·XII Specification Working Group. This ·XII members-only working group maintains the ·specification and develops foundation-level modules and participates in the development of modelling rule-level documentation.
·syntax	The structure of a language, according to a set of rules. The syntax of ·XBRL is defined by the ·specification, as well as a number of other ·XML specifications, including several important *W3C* standards: *XML Schema*, *Xlink* and *Xpath*.
·stylesheet	See ·XSLT.
·tag	Another (less precise) term for an ·element. "Tagging" means to associate appropriate elements with the concepts in a business report.

XBRL Terms Definitions	
Item	*Definition*
·**taxonomist**	A professional ·taxonomy developer concerned primarily with the logical organization of reporting concepts that exist in a particular domain, whether that be at the level of group internal reporting, external corporate reporting, the capture and definition of industry key performance indicia, or an accounting framework promulgated by an accounting standards setter.

Source: Richard Oppenheim, The Oppenheim Group. Created by the XBRL consortium http://www.xbrl.org/technical/SGS-PWD-2005-05-17.htm

¶ 1015 Security: The Hidden Vulnerabilities of Technology

As accountants, we have access to our clients' most sensitive financial information and personal data. Ensuring the security of this information has always been an awesome responsibility, but the ease with which this data is transmitted over various electronic media raises it to an unprecedented level. Consequently, it is vital that your firm have strong, clear policies, procedures and safeguards in place for the transmission of documents.

With the enactment of the new IRS rules under Code Sec. 7216, firms must rewrite their policies regarding the transmission of documents, and it is likely that firms won't be transferring as much to clients or third parties (e.g., bankers and attorneys) via e-mail. Firms that do will have to get approval beforehand. In any case, encrypted e-mail (Verisign, PGP, CertifiedMail, Amplock SmartSoftKey, Google Encryption) or more likely a portal system tied to their document management system is the safest way to transmit such documents. More detailed information is available on *SANS.org* or the *IRS.gov*.

Many of us mistakenly think that our firm's intranets are safer from intrusion than the Internet. That is true only if we can ensure the safety of the information we store on our servers, send to our clients, receive from our clients, and used by our remote access users. Think about the headlines you've seen about the security breaches experienced by our banks, retail stores and even the federal government. Our IT professionals are responsible for a lot more than making sure computers are properly networked. Ultimately, they are responsible for making each wireless access point as secure as the network servers.

Computer security has three essential goals: confidentiality of information, integrity of the system, and availability of the data. In terms of security, this often translates to monitoring access to the system. Because of the security hierarchy built into the software we use, an initial step is assigning every job classification a specific level of access appropriate to that position. For example, your firm administrator or human resources professional may be given access to the partners' remuneration, but the department's secretary may be barred from seeing that information. Here's another example: your firm's Web master, who may also be the marketing director, may be the only person at the firm with access to post approved changes on the firm's Web site.

Once the firm has a client portal, as many firms do, the security issues get even more complicated. The system must be sophisticated and secure enough to ensure that clients who sign in with their password can view only their own information.

E-mail presents its own complications, ranging from spam to the potential for viruses. Programs like Postini scan incoming e-mails and use key words (e.g., pharmacy, male, female, sale, etc.) to filter and quarantine messages that seem inappropriate. They then send a separate "quarantine report" to everyone at the firm. Each recipient has the capability allowing the e-mail or deleting it.

Another security measure is preventing messages from being previewed. This is designed to prevent the recipients from opening infected e-mails.

In addition to putting a system in place to limit access to sensitive information, certain other precautions can help defend against the common vulnerabilities presented by the Internet, intranets, and remote access, including:

- Firewalls and antivirus software.
  - Make sure firewalls are properly configured.
  - Make sure antivirus software is current.
  - Use Virtual Private Networks (VPNs) to safeguard remote access.
  - Ensure that firewall and antivirus software you choose won't conflict with other programs used in your practice.
- Encryption.
  - Use secure server/client software.
  - Authenticate log-ons.
  - Encrypt sensitive information.
- Passwords.
  - Have employees change their passwords on a regular basis (e.g., every three months).
  - Don't allow the same password to be repeated for a period of time (e.g., two years).
  - Require the use of a combination of letters, numbers, and symbols.

— Make sure passwords are kept hidden (e.g., in a desk drawer) and not in plain sight.

- Software audits.

  — Have your IT professional or an outside third party periodically check the security of your systems.

- Crisis communications plan.

  — Have a crisis communications plan in place in the event your server becomes vulnerable and client data is hacked.

- Disaster recovery plan.

  — Reliance on computers has made us all susceptible to the loss of data. A disaster recovery plan will allow your firm to be back in business shortly after a disaster, whether that is manmade (e.g., crashed server or communications failure) or natural disaster (e.g., a fire, hurricane, tornado, or earthquake).

Figure 10.3

Disaster Recovery Plan

- Business impact analysis:

  — Determine what you will need to be up and running immediately.

  — Make it a company policy for everyone with client contact responsibility to leave for the day with an updated calendar.

  — Have written documentation of the firm's computer back-up procedure; update it as necessary.

  — If there is a server on the premises, make it a formal procedure that the person doing the backup sends a copy of the backup to a secure, remote location on a daily basis.

- Establish a chain of command. The managing partner should have a list of key personnel, their contact information, and the roles they will play in the event of a disaster. Ensure the list is updated frequently.

  — IT

  — HR

  — Marketing/public relations

  — COO/facilities manager

- Prepare a list critical company functions.

  — What is the order in which they need to be reestablished?

  — Can these functions be performed from home? For how long?

  — How quickly does an alternate work site need to be functional?

- Ensure that any critical hard copy documents are stored in a safe place.

- Prepare a list of personnel, their contact information and their job functions

  — How will they be notified of the emergency?

  — How will they be updated?

- Prepare a client list organized by importance to the firm.

  — Under what circumstances will they need to be contacted?

  — Who will be responsible for contacting them?

- Prepare a list of equipment needs of critical personnel.

  — Have a list of vendors that can replace this equipment immediately

- Establish a recovery task list that documents accountability.

- Create a crisis communications plan for clients, employees, community, and the media.

¶ 1020 The New Cooperation

Before the enactment of SOX, if you asked a client who their accounting firm was, they'd invariably name a single firm. Big Four firms rarely worked closely with their smaller counterparts. Accounting firms that share geographic markets or niche specialties rarely shared a client. SOX challenged the historical one-accountant-per-client mentality and caused firms to develop the symbiotic and cooperative relationships that we see today. These relationships are likely to deepen and new relationships formed as we move forward and new changes evolve from the fallout of the perceived root causes of the current economic crisis.

SOX changed the old paradigm by limiting the types of work that primary auditors can perform for the estimated 33,000 public companies worldwide that may seek their services. As a result, these potential clients began hiring multiple firms for various, specific engagements. Today, an accounting firm can work for dozens of public companies without doing any registrant work—a phenomenon unheard of in pre-SOX days.

Big Four firms had to partner and form alliances with smaller firms on a national and regional basis, and on a scale never seen before. They aligned with local regional firms and worked with them, each taking the lead on engagements best suited to their respective core strengths and the regulatory constraints involved. For example, a Big Four firm may do the primary audit work, while its smaller local partner handles internal audit responsibilities.

Forward-thinking firms saw the opportunities SOX presented for increasing their client base and worked to forge relationships with the Big Four firms in their geographic area who represented public companies. They set up meetings with these firms where they basically said, "Your public client needs to hire a second CPA firm. We'd like to work with you and be your clients' other firm. We're no threat to you, but if another Big Four comes in, they might be." For many, it worked like magic!

In addition, like-sized firms frequently collaborate informally as well as through national and international networks, associations, and alliances. These are becoming increasingly important as member firms work together on shared engagements. Some work requires professionals to be in place at multiple locations, and alliances through association memberships can be a seamless solution for small and mid-size firms that might otherwise be overwhelmingly burdened by an engagement's geographic demands.

Associations and alliances can also be a linchpin on proposals. These groups can help a firm demonstrate access to expertise, resources, and global reach that, on their own, would cost millions of dollars to develop. One firm may do the part of the work that happens in the United Kingdom, another does the part necessary in California, another in Florida, and another in South Africa.

Due to the changing nature of competition over the last decade (and for the foreseeable future), access to global resources is now essential, and it's one factor driving the increase in alliances and associations. The AICPA is deliberating about the nature of these alliances that may lead to more structure going forward.

Figure 10.4 ———

AICPA's Professional Ethics Division Interpretation on Networks and Network Firms and Proposed New and Revised Related Definitions: Exposure Draft

EXPOSURE DRAFT

Proposed New Interpretation

Interpretation 101-17 under Rule 101: Networks and Network Firms

Proposed New Definitions of Network and Network Firm and Proposed Revised Definition of Firm

ET Section 92

Executive Summary

CPA firms frequently form associations with other firms and entities and cooperate with them to enhance their capabilities to provide professional services. The proposals specify that when firms and entities in such associations share certain characteristics, they are considered to be a network and must be independent of certain attest clients of the other network firms. Under the proposal, those shared characteristics are:

- The use of a common brand name in the firm name
- Common control among the firms
- Profits or costs, excluding costs of operating the association; costs of developing audit methodologies, manuals, and training courses; and other costs that are immaterial to the firm
- Common business strategy that involves ongoing collaboration amongst the firms whereby the firms are responsible for implementing the association's strategy and are held accountable for performance pursuant to that strategy
- Significant part of professional resources
- Common quality control policies and procedures that are designed and monitored by the association and that the firms are required to implement

The proposal extends the independence requirements imposed on network firms to any firm or entity that a network firm (a) controls (either by itself or through its owners), (b) is controlled by, or (c) is under common control with. It also notes that if only a subset of firms within an association share one or more of the characteristics of a network firm (for example, a common brand name), only that subset of firms, rather than the entire association, would be considered a network for purposes of the proposed interpretation.

Under this proposal, network firms should be independent of all other network firms' audit and review clients for which a general use audit or review report is issued (that is, use of the report is not restricted to specified users).

For all other attest clients (for example, compilations), a network firm should consider any threats that the firm knows or has reason to believe may be created by other network firms' interests in and relationships with the client and, if those threats are not at an acceptable level, apply safeguards to eliminate the threats or reduce them to an acceptable level.

The committee believes the proposals are consistent with the guidance set forth in the International Federation of Accountants Code of Ethics for Professional Accountants and therefore will assist the Committee with its efforts to harmonize the AICPA's ethics standards with international ethics standards.

¶ 1025 The Globalization of Competition

.01 The Internet Levels the Playing Field

In many ways, the demand for global access is becoming a competitor, just as technology did. The Internet has leveled the playing field by giving everyone equal access to sources of information. Potential clients conduct due diligence investigations too. So, if your firm's Web site, for instance, doesn't state your expertise in the particular industry or service area niche a potential client is looking for, your firm may be ruled out. It may not matter that you were referred because of your knowledge in the area. That means clients who once hired a firm because of its local market now may hire firms from around the globe due to their specialties and niche expertise. Firms around the world may be competitors. It's very possible that, on any given engagement, your competitor is a firm you've never heard of, headquartered in a place hundreds or even thousands miles away.

.02 Outsourcing

By the same token, manufacturing companies and service centers aren't the only companies moving jobs overseas. Professional services firms are too. For example, tax returns that were once completed in-house may be outsourced to India, Pakistan, or China. In some cases, the labor for these services is 90 percent lower when they're outsourced overseas. When competitors are outsourcing to countries where work can be performed faster and cheaper, your firm may be at a pricing disadvantage if it doesn't do the same.

Outsourcing professional services work overseas isn't without risks, but many clients have become savvy enough to understand and accept those risks. The biggest risk, perhaps, is dependency. Because the American firms that outsource the work share the same skills as the overseas firms to whom they outsource, the work can always be brought back to American soil. But the risk is that American firms become dependent on the relief and efficiencies that outsourcing provides. Here's an example:

> A Virginia firm has 10 people working on 1040s and moves all that work to India. It doesn't need all 10 of those people anymore and lets six of them go, saving $250,000 in costs. But six months or a year later, the Indian company goes out of business. Suddenly, the Virginia firm is in big trouble. It needs those six people back—pronto! But they're long gone.

Aside from the attending security and philosophical issues related to outsourcing (for example, is outsourcing unpatriotic?), American firms risk losing skills sets to perform the services they outsource. The value of retaining those skills in-house is something each firm must assess individually. If tax work accounts for six percent of your business, how much time do you want to devote to it? If 80 percent of that 6 percent is compliance work such as 1040s and doesn't generate top dollar, is the work clogging efficiencies throughout your firm? Are good clients receiving lesser services because lower-end 1040s are disrupting your ability to service them? If so, how important is retaining skills to perform 1040s?

Outsourcing works best for compliance work. One advantage for American professionals is that the work is done while they sleep. They wake up, go to the office, and find that the work was finished in India or Pakistan while they were entertaining the sandman. Outsourcing offers a lot of benefits, but it also opens the door for other countries to eventually lure away higher value work as well. As the world gets flatter and smaller, firms in places like South Africa or India may go directly to our clients just as the owners of TurboTax did.

The new Code Sec. 7216 regulations have put a real crimp in outsourcing. Because there was an ongoing debate about whether clients had to be informed that their tax return might be outsourced, this, along with the anticipatory loans touted by wholesale preparers like H&R Block, became the face of the reason Congress backed the new regulations. Clients must expressly consent to having their returns outsourced.

We believe this is patently unfair: there is no other business that has to tell its clients where every part of its business is done. American car manufacturers, for instance, don't need to tell buyers where the vehicle's plastic cup holder was manufactured. Nevertheless, it is the rule, and firms must be in compliance.

¶ 1030 The Shift in Client Priorities

Another area of competition is client priorities, which have changed over time. The age of the general practice is over as clients look for firms that are familiar with their business or industry. And these clients are willing to pay a premium for expertise.

This fact is why differentiation, as discussed in an earlier chapter, is so critical in this environment of chaos. It is rare these days to pick up a new client on the mere say so of a referral source and without being vetted through a proposal process. The proposal process itself is far from pro forma. It is an exercise in showcasing your firm's experience and knowledge in the niche or service area by illustrating your awareness of the challenges their business and their industry are facing. Personally researching a client or a prospect is one way of doing this. Many firms have marketing and business development departments that are charged with doing this. In addition, companies like First Research, Inc., which provides industry-centric information appropriate for every stage of the sales cycle, and ProfitCents, which performs sophisticated financial analysis including financial projections and analytical procedures, have come on the scene to buttress the proposal process. These tools, and others like them, can be very cost effective methods of educating clients and enhancing their level of satisfaction with your firm. They are part of a marketing arsenal that is needed to keep your firm in step with what your competitors are doing.

.01 *Know Your Competition*

One key to successful proposals in this chaotic environment is identifying the firms who are competing against you for the work. If competitors bidding against you on a project are smaller firms with more limited resources, it's fairly safe to assume that the prospective job will be more price-sensitive. Conversely, in situations where larger firms are proposing, the work will be less price-sensitive. Demonstrating expertise and specialization in those cases will be more crucial. Either way, examining who the competition is can provide some insight into the prospect's hot buttons. It's important to be able to answer the question: "Who are we competing against?"

.02 *Keeping Track of Wins and Losses*

It is important to keep track of the number of proposals you sent out, which you win and which you lose, as well as the industries in which the target businesses operate. Over time, tracking allows you to evaluate where the marketplace perceives your strengths. If it becomes necessary, you can reevaluate your strategic growth plan to accommodate your strengths. Unless you are prepared to commit the marketing budget needed to convince the market otherwise, it may not make sense to continue pursuing business in an area that does not seem to see your value in the same place you do. Figure 10.5 shows a sample proposal log that will allow you to measure where your marketing efforts are paying dividends.

Figure 10.5 —————————————————————————————

Sample Proposal Log

							Mktg. Touches (date and type)		Fee Breakdown					
Date Entrd in Sys.	Date Updtd.	Client/Prospect/Target	Source	Industry	Eng. Ptr.	Eng. Team	Mktg. Touches (date and type)	Total Fee	Audit	Review	Tax	Consulting	Status	Comments

Proposal Log: June 2008-July 2009

	Total		Audit	Review	Tax	Consulting
YTD $ Value of Proposals						
YTD % Value of Industry						
YTD % by Service						
$ Value Open						
$ Value Lost						
$ Value Won						
Total Number of Proposals						
Open						
Lost						
Wins						

.03 Carving a Profitable Niche

As firms diversify and offer a wider variety of services, they also encounter competitors they've never seen on the front lines of traditional services. For example, firms offering staffing services are competing with professional recruiting firms. Firms that provide technology services face off against technology companies. Accounting and law firms with estate and financial planning practices vie with stockbrokers and financial planning companies. If a niche is narrow enough, competition can be practically eliminated. For example, SS&G Financial Services of Cleveland has a healthcare consulting niche that manages the business side of physicians' practices for them. The skills required to run a physician's practice today are very difficult to find in a single person: insurance savvy, negotiation skills, office management, human resources expertise, telephone skills, medical coding, tracking continuing education, and managing waiting times—to name a few. SS&G charges the client $50,000 to $100,000 per year for the service, but performs all practice management functions, from hiring and firing to strategic planning. The niche has grown to employ 100 people within 10 years. It's headed by a pharmacist, and the two key lieutenants are a nurse and a CPA. Who thought an accounting firm would ever employ pharmacists and nurses? Clients buying these services are scattered throughout the nation. It's differentiated to the point where it has few, if any, competitors. One of the firm's key challenges is managing the travel schedules of these employees to prevent burn-out, because the clients are so far-flung. Another firm, The Cornerstone Accounting Group in Roseland, N.J., which has a national real estate specialty, employs a full-time travel professional to manage its experts' cross-country commitments.

¶ 1035 Financial Issues: Partner Compensation

Partner compensation is a sticky issue. Yet all firms need to come to grips with how their partners will be compensated while they are active partners as well as when they retire. Each compensation model—and there are many—has different pros and cons. Generally speaking, smaller firms tend to follow the traditional models that rely on tangible metrics, such as ownership percentages, while larger firms are more prone to consider intangible factors, such as leadership potential, business development, and partner evaluations.

There are certain universal truths about how partner compensation must be viewed by the partnership in order for the firm to operate at its most effective:

- All partners must perceive the agreement as fair. This includes nonequity partners, who should be fully aware of the guidelines for transitioning to equity partner.

- The partnership needs to be open to amending its compensation plan as events warrant. For instance, circumstances like a merger or acquisition or the addition of another layer of equity partner may require a change in the plan.

- The payout to retiring partners may need to be amended so that the firm remains solvent.

- Partner compensation needs to be based on a set of performance-based factors. As long as the parameters for compensation are transparent, it is okay if this means that rainmaker partners may earn more than quality control partners.

- The partnership needs to agree to either open or closed compensation. With open compensation, every partner knows the compensation of every other partner. There are valid arguments for each model, but the trend is toward the transparency of open compensation plans.

¶ 1040 Capital Contributions

.01 Immediate Capital Contributions

Other factors that need to be considered include whether new partners will be required to make a capital contribution upon admission to the partnership. Using this model, each partner purchases a fixed number of partnership units at a per-share price fixed by the firm. Additional shares may be assigned or sold to partners in the future on the basis of certain events (e.g., the retirement of a partner) or performance (e.g., leadership potential). In many firms, certain triggers reset the share price; some firms set a permanent price per share.

Some firms finance the purchase themselves; others require the new partner to obtain his or her own financing. Interest may or may not accrue on the contribution. However, it must be made clear to the partners that their capital contribution is essentially loan capital, not a profit-sharing account.

.02 Graduated Capital Contributions

Using this model, each new partner purchases a fixed number of partnership units, but he or she can pay the amount over time through deductions from their compensation. As a general rule, the payout term is five years. Additional shares may become available under the same circumstances described above.

¶ 1045 Annual Compensation

Not unexpectedly, there are many compensation models to choose from. Many firms are moving toward performance-based systems, where partners are paid a guaranteed salary plus a bonus based on performance. Any remaining profits are paid at the end of each year based on the partner's ownership percentage in the firm. Some firms set aside a certain percentage of the annual profits to be distributed at the partners' discretion to nonequity partners and staff on the basis of performance. There are no surprises under these arrangements: the managing partner or the executive committee set each partner's performance objectives at the start of the year; everyone is aware of what is expected of them. Firms that use this type of balanced scorecard approach tend to have a firm culture that views the firm as a holistic team in which everyone contributes to the firm's success.

Traditional partnership compensation models don't have a guaranteed salary. Instead, partners are compensated from the firm's projected residual income according to their percentage of ownership. Partners receive periodic distributions throughout the year, and at the end of the year, the projected amount is reconciled with the firm's true residual income.

¶ 1050 Payout for the Baby Boomers

It is coming. The wave of partner retirements is upon us, and firms that haven't adequately planned for their firm's future are scrambling to figure out how they will be able to pay their retiring partners.

Most partnership agreements provide for either funded or unfunded retirement. Under funded arrangements, each partner has an individual account set up in his or her name. Partners each contribute a certain amount (usually a percentage of pay or a set amount) to his or her retirement fund. The partner's contributions are periodically included in taxable income, so that post-retirement income from the fund, other than income from current interest, is tax-free.

In an alternate version of this arrangement, which a number of firms follow, the firm calculates a defined death benefit for each partner on the basis of his or her ownership percentage and then contributes to the fund to meet this amount. Upon retirement, the partner's withdrawals are taxable income. However, the partner generally is in a lower tax rate when the distribution occurs.

¶ 1055 Mandatory and Minimum Retirement Ages

Many firms have both mandatory and minimum retirement ages. Partners generally are required to give ample notice of their projected retirement date to the firm. Most firms ask for two years notice so that there is enough time to transition clients.

Often, there are financial penalties for partners who leave before the minimum retirement age, up to and including forfeiture of their capital contribution. We should note that the "minimum age" may not be a chronological age; it may be tied to minimum length of time the person must have been a partner at the firm.

¶ 1060 "Fired" Partners

Firing partners from a CPA firm partnership is something like Congress talking about changing Social Security. There is no set formula for paying out partners who are dismissed from a partnership. Partners who are let go because they have violated the law of ethics of the profession might not be entitled to any compensation, possibly even including the return of their capital contribution. Partners who are dismissed for other reasons, such as nonperformance, are entitled to the return of their capital contribution, generally paid out over a period of several years, as well as some sort of severance package tied to a noncompete agreement.

Figure 10.6 ―――――――――――――――――――――――――――――――――――

Measuring Partner and Professional Staff Marketing ROI

Marketing to Existing Clients

- Number of client meetings where feedback is sought to establish client satisfaction.
- Number of routine status calls made to existing clients.
- Number of follow-up calls to check status of ongoing client issues.
- Number of nonbillable client meetings to probe for new business opportunities.
- Number of "stay in touch" phone calls to inactive clients on A or B client list.
- Number of "touches through the year (e.g., newsletters, articles of interest, personal notes, etc.).
- Number of referrals from existing clients.
- Number of referrals from other centers of influence.

Marketing to Prospective Clients

- Number of phone calls to arrange marketing meetings.
- Number of marketing meetings/networking events.
- Number of contacts with school and staff alumni.
- Amount of preparation time for business development meetings.
    - Visits to prospect's Web site
    - Meeting with marketing director to get information about prospect.
    - Speaking with others who know prospect to gain additional insight.
- Number of speaking engagements to audiences filled with prospective clients or referral sources.

- — Number of follow-up calls made within three-five days of speech.
- — Number of follow-up meetings scheduled.
- Number of articles written.
  - — How published article was used to bolster marketing efforts.
- Number of networking meetings:
  - — Within the firm, with partners and others you don't ordinarily interact.
  - — Outside of the firm.

Training

- Number of training sessions:
  - — Proactively initiated.
  - — Initiated at managing partner's request.
  - — At request of marketing department.
- Type of training:
  - — Networking.
  - — Leadership.
  - — Business writing.
  - — Dress for success.
  - — Executive coaching.
  - — Life coaching.
  - — Technical.
  - — Other (specify).
- Training sessions at which partner/professional led the session.

Chapter 11
Partnership and the Evolution of Firm Structure

¶ 1101 Emergence of the C-Suite

As firms struggle to manage the chaos that surrounds them, the traditional governance structure upon which most accounting firms were founded teeters precariously. Many of the most visionary firms either have or are in the process of transitioning from the historically revered one-partner-one-vote model to a more fluid model that centers leadership in a few key people who can react quickly and decisively to changes in the business environment. The difference between successful firms and mediocre ones will hinge on the firms' capacity to rely on the decision-making ability of a core team that is knowledgeable about the marketplace and the firm's core clients in particular.

In theory, the switch in management style makes a lot of sense. Adopting a decentralized C-suite style of governance whereby CEOs, CFOs, COOs, and CMOs run the internal business of the firm and everyone else is asked to focus on their individual pieces of the business recognizes the individual strengths of the partners: some are natural leaders, others are rainmakers, and still others are talented technicians. A firm that plans to be in business over the long haul needs partners in all of these categories. The challenge lies in finding a way to make the change—which ultimately is for the betterment of the firm—without fostering feelings of disenfranchisement among the partners who will be losing their ability to vote on every issue.

Change, whether positive or negative, is difficult. A change of this magnitude requires extra care, or the firm can implode. Every partner must believe that he or she still is valued and will know what is happening in the C-suite even without a formal role in the decision-making process.

Make no mistake: deciding on restructuring the firm in this way can be a make-or-break moment for the firm. If it isn't handled with skill and tact, the result can be an insurmountable schism. This is one of those times that working with a consultant to initiate and organize the new firm structure and cultivate the buy-in of all the partners can pay huge dividends. Giving all the partners a safe place to provide their insights and express their feelings can result in a stronger team.

¶ 1105 The Concept Isn't New

The Big Four and other large firms were the first to adopt a corporate-style structure. Believe it or not, these arrangements were firmly entrenched at the megafirms by 1985. These firms were the first to understand the need for a more manageable way to facilitate firmwide business.

The corporate model works equally well for significantly smaller firms, and partnerships across the board are recognizing its appeal and adopting it. Even a partnership with three or four people isn't effective when everybody has equal say. Organizations with lots of input in the decision-making process move more slowly, which can lead to missed opportunities. Keeping decision-making in the hands of a few has become the acceptable and smart way to manage. The corporate-style model originated by the Big Four is moving downstream.

¶ 1110 When Should a Corporate Structure Be Adopted?

Firms no longer have the luxury of extended debate among the partners, so decisions like whether to start a new niche, start a blog, or sponsor a seminar can no longer stretch to months or years. Any governance style that hinders the ability to act quickly is unacceptable. A successful professional services firm today needs both the strategic mind of a coach and the strategic athleticism of a quarterback.

There is no magic formula for determining when the time is right for implementing a corporate-style structure, or even if it ever will be right for your firm. Sticking to a traditional partner structure can continue to work well for your firm, as long as quicker decision-making is facilitated by taking some of the bloat out of the system. Adopting a streamlined structure that delineates responsibilities can help even a small firm to increase its profitability. For example, a three-partner firm can save a lot of time and resources by simplifying the way it votes on day-to-day matters. Is it really necessary to have all three partners vote on which postage machine or copy machine to purchase? Wouldn't it be much more efficient to hold a partner meeting to determine which partner will handle the administrative responsibilities, which will oversee marketing, and which will handle HR? Each partner should be given the authority to run his or her area without input from the other two for all day-to-day decision-making. The meeting agenda should include setting budgets for each "department" and scheduling monthly partner meetings that focus solely on the three areas of firm administration.

Figure 11.1 ——

Sample Organizational Chart

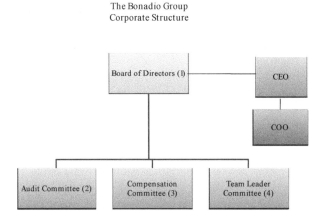

The Bonadio Group
Corporate Structure

(1)   Comprised of CEO (Managing Partner), COO, and eight (8) senior partners
(2)   Comprised of CEO, COO, Dir. of Finance, Controller and three (3) non-BOD partners
(3)   Comprised of CEO and six (6) BOD partners
(4)   Comprised of CEO, COO, and eleven (11) partners/team leaders; six (6) are BOD partners

Source: The Bonadio Group, Pittsford, NY.

Figure 11.2 ———

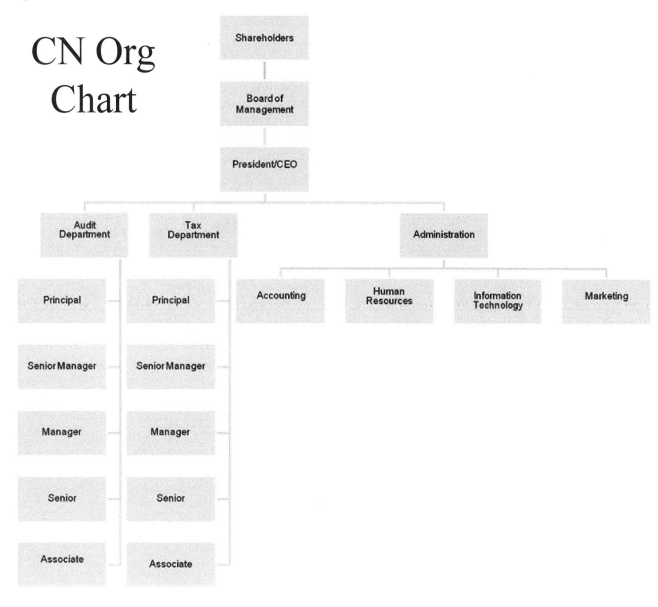

Figure 11.3 ———

Case Study: The Management Style of Tom Marino, CEO, J.H. Cohn LLP

Tom Marino, CEO of Roseland, NJ-based J.H. Cohn LLP, is well-positioned to comment on the C-suite trend in CPA firms. Marino has taken the firm from a $70 million firm to a $250 million firm, from a firm with a local profile and offices only in New Jersey to a nationally recognized firm with offices in New Jersey, New York, Connecticut, California, and the Cayman Islands. The firm's growth was strategically planned, and took planning, flexibility, time and resources.

And, according to Marino, it also involved some difficult choices. "One of the choices we made was to consciously define the seats on our bus and fill them with the best possible team we could hire. At times, that meant 'reseating' or replacing people so our firm could make the highest use of their individual talents. Most found that their new seats suited them very well. Others chose to align with other firms because they were unhappy with our decisions. It may sound insensitive, but those mostly talented and smart individuals just didn't fit our culture, and that mitigated their contributions to our firm's success."

Another choice made by the firm was decentralizing management and making each office location responsible for its performance under an office managing partner. "It goes back to our 'seat-on-the-bus' example," said Marino. "When the right people are in place, your success rate goes up exponentially." Performance is measured by a number of elements, and the bottom line is only one of them. The office's turnover rate is a big factor since the cost of hiring and training is so high. The firm doesn't scrimp on training, either. They view it as an investment in their people that will come back in many ways. "Whatever the circumstances, we don't plan on cutting training. The strength of our people is our most important asset. We tell them that, of course, but that's not enough. We need to treat them in ways that show them how much we value them. We can find other ways to trim our budget if we need to."

The firm has two levels of partner, equity and partial equity, and each has one vote. (There are a few contact partners, but they are rare. Partial equity partners don't vote on compensation or retirement matters, and they contribute less capital. Based on performance, partial equity partners can move to equity partners. No time constraints are attached, which recognizes their contributions while moving along on a slower track that enables them to meet family or other obligations. The partner compensation process is a hallmark of the firm's management philosophy. The firm's management committee determines a budget for each office. It is the responsibility of each office's managing partner to allocate the amount of each partner's compensation based on a set of established criteria. "We believe that office managing partners have earned their positions, and making them financially autonomous in certain areas lets them manage and compensate their people in a way that makes sense for them in terms of factors such as the services the particular office provides," says Marino.

"My door is always open," Marino continues, "and partners, including office managing partners, can come to me for help. The only thing we have a problem tolerating is partners who act like they're already retired. We work hard with any underachieving partners, giving them the training and other support they need to bring up their performance. In my 12 years as managing partner, this approach has worked virtually 100% of the time."

"We certainly haven't done everything right all of the time, but we've learned from our mistakes. We've learned that mergers should only be made because of the quality of the people we are taking on. Just adding to the number of people we employ isn't a productive strategy. Another lesson was that successful mergers take a lot of time: we now schedule a long rollout that includes relocating some of our staff to the new office, nurturing new partners and staff, and educating them in J.H. Cohn's philosophy and culture. We don't want any stepchildren.

"In the 'did-it-right' column, we've always focused on building trust in our partners, and that has paid-off big time. As Jim Collins said in *Good to Great*, "The moment you feel the need to tightly manage someone, you've made a hiring mistake. The best people don't need to be managed. Guided, taught, led—yes. But not tightly managed."

"The result is that my role has become much less hands on: I have 100% faith in the people running the individual offices. Most of my time is spent overseeing opportunities and deals, keeping our firm's name in front of clients and potential clients, paying attention to partners and strategizing for the future."

¶ 1115 Utilizing a Committee Structure

Some firms find that forming committees to oversee the firm's executive and marketing functions is another way to trim the time it can take to make decisions. The CEO or managing partner has the authority to make a final decision on whether to go ahead with the proposed plan, but all of the preliminary evaluations—the weeding through various ideas and proposals and doing due diligence on them—have already been taken care of in committee.

The most prevalent committees in firms today are the executive committee (also called the management committee), which oversees the firm's operational and strategic initiatives such as developing a new niche, initiating a merger, and leveraging new technologies to meet client needs; and the marketing committee, which oversees the firm's marketing and business development initiatives, such as creating a professional development training program and overseeing partners' practice development programs. In larger firms, these committees may be broken into smaller groups, such as the technology committee, the diversity committee, or the continuing education committee, for instance.

Other committees exist as well, including diversity committees, client advisory/business advisory committees, and staff advisory committees. Each of these committees offers a different set of challenges. In one sense, they are voluntary because they don't directly concern the firm's operations. In another, they can provide vital measurements of how the firm is viewed from outside management's ivory tower: they require input and feedback from random people who generally don't have direct-line reports to top management and who might say things about the firm that management may not want to acknowledge. Establishing any of these committees requires the firm's leaders to be responsive to and accountable for acting on at least the committee's major findings or risk a negative impact on the firm's culture.

Diversity committees are responsible for ensuring that the firm is giving qualified women and minorities the opportunity to become partner. Initiatives that foster diversity include mentoring programs, leadership coaching, facilitating a slower partner track, networking within the firm, and providing work assignments that enable the employee to learn and grow. This committee gains credibility if it is lead by top firm leaders.

Client advisory/business advisory committees garner feedback from the firm's clients. They are living, breathing client satisfaction surveys. It takes a management team who are willing to hear criticism for them to be effective.

SS&G Financial Services takes this concept a step further: for the past 11 years, the firm has met semi-annually with an outside advisory board charged with evaluating how the firm can improve and reinforcing the firm culture. Typically, the committee is comprised of a CPA, an attorney, and a businessperson who are specialists in specific industries or service areas but with no ties to the firm. This committee, which rotates members as necessary, comes up with a list of between four and seven strategic initiatives and an implementation plan for each. A committee person is assigned responsibility for following up on each initiative. The list is reexamined at every meeting, with some initiatives completed, some given more time, and some taken off the list. The board's goal is twofold: (1) to provide visioning and (2) to give the firm unbiased feedback that will bring value to the firm and support its firm culture, growth, and profitability.

Canadian Chartered Accounting firm VanParys Micacchi Shippey & Warnick (VMSW) has taken a different route to enhancing its services. The five-partner firm embarked on a customer experience program geared toward increasing the loyalty of the firm's existing clients. The program reinforces the firm's belief that loyal customers tend to stay longer, buy more, and share their great experiences with others. In a nutshell, the program identifies every point at which clients interact with VMSW and examines how clients perceive the experience. The information from these analyses is used to improve and enhance that experience, referring back to the firm's brand promise as the benchmark. This program, several-year-long, was introduced at a meeting entitled *Together We Can Achieve the Extraordinary*. The program is anchored by this proverb:

> The high road to service is traveled with integrity, compassion and understanding . . . people don't care how much we know until they know how much we care.
>
> —Author unknown

Not all firms have or want to operate within a committee structure. Those firms prefer to have all firm leaders report directly to them. Depending on the size of the firm and the firm culture, that can, in fact, be the best option.

¶ 1120 Ability To Run a Tight Meeting Is Key to Successful Committee

The key to successful committees is a structured meeting run by a chair who guides the conversation and steers away from tangential discussions. (We've all been in meetings that go on seemingly forever and don't accomplish much.) There are some tried-and-true guidelines for running an effective meeting:

- *Set an agenda—and stick to it.* Before the agenda is set, ask the committee members if there are any particular items they want to address. A certain amount of flexibility encourages creativity, but that doesn't mean a long discussion of an ancillary item.

- *Hold interim meetings.* The chair should meet with team members who are accountable for accomplishing certain tasks before the full committee meeting. This allows the chair to adjust timelines or specific goals if that becomes necessary.

- *Start and end on time.* People hate to feel they are wasting their time. If you haven't gotten to some of your agenda items, you can either carry them over to the next meeting or ask everyone to send you their updates so you can summarize their input and issue a report.

- *Foster team spirit.* Allow everyone to have input. If the actual meeting time is limited or if certain members will be unable to attend, the committee chair can use the firm's intranet or e-mail to contact members and gather their input on specific issues.

- *Notice who is and isn't participating.* Be sure to involve everyone on the committee. Understand their personalities, and watch their body language. If someone is shy, help draw them out by specifically asking for their opinion. If someone who always speaks up is silent, ask for their thoughts as well. It may be that they disagree with something and are holding back on saying so. You are much better off facing dissent head on instead of having it leave the meeting and be aired across the firm.

- *Handle dissent with care.* If there is dissent, be sure that it is on the merits of the decision and not a personal attack. Personal attacks can seriously undermine the firm.

- *Control difficult people.* Many committees have a member who insists on making everything personal or arguing every tiny point. This type of disruptive behavior should not be tolerated. The chair needs to meet with such a person individually and explain that his behavior needs to be modified and that he will be held accountable for making the necessary modifications.

- *Summarize the conversation.* At the end of a discussion or at a natural stopping point, the chair should summarize what was said, clarify the committee's decision, and state the next steps.

- *Have someone take notes.* After the meeting, these notes should be formalized in a document and distributed to the committee members and firm leaders. This is a good way to measure progress and accountability.

¶ 1125 Good Communication Is Critical

Executive committee members are empowered to make important decisions, but they're *not* empowered to withhold communication about them. Merger discussions are a good example. If a partner hears through the grapevine that the firm is discussing a merger, and if the executives with decision-making power on merger issues haven't informed the partnership of those discussions, then the partner who learned of the merger talks through second-hand sources might be justifiably incensed. That's not to say that a momentary, off-the-cuff and inconclusive merger discussion must be broadcast to the entire partnership, but all partners have a right to expect that they'll be informed about serious directive matters.

A corporate-style governance structure isn't a license to disenfranchise partners. It works best when leaders give all partners as much respect and sense of inclusion as possible. A whole new cluster of headaches arises when partners sense that the firm is taking away what they expect in a partnership. Regardless of the management structure, partners must have great lines of communication and be respectful of all other partners if the firm is going to thrive.

This holds true for more traditional firm structures as well. It is an undeniable fact that even in the most democratic partnership not all partners are treated equally. In all but the smallest partnerships, the managing partner seeks the insights of some partners and not others. The truth is that partnerships are somewhat like a high school cafeteria: the leaders all sit at one table, the math whizzes at another. To function at maximum efficiency, the firm needs everyone, and the important thing is that everyone knows that their particular attributes and contributions to the firm are appreciated.

That is why good communication among partners is so essential. A one-culture firm depends on it. In larger organizations, there may be hundreds of partners. They may not know each other; they may not be located at the same location; the annual firm retreat may be the only time all year they are at the same place. Good communication channels—whether through in-person meetings, teleconferences, conference calls, e-mail, or some other method—are the only way of letting partners know that they have a stake in all the issues of the firm. (Remember how Andersen tax partners in, say, Miami and Las Vegas, were affected by the decisions of a few audit partners working on Enron in Houston?)

Communication is just as important in smaller firms. The partners need to know they have open access to the managing partner, CEO, and executive committee.

For their part, managing partners and CEOs should go out of their way to keep a pipeline of information about what's happening in their firms flowing to the partners. All of the partners don't need to know that the firm purchased a new copier for the Boise office, but they must be kept informed about whether the Boise office was granted an infusion of additional capital because it exceeded its budget.

Other avenues of communication include partner dinners, visits to different offices, and informational meetings. Prepare agendas to go over with them to keep them in the loop. Explain what's happening in other offices. Listen to their agendas and concerns with the same level of interest and attention you would give your best clients—your partners are your best clients; they influence the internal workings and mood of the firm on a daily basis.

We predict that professional services firms of all disciplines will increasingly adopt and expand the C-suite style of governance. In addition, professional CEOs, CFOs, and COOs who aren't lawyers or CPAs will become increasingly significant authority figures and decision-makers at firms of all sizes.

Figure 11.4 ————————————————————————————————————

Taking Internal Communications to New Heights LBMC/Nashville

Having an effective communication process across a firm is critical to success. Accounting firms are no different from any other business when it comes to this statement.

At LBMC, we had been using an intranet to communicate across the firm for several years. Our Intranet had all the basics—helpful links, press releases and announcements, tech support, and an occasional article of interest. We recognized that the site was imperfect: it had no real "owner" and there was no consistency in when or why new information was posted. We also knew that the need for a new internal communication process meant migrating away from the existing platform and finding something new that would be scalable as we continued to grow.

As we brainstormed what we wanted in our new system, it became clear we wanted an innovative communication tool that would allow us to share information about the firm, reduce the time on key areas (marketing, human resources, internal accounting, and IT), and provide a centralized location for the day-to-day information the firm's leadership deemed important. In addition, we needed to have a communication tool that was easily edited by various departments, and an interactive way to communicate with personnel would enable and increase the use, making it a staple of operations. In essence, we wanted a tool that would drive LBMC personnel to the site daily, provide them with needed information, and be a sustainable platform for communicating between departments.

The Tool of Choice

We decided to utilize a Microsoft tool called SharePoint, an infrastructure for collaboration and a foundation for building Web-based applications with Windows. SharePoint provided us with a people-driven platform that fostered teamwork and information sharing and provided an interface with programs such as Outlook and forms products. We felt it offered us five key benefits:

1. *Empowers our teams/departments* by providing an easy tool for sharing information while maintaining an access hierarchy that prevents unauthorized changes to the site. The Intranet home page (see the sample below) that comes up when any computer in the firm is turned on.

2. *Provides connection through portals* that limit access to confidential information by separate portals for discreet information. For example, partners have their own password-protected portal on the Intranet.

3. *Builds departments/communities* based on common interests and is utilized as a work accountability tool. For example, industry segment teams can use pages for materials, discussions, meeting planning, resource sharing, next steps, etc., all with a tool built on Web parts that are easy to use.

4. *Windows-based application* that is not intimidating, even to team members with minimal skills, allowing all LMBC employees to participate.

5. *Controlled cost* that leverages our existing IT investments, but is scalable and interfaces with our other systems, which ultimately reduces cost.

The Implementation Process

Our internal and external IT teams worked together on the infrastructure of the product and roll out to the firm. Marketing was involved to give the tool a personality and make it compliant with overall firm branding standards. To make it fun and get people's attention, we even created a firm mascot as part of LBMC@WORK portrayed as a super hero who had all the answers. He was an immediate hit.

Implementation was fairly easy and fast. However, we continue to find innovative ways to grow the site.

Over the last year we have looked for ways to build the site well beyond our original plan. At first, it was a communication tool for our internal groups: accounting, human resources, marketing, and IT. Then we added sites for industry work teams and departments. Ultimately, our goal is to have individual sites for everyone in the firm, which will allow us to more systematically organize and disseminate information. We feel that this is a scalable tool and a necessary communication vehicle that will continuously propel us forward as a firm. We have even added a Monday video, titled "Monday's with Mike and David," named after our managing partners, Mike Cain and David Morgan. We host video segments on services, new appointments or designations, and further share information about LBMC.

We are in the process of adding a "Client Spotlights" feature, where we will host a client video and help everyone at LBMC better understand who our clients are and what they do, and are anticipating the addition of employee recognition for outstanding performance, case studies of "won opportunities," client satisfaction results, and more video enhancements.

Reporting

We added a reporting page to the site and set up the most frequently requested reports (e.g., revenue by industry, revenue by department, realization, and utilization of resources). Through a collaboration between SharePoint and our time and billing system, we can run "up to the second" reports on industries, service lines, year over year comparisons, and even drill down to specific services we provide on client-by-client basis. Historically, this would have taken time, especially in situations in which a client engages us for multiple services through different departments. Using SharePoint, the process is painless and provides us with more exact information about revenue, realization, and utilization.

Results

LBMC's intranet has become a centralized source of information that is integral to our daily operations. This tool has moved communications at LBMC to an entirely different level, and we are continuously looking for ways to increase its efficiencies across the firm.

Source: Exerpted from CPA Practice Management Forum (April 2009).

¶ 1130 Are Ancillary Companies and Non-CPA Partners the New Normal?

Just as many CEOs, CFOs, and COOs aren't CPAs, many partners aren't either. As firms offer a greater range of services to their clients, they're increasingly hiring partner-level executives from outside their profession to run those practice areas. Financial planners, staffing professionals, risk management experts, pension and benefits administrators, medical professionals, and others increasingly are finding a seat at partner meetings.

The changing mix of credentials among partnerships goes hand-in-hand with firms' move toward more ownership of ancillary companies. These companies commonly have different ownership than the firm itself. Of the 100 largest non-national accounting firms in the country, 38 percent reported owning a related company in 2006. Among the types of companies they own are those specializing in wealth management, financial services, real estate, benefits consulting, training, claims administration, technology, human resources services, nonprofit foundations, investment services, staffing and recruiting, health care consulting, and insurance-related services.

The diversification of expertise among professional services partnerships is one of the reasons that the traditional partnership model itself is in chaos. Another significant reason is that so many young professionals have no desire to become partners. The hours, years and risks required for partnership are turn-offs to younger generations who value time over money and personal goals over professional ambitions. Traditional partnership structures are losing the numbers game. Approximately 50 percent of all accounting firm partners are over age 50. Partners who are retiring or otherwise moving out of their firms outnumber those that are entering partnership, and that trend will continue for the foreseeable future.

The numbers beg the question: How are firms going to succeed in the long term when half their partners are approaching retirement and there aren't sufficient numbers of successors to replace them? Demographics and trends simply don't support the traditional partnership model. We forecast that, because of these trends, mid-sized firms that generate $20 million to 60 million in annual revenue will grow exponentially, swallowing up their smaller counterparts along the way.

Delegating and empowering staff becomes more crucial than ever when the numbers are so off-kilter. The three ingredients required to effectively delegate and empower others—trust, treating mistakes as learning experiences, and blocking the efforts of those who don't want others empowered—is very different from the formula used for creating the traditional partnerships and practices of the past.

¶ 1135 What Qualities Make a Good Partner?

Historically, firms were interested only in hiring people with at least one of three traits: high technical skills, rainmaking talent, and worker bees who could turn work around and get it out the door. Those criteria are very practical, but they don't work in an environment where the availability of skilled professionals is so limited that it restricts a firm's ability to seize the volume of work available to it or where they conflict with the needs and aspirations of the diverse populations and Gen X and Gen Y professionals firms need to remain competitive.

The same three categories of professionals are needed, but they can't be applied in the same paternalistic, formulaic manner that worked in the past. Firm leaders need to switch to a model that focuses on delegating tasks down to the lowest level professional that can perform them, empowering everyone at the firm to contribute to the firm's success, and communicating as much information about the firm's achievements and failures as possible without breaching its security. The last 10 to 15 years have seen so much consolidation, growth, and diversification that clinging to the old firm paradigm almost guarantees obsolescence. Professional services firms have greater opportunities than ever, as well as an unprecedented ability, to deliver services on an international basis. The criteria and requirements for partnership should mirror the traits valued in a business that operates in this macro environment.

Figure 11.5

The Five Non-Negotiable Characteristics of a Partner

1. *Leadership.* Leadership means the ability to motivate, develop, and be respected by partners and subordinates; to conceptualize a problem; to be innovative and creative in developing solutions; to inspire clients; to take a positive and aggressive attitude in approaching one's own responsibilities; to assume responsibility and discretion with discretion and judgment; and to effectively manage one's own time and that of subordinates.

2. *Honesty and integrity.* It is not overstating anything to say that having a firm leader without these two attributes would be like having a firm with no strength of character. Good leaders have to know a lot of things, but at the core they have to be able to believe in what their gut is telling them. A true leader will follow the right path for his or her firm even when that means doing something that is not terribly comfortable, such as firing a lucrative client who is not being straightforward. One need look no further than the current Ponzi scheme scandals or peanut butter recall to see what could happen to a firm whose leaders lack honesty and integrity.

3. *Technical competence.* Technical competence requires an acquired body of knowledge in a field of specialization coupled with the ability to apply that knowledge in reaching sound business decisions for clients and the firm, keeping current with new technical developments; demonstrating technical competence to clients and the public by one's expressed comfort with technical matters, and having a breadth of knowledge about all services offered by the firm to ensure optimal client service and resulting in firm profitability.

4. *Ability to contribute to growth.* This ability requires being aware of and encouraging existing clients to use all of the firm's applicable and relevant services; being alert to opportunities to obtain new clients; making high-quality, successful presentations; bringing in new clients; and making positive contributions to the firm's recruitment, education, development, and staff retention efforts.

5. *Business sense.* Every partner uses sound business knowledge and judgment on an ongoing basis, makes sound business decisions about client acceptance and retention, applies good strategy in setting fees, is profit oriented, is timely and aggressive in billing and collection efforts, is efficient and effective in performance of administrative activities, and is mature in his or her outlook toward business reversals.

6. *Executive presence.* Executive presence is the image an individual portrays in the company of others. A partner has individual stature, integrity, moral courage, and leaves a lasting impression in the minds of others; he or she demonstrates a positive, enthusiastic outlook toward the firm, his or her own personal conduct and grooming, and the development of subordinates. And effective executive's subordinates seek his or her advice and counsel, while superiors seek his or her opinion.

¶ 1140 Reasons New Partners Are Admitted: The Good, the Bad, and the Ugly

Firms admit new partners for a variety of reasons, both good and bad. Good reasons to admit new partners are to provide sustained growth, to bring continuity of the firm's existence, to provide new ideas to solutions and problems, and to ensure a structure that finances the retirement of older partners. Other good reasons to admit a partner are to broaden existing partners' expertise, to broaden the age mix among the partner group, and to retain a strong candidate who meets the qualifications and has the characteristics of a good partner.

But firms admit new partners for a number of bad reasons too, including:

- Keeping a staff member from leaving, even when his or her qualifications don't measure up to the standards of partnership.
- Avoiding hurt feelings by simultaneously admitting two or more partners with similar lengths of service when only one meets the firm's criteria for partnership at the time of admission.
- Promoting a staff member because of his or her strong relationship with a group of clients whom the firm fears losing.
- Acknowledging and rewarding faithful and loyal service to the firm.
- Because of seniority.

Prior to admission, all prospective partners should execute and sign any documents to which existing partners are parties, such as the existing partnership agreement and buy-sell agreements. Establish percentages of equity beforehand, and establish the price for equity or stock and the terms of payment.

Figure 11.6

Competencies Required of Future Partners

The following criteria are not listed in any order, but they follow two central themes: trust and compatibility. Trust and compatibility are binding forces that hold firms together while other firms struggle.

Technical Competence

- Keep abreast of changes and adjustments in accounting.
- Become a regular reader in technical areas and become an expert in your chosen specialty.
- Maintain strict quality control standards.

Practice Development

- Show the ability to bring in new clients and to provide additional services to existing clients.
- Demonstrate the ability to handle the firm's clients.
- Perform assignments within budget.
- Handle billing and collections in a timely fashion.
- Show good organizational and time management skills, including the ability to meet deadlines.

Staff Relations

- Show the ability to train and develop staff.
- Counsel and motivate those you are supervising.
- Contribute to maintaining high staff morale.

Personal Development

- Exhibit honesty and integrity.
- Exercise good communications skills.
- Demonstrate effective delegation skills.
- Maintain good relationships with peers and partners.
- Demonstrate maturity.
- Maintain a professional appearance and good grooming habits.
- Demonstrate involvement in professional organizations such as local chapters of state CPA societies and bar associations.

- Participate in firm committees and voluntary intrafirm services that indicate you would be a well-rounded partner.

Community Activities

- Demonstrate involvement in civic, religious and social organizations to offer public service and create an awareness of the firm and the quality of its staff.

Support of the Firm

- Be publicly and internally supportive of the firm's decisions.
- Effectively communicate the firm's position to other staff, and be a team player in general.

We recognize that no individual can meet all of the above criteria 100 percent of the time. But partners and future partners should try their best to operate at as high a level within each of the categories as possible.

¶ 1145 The Rise of the Non-Equity Partner

Partnership isn't for everybody. It never has been, but young people today certainly don't view it as the brass ring that it once was. Generations whose value systems prize work-life balance and immediate gratification over single-minded ambition and future rewards don't look at partnership the way their elders did. In the minds of many young professionals today, partnership simply isn't worth the cost of long hours, capital contribution, and potential liabilities. But professionals who either aren't partner material or who have family obligations that prevent them from advancing to equity partner along the usual path still can bring value to the firm. As a result, professional services firms have been redefining their partnership structure.

This new way of thinking about what it means to be a partner is quite a shift from the up-or-out mentality we were used to. That system discarded valuable, talented professionals without a whole lot of thought. The quality of life issues, staffing issues, and general chaos we currently find ourselves in caused firms to realize that talent can be recognized in many ways, not just through equity partnership. Professionals with strong client services skills, great technical skills, and valuable client relationships can be rewarded with non-equity partnerships that allow them to have visible, high-status positions that give them career satisfaction and encourage them to have long-term careers with the firm even though they never will be equity partners.

Outside of partner meetings, most firms don't distinguish between equity and non-equity partners. They want non-equity partners to be held in high regard by the outside world and to feel empowered. The non-equity status is acknowledged only internally, and often only by equity partners behind closed doors. Staff may not even know that certain partners don't have equity ownership.

Non-equity partners are basically salaried employees who share in the bonus pool. Their formal title may be partner, principal, director, or something else. Law firms pioneered the design of non-equity partnerships when they developed counsel positions years ago. Now the model has been adapted by large and mid-size accounting firms and is moving downstream to small firms. A 2005 study showed that 19 percent of all partners at accounting firms did not hold equity. These positions are a lot more commonplace now, but they amounted to a huge change from the systems in place 30 years ago, when up-or-out career tracks were practically carved in stone.

Non-equity partners generally are given the same decision-making parameters regarding how they manage practices or how they service clients. However, they may not have the ability to vote on issues such as admission of new partners or mergers and acquisitions. They're generally not entitled to deferred compensation and don't buy into the practice or get bought out of it. If the firm is sued, they don't bear the same liability burdens as equity partners.

At some firms, non-equity partnerships serve as stepping stones to equity partnerships, but in most cases, they're a final destination. Some firms even allow non-equity partners to have a token share of ownership—usually less than 1 percent—but these partners generally have no voting power.

¶ 1150 The Partnership Agreement

It is amazing to realize that many firms operate either without partnership agreements or with outdated or non-uniform agreements. With smaller firms, the partners sometimes feel there is no need for a formal agreement: things will just work themselves out as they arise. As firms get larger and new partners join the partnership through promotion or merger, some new partners sign agreements that are slightly different than already existing agreements and others don't sign any agreement.

The consequences of not reviewing your firm's partnership agreement on a regular basis can be severe, especially since the primary purposes of such agreements touch the three most potentially controversial areas of the partnership: the resolution of problems, partnership termination or dissolution, and financial arrangements. There are many horror stories about partners ending up in litigation because their agreements weren't explicit enough about what would happen in these circumstances. Even when a firm survives, it takes time to recreate a positive culture—which is an area of chaos that is avoidable.

Partnership agreement forms are readily available online, but it is not advisable to use them. It is far better to have an agreement drawn up by the firm's attorneys, who are familiar with the firm and its culture. They will know the right language and clauses to use.

All partnership agreements have some boilerplate clauses, but there are other topics that need to be addressed as well, including:

- *Mandatory and minimum retirement ages.* This clause should cover more than a chronological age. Among other things, it should address the timespan for the process, client transition issues, eligibility for a payout, and the terms under which a retired partner can stay on.

- *Termination of a partner.* The types of behaviors that will result in this drastic action should be outlined, as should the number of votes it takes to carry out the termination and whether there will be a severance package. Actions that put the firm at risk, debilitating illness, and underperformance are examples of areas that should be addressed. In addition, it is becoming more common for partnerships to want to "fire" partners without cause, as they can do with at-will employees. This, too, should be considered in the partnership agreement.

- *Dissolution of the firm.* The partnership agreement needs to stipulate what will happen if the firm is acquired as well as if it dissolves.

- *Partner capital contributions.* Language should be included in the agreement that sets out the terms under which partners will be required to make a capital contribution to the firm (e.g., immediate, never or over a period of years; guidelines for a request for additional capital). Recently, Chicago-based law firm DLA Piper announced plans to ask U.S. income partners to contribute capital to the firm for the first time starting next year and to reduce monthly payments to some top U.S. equity partners. The firm is seeking to reduce its reliance on bank credit and simplify its compensation structure. Some large CPA firms may well follow suit.

- *Partner compensation.* This issue is not as straightforward as it was when all partners were equity partners. Now, the various levels of equity and non-equity partner may have a stake in the firm's profitability through a non-traditional structure such as an income pool consisting of a percentage of profits. Any performance-related activities and goals tied to compensation should be included in the agreement.

- *Retirement benefits, pensions, and disability payments.* The agreement should detail the payment schedule of a retiring partner, how a disabled partner will be paid and for how long, and what happens if the assets in the firm's pension plan fall below established levels. No agreement can cover every possible eventuality, but an experienced attorney familiar with CPA firm partnership agreements can help minimize the firm's risk exposure.

- *Firm management issues.* The election, terms, authority, and responsibility of the managing partner should be formally set out in the partnership agreement. If the firm has adopted a corporate and/or a committee structure, the parameters under which they operate should also be set out. This is especially important in today's firm environment where the C-suite is likely to formulate important strategic initiatives before asking the equity partners to vote—if the matter even is one that the partners are required to vote on.

- *Non-compete agreements.* This clause protects the firm from the sudden loss of income if a partner with a large book of business leaves. Penalties should be attached to violating this clause, and those penalties should be clearly set out in the agreement.

- *Confidentiality agreement.* In addition, this clause protects the firm against the premature disclosure of merger plans, the signing of a big new client, and so forth.

- *Dispute resolution.* No one likes conflict, but it can arise despite the best of intentions. Mediation and arbitration are far better alternatives than the courts, but the partnership agreement needs to spell out the progression.

The foregoing is not an all-inclusive list, and the advisability of consulting an attorney can't be over-emphasized. Writing a partnership agreement that will protect both the firm and the partners can be time-consuming and expensive, but the benefit of a well-crafted agreement far outweighs the cost.

¶ 1155 Partner Compensation

Partners are compensated in a variety of ways. Traditionally, partner compensation was based on a combination of equity share, book of business, and longevity. That, like most other things related to firm management, has changed. Forward-thinking firms today use compensation models that reward top performers, much like corporations. For the most part, firms use some combination of annual pay plus bonus and a share of profits. However the pay scale is formulated, the goal is having all partners—both equity and income—come away with a feeling of fairness.

¶ 1160 The Myth of Lifelong Partnership

The historical notion of "once a partner, always a partner" is as relevant as the rotary-dial telephone. Dead weight in partnerships is more expensive and damaging than ever. Firms should have zero tolerance for it. By tolerating dead weight, firms are asking productive partners to subsidize the livelihoods of their less able, less competent, less motivated peers. Seniority isn't a job qualification. Partners who drive away staff, who argue with other partners, who spend more energy resisting change than helping the firm, who don't maintain and build on their skills, who don't get quality work out the door for clients - these are partners who drain the blood of the firm drop by drop, inch by inch. They're not worth it. They're too expensive, both psychologically and financially. All firms should have policies that define, in writing, partner expectations, partner codes of conduct, and standards for becoming a partner.

.01 Partner Performance Review

The five primary characteristics a person should have before they're considered to be eligible for consideration as a partner were outlined earlier in this chapter. In addition, every partner should be reviewed annually for his or her ability to:

- Give and receive information and maintain meaningful relationships with others;
- Link data, knowledge, and wisdom to provide quality advice;
- Identify market trends and meet the changing needs of clients better than competitors can;
- Interpret financial and non-financial information as they interact with each other, staff, and clients; and
- Use and leverage technology.

Make sure all partners are aware of what is expected of them. Have an annual performance evaluation process in place so partners know when they're falling under par. The annual review can be accomplished by a peer review or an upward evaluation. The managing partner or CEO should meet with every partner personally to discuss the results of the review process.

.02 Preparing for a Meeting To Discuss a Negative Performance Review

If the review is good, the meeting is simply an open and honest discussion between colleagues. The meeting can be difficult if there are deficiencies that need to be addressed. It's not easy to explain to a peer or mentor that his or her performance is substandard. There needs to be a fair amount of preparation for such meetings, both emotionally and intellectually.

Figure 11.7 ───────────────────────────────

Preparing for a Negative Partner Review

- Ensure the meeting will be private and uninterrupted.
- Clearly state the issues.
- Be prepared with a plan for remedying the situation (e.g., coaching and mentoring) as well as a timeline for measuring progress.
- Keep the lines of communication open. Begin the conversation by saying something like this:

  Thank you for taking the time to meet with me. As you know, it's time for your annual performance evaluation. I've become aware that there are some problems which I'd like to discuss with you. My understanding of this comes from the comments made on the review. I'd like to tell you about that and then give you a chance to tell me how you see the situation and clarify any misunderstandings. Then we can look at what needs to happen next.

  It's my understanding that . . . . . .

- Be alert to how the partner is reacting to what you are saying. Look for verbal and nonverbal responses. Allow as much time as necessary for the partner to respond, but don't allow any personal attacks. If the atmosphere of the meeting turns nasty or threatening, adjourn the meeting to another time.
- Take notes while the partner is responding to what you have said. This will form the basis of your summary of the discussion. If necessary, ask for further explanation or clarification.
- Once all of the issues and concerns are laid out, ask what the partner thinks the next steps should be. Tell the partner what you envision as the next move.
- Agree on the goals and a timeline.
- Set a date for a future meeting.

───────────────────────────────

¶ 1165 The Third Rail of Firm Management: Firing a Partner

There are times when it just doesn't work out. A partner at the firm is so difficult that the atmosphere feels thick with tension. Warnings, coaching, and mentoring don't work. If something isn't done to alleviate the situation, the firm may find itself divided between fans of the toxic partner and opponents of that partner. Anyone who has ever been in that position never forgets it.

The managing partner of the firm needs to take the lead. It is far from an enviable position, but no one said being a leader was easy. There are certain facts that need to be determined:

- If the ultimate step is taken, will the toxic partner take any allies with him or her?
- What will the loss mean to the firm in terms of book of business and staffing?
- How are the other partners likely to be impacted?
- If the toxic partner led a niche, is there someone else who can pick up the slack?
- How will the decision be communicated to the partners and staff? Clients? The community?
- What legalities are involved?

- Should there be a timeline?
- What does the partnership agreement say about these situations?
- How much will it cost?
- How will rumors be addressed?
- How will firm morale be nurtured?

Good communication is key. It is amazing how quickly word will spread, especially in the type of situation where ego and hurt feelings can make people speak out before they should. It is very likely that even though many at the firm view the partner as toxic, the partner believes he or she was acting in the firm's best interests. It is a very touchy time for any firm.

That is why it is a good idea to hire a consultant to work with the firm from the time the idea of terminating the partner is first brought up to the rebuilding afterward. The extreme difficulty of this kind of scenario makes it imperative for the partners to be able to talk to someone who can be objective.

The fact is that partners are not fired very often. When it does happen, there will be a knee-jerk negative reaction before there is a collective sigh of relief that tension and dissent are no longer part of the firm's "subculture."

We believe that as firms emerge from the current chaotic environment, termination will become more common. Surviving the chaos of a global business environment, an economic roller coaster, a generational divide, and a new practice paradigm will result in firms being less tolerant of nonperforming partners.

Chapter 12
The Chronic Headache of Risk Management

¶ 1201 Risk versus Reward

The threat of litigation is escalating to take a significant percentage of time for the top executives at professional services firms. All sectors of the business world wrestle with the implications and potential threat of our increasingly litigious society, and professional services firms are no exception. Litigation against the firm and the threat of it, sucks away time and money that otherwise could be used to benefit the firm. It's also frustrating. In most cases, there are no grounds to sue the firm, and claims against it are meaningless. But defending the firm is tough. It takes an amazing amount of time and financial resources to defend the firm and its professionals against lawsuits. In some ways, it can really overtake the practice. Executives suddenly find themselves going to depositions, discovery processes, and negotiations instead of running their firms. The most miniscule and trivial seed can plant a lawsuit, and it then grows out of control. Risk management and litigation are another big, new log on the fire when it comes to factors that fuel the chaos of managing a professional services firm in the 21st century.

Until 15 years ago, litigation, and the energy required to avoid it, wasn't the migraine-maker that it is today. Professional malpractice insurance was inexpensive. Firms weren't often sued. Lawsuits weren't as complex, and firms could just go buy insurance without any hassle. Not anymore. The application process simply to acquire insurance usually takes three to five weeks. It can be an intricate, intense, detailed, and burdensome process—and a trying exercise in negotiation. The insurance companies are much more thorough, inquisitive, and strict. Often there are fewer carriers to choose from, and the options are more limited. Because of the increasing threat of litigation, firm executives today spend a lot of energy managing their relationships with malpractice carriers.

But preventing litigation also improves practices in many ways. For example, the new emphasis on client selection was originally intended to improve the profitability of a firm's client base, but it has also become an essential risk management tool. Historically, firms didn't really investigate whether they were taking on an appropriate client. They didn't look at whether the client sued its previous accountants or lawyers. They didn't look at prior legal filings, the client's history of dishonesty, whether they were paying payroll taxes, and other issues that become important to a litigation-wary professional services firm. Due diligence and research with regard to client selection take a whole new importance in this chaotic environment.

The litigious environment is having a huge impact not only on which clients firms accept, but the specialties and engagements they choose as well. In the post-SOX era, many accounting firms won't audit public companies because of the risks involved. Others have made public company audits a niche specialty and charge top dollar for the service, in part to help hedge the increased risk. Those higher fees are justified. The total risk is overwhelming compared to the insurance available. The maximum coverage that accounting firms are picking up for SEC audit work is in the $20 million to $30 million range, and the market cap of a small public company definitely exceeds that. Many small firms do SEC work, and many of them can't get enough insurance to cover the potential liability of their engagements.

Much of the reason for such limited availability of coverage can be traced not to Enron and WorldCom and their ilk, but to SOX and the staffing shortage, according to Camico Mutual Insurance Company of Redwood City, Calif., one of the leading providers of liability insurance for CPAs. The work cascading to smaller firms from the Big Four in response to SOX, and the lack of staff to handle the work, have created a business environment where too many firms are accepting work for which they're not qualified, says John Raspante, CPA, an advisor with the insurance company. The opportunity to bring in new clients and increase their billings is too tempting to pass up for many firms, and they overlook the importance of their risk to exposure.

All firms are vulnerable in the litigious environment of the 21st century, so risk assessment and risk management become critical. Some consultants advise firms not to worry about litigation. They say that as long as firms have respectable insurance, they'll be sued only for the amount of coverage they carry. We're not so sure. We've yet to see a plaintiff offer that guarantee in writing, so we believe that risk assessment, risk management, and prudent client selection are critical to good practice management.

Figure 12.1 ——

Types of Coverage Firms Should Consider

- Directors and Officers Liability Coverage
- Errors and Omissions Coverage
- Prior Acts Coverage
- "Tails" Coverage for Retiring Partners
- Fiduciary Bonds—Employee Dishonesty Coverage
- Investment Advisors ERISA Bonds
- Registered Investment Advisors Errors and Omissions Policy
- Registered Investment Advisors Fidelity Bonds
- State Surety Bonds
- Privacy and Network Liability Policies
- Employment Practices Liability Insurance

Figure 12.2 ——

Special Coverage: An Attorney's View

According to Richard L. Steer, a partner at New York's Tarter, Krinsky & Drogin LLP, accountants might consider asking for the following clauses to be included in their malpractice policies:

- *Defense costs to be in addition to the policy limits.* In such event, the policy limits would be available to indemnify for claims.

- *Having the aggregate loss apply to the deductible.* For example, in such event, rather than have each claim have its own deductible in a policy year, each claim in that year would be added together in determining whether the deductible is met.

- *An aggregate loss only deductible, which reserves the deductible only for indemnity payments paid for losses during the policy year.* Under such a provision, the insurance company and not the policy holder would ordinarily be responsible for payment of defense costs, which in many claims makes up a large portion of the expense of such a claim.

¶ 1205 The Lawsuit Against You: It's a Matter of Time

Law firms, to some extent, are victims of their own success. Tort reform in recent years limits the liability of physicians. Where are the litigators who so successfully once sued physicians going to drill for new oil? Professional services firms are seeing a lot more corporate litigation, because litigators have redirected in their practices in response to new limits on liability in the medical community.

If your firm hasn't been sued, it probably will be at some point. Fifteen or 20 years ago, if a Top 100 accounting firm was sued, it was the exception unless it was a Big Six or Big Eight firm. Today, most if not all of the Top 100 accounting firms have been sued. It's a total paradigm shift. Practically all of the large accounting firms in the United States currently have active lawsuits against them, and managing them is now part of their business. The firms will settle one or two, and the next lawsuit then will come along. These lawsuits are aggravating nuisances that rarely have merit, but they're so disruptive that they add significantly to the chaos of firm management. Large and mid-size firms are learning to minimize the disruption of litigation by letting to one or two executives handle the distasteful business of lawsuits against the firm, but the accused parties are still dragged away from their work to answer questions and attend required legal proceedings.

The nature of our work also leaves us vulnerable to lawsuits. As accountants and lawyers, we deal on a daily basis with people's fortunes, their futures, and their retirements. We handle the most sensitive and critical aspects of their financial lives. In addition, our clients often don't understand what we do. For example, they can't reasonably expect their accounting firm to know if their bookkeeper is stealing money from them, but when bookkeepers embezzle, accounting firms are sued anyway. And although the firm isn't at fault, nine times out of 10 it settles. Dealing with litigation and avoiding it are just part of doing business today.

Figure 12.3 ——

The Madoff Scandal: The 800-Pound Gorilla

When news of the $65 billion Ponzi scheme engineered by former NASDAQ chief Bernard Madoff broke into the headlines, a tremor shook the financial community. Then other such schemes surfaced and made more headlines. Thousands of investors lost their savings in crimes committed by their fiduciaries. Relatively speaking, the fallout is still in its infancy. So far, lawsuits have been filed against McGladrey & Pullen, KPMG, Ernst & Young, and BDO Seidman. These suits allege that these accounting firms failed to detect problems when they performed their audits.

The SEC is another likely target of potential lawsuits since it failed to detect the fraud even though there were at least two red flags: (1) it was approached by a whistleblower on several occasions and (2) Madoff's firm was audited by David Friehling, who operated what was essentially a one-person firm, since the early 1990s and who acted as his own bookkeeper. Friehling has since been charged with a six-count criminal complaint that accused him of one count each of securities and investment advisor fraud and four of making false filings to the SEC. In addition, the SEC filed a civil enforcement action alleging that Friehling "did not perform anything remotely resembling an audit." So far, Friehling is the only person other than Madoff to be indicted, but it is unlikely that he will be the last.

Even if no changes to the accounting rules or additional oversight rules are imposed, this is a cautionary tale: all of us need to be extra diligent if we are to maintain our status as trusted advisor.

¶ 1210 Minimize Your Firm's Risk

Firms are most at risk when they expand into new service niches without adequate preparation, according to Camico Mutual Insurance Co. of Redwood City, Calif., one of the leading providers of professional liability insurance for CPAs. Rather than dabble, refer clients to other practitioners who have sufficient expertise, or consult with other practitioners to acquire the expertise needed for a specific area. Competency includes the ability to identify risk points in an engagement, which requires a thorough understanding of the client's business and industry.

Firms should screen all of their clients annually. They should also define the scope of their practices by writing a clear statement of what they can do and what they can't do, according to John F. Raspante, CPA, and advisor for Camico. Establish policies about the types of work your firm won't accept because of its lack of expertise in that area. If the firm has clients who don't fit within the scope of its services, weed them out and refer them elsewhere. Provide ongoing training so that employees understand the firm's appetite for risk.

Raspante also recommends that firms become adept at setting and documenting client expectations so that there's no perception gap that can lead to a lawsuit. Document all conversations and communications with clients, and keep engagement letters current. Create a team to evaluate new engagements to ensure quality of the work product. Perform due diligence in vetting other professionals you'll be relying on, such as actuaries for the pension plan you're auditing. Disclose to clients how the firm is paid and its relationships with third-party providers. When your firm partners with third parties, control the communications between the third party, your firm, and the client to avoid misunderstandings. Exercise added caution and due diligence in tax areas, because it often carries the highest risk of exposure. Other high-risk areas are financial statements, investment fraud, and defalcation.

According to Raspante, these practitioners should take the following steps to gain competence in a specialty and to minimize the risk of litigation to themselves and the firm:

- Acquire CPE in the specialty area.
- Read the professional literature.
- Acquire a designation in the specialty.
- Consult with a practitioner who is current in the specialization.
- Join a professional society's committee on the specialized area, or join an association that focuses on that specialty.
- Join an association of other firms to facilitate consultations, cross-referrals, and the exchange of expertise and information as part of the learning process.

Figure 12.4

A Circular 230 Primer

In an effort to combat tax shelters and in response to the impact that these tax avoidance structures have on the public's confidence in the honesty and integrity of tax professionals and the fairness of the U.S. taxation system, in late 2004 the IRS significantly altered Circular 230, which imposes standards upon tax practitioners who render tax advice (though Circular 230 does not contain all such standards) by deleting the old requirements concerning "tax shelter opinions" that tax professionals practicing before the IRS had previously followed in favor of new regulations intended to apply to all written tax advice (including those delivered by electronic means).

These regulations (in force since 2005) divide tax advice into two distinct categories: "covered opinions" and "other written advice." The former category is subject to a rigorous set of regulations while the latter category is governed by lesser requirements. Determination of whether a communication is a "covered opinion" or simply "other written advice" is a factual analysis to be undertaken by the tax professional. In addition, the scope of what constitutes a "covered opinion" is not clearly defined. A tax professional runs the risk of being sanctioned or even disbarred in the event of noncompliance.

In addition to the challenge of identifying what may constitute a "covered opinion" and the attendant practical problems of (a) undertaking this process for every tax-related communication and (b) billing your client for the time it takes to discern whether or not your communication is one, the new regulations also present problems with the traditional role of a tax advisor.

For example, prior to the 2005 regulations, a tax professional could (in a non-tax shelter transaction) counsel a taxpayer utilizing a "realistic possibility of success standard" which allowed the tax professional to give advice so long as a good faith effort was made to determine the validity, scope, meaning, or application of the law. Because the advice pertains to the complexities inherent in the Internal Revenue Code, this standard gave tax professionals comfort that if they properly researched the issue and made sound recommendations to the taxpayer, then they would be protected from IRS penalty even if the positions taken were not sustained. In addition, the taxpayer could rely on the written advice without fear of penalty from the IRS so long as the taxpayer showed a good faith assumption of the validity of their position. Presently, Circular 230 standards require tax advisors to have a higher degree of certainty in their opinions and the resulting fear of IRS sanctions (and the inability to shield their clients from possible penalty for relying on their advice) has made tax professionals wary of giving opinions and has promulgated the widespread use of Circular 230 disclaimers in an effort to give tax professionals some form of self-protection.

Based on the foregoing, if the written advice is construed as a "covered opinion" by the taxpayer and relied upon then notwithstanding the tax professional's intention, he is at risk for running afoul of the Circular 230 regulations. Accordingly, we recommend utilizing a Circular 230 disclaimer, where permitted, in any written communication that could possibly be viewed as written tax advice in an effort to clearly advise the taxpayer that the written advice is not intended to be a "covered opinion" and therefore cannot be relied upon by the taxpayer for the purpose of avoiding penalties resulting from federal tax positions taken by the taxpayer in the subject transaction.

As to the Circular 230 disclaimer itself, the 2005 rules require such notices to be "prominently disclosed," i.e., "readily apparent" to the reader. The notice must be in a separate section (but not in a footnote or as "fine print") of the correspondence. The typeface used must be at least the same size as the typeface used in any discussion of facts or law.

Below is a typical Circular 230 disclaimer though we are not aware of any standardized format:

"IRS Circular 230 Disclosure: To ensure compliance with requirements imposed by the Unites States Internal Revenue Service, we inform you that any U.S. tax advice contained in this communication (including any attachments, enclosures or other accompanying materials) is not intended or written to be used, and cannot be used, for the purpose of (i) avoiding penalties under the Internal Revenue Code or (ii) promoting, marketing, or recommending to another party any transaction or tax-related matter addressed herein."

Source: Thomas G. Huszar, Counsel at Tarter Krinsky & Drogin LLP.

Figure 12.5

Sample File-Retention Policy

1. Existing client files may not be purged. At the end of each engagement, original client documents are returned to the client and copies of key documents are retained.

2. Former client files are kept intact for seven years after termination of the client relationship. At that time:

   - Original client records are to be returned to the former client.
   - Essential files and summaries are to be retained in a permanent file.
   - All other files are to be destroyed, preferably by shredding.

3. After 10 years, permanent files for former clients are to be destroyed, preferably by shredding.

Under this policy, the essential records of former clients are retained for 10 years. The risk of liability is sharply reduced beyond that time. If a claim is made against the firm during that period, the firm must follow the instructions of its malpractice insurer.

Also, it is important to be sure your firm's records retention policy complies with all federal and local laws and regulations. The best way to ensure your firm is in compliance is to consult with an attorney or the state society.

Figure 12.6 ———————————————————————————————————

Firm Culture Impacts Level of Risk

Good firm management—with top-down accountability and good systems and procedures in place—can contribute significantly to reducing a firm's level of risk. The firm's level of exposure lessens with the adoption of each of the following:

- Written partnership agreement that includes the following:
  — Acceptable standards of behavior.
  — Explanation of behaviors that are cause for termination.
  — Definition of compensation system, including;
    - Mandatory and minimum retirement.
    - Payout system for retiring partners.
    - Payout formula(s) for partners who leave for any reason other than retirement.
    - Key person insurance.
  — Clarification of expectations for new business development.
- Client acceptance process and procedure.
- New hire process and procedure.
- Employee handbook.
- Ongoing CPE.
- Culture that nurtures team mentality and discourages silo (or eat-what-you-kill) behavior.
- Succession plan that is communicated to everyone at the firm.
- Disaster plan that is communicated to everyone at the firm.
- Emergency action plan in the event of a fire, sudden illness, or the like.
- Ability to effectively monitor productivity, WIP, collections, and due dates.
- Comprehensive system of checks and balances that provides oversight and prevents fraudulent activity.
- Established communications systems tailored to various constituencies:
  — Internal firm communications.
  — Clients.
  — Target clients.
  — Referral sources.
  — The public.
  — The media.

———

¶ 1215 Employee Handbooks

To protect the firm against lawsuits, it is a good idea to create an employee handbook that outlines the firm's workplace policies. The handbook should be distributed to every new hire, whatever their level, at orientation. Its goal is to set up expectations about workplace policies and procedures, including what the employee should expect from the firm, and detail what happens if the employee has a complaint.

All of the policies in the manual must comply with applicable federal and state laws, and management must agree to be bound by the document. Failure to consistently apply the policies and procedures in the manual leaves the firm open to discrimination litigation.

Because the laws may vary from jurisdiction to jurisdiction, an attorney specializing in these matters should be consulted for advice and guidance before the manual, or any addendum, is distributed to employees and annually thereafter. The entire manual should be reissued if there is a major organizational change or if the law changes.

One other important note: to help avoid having the courts construe the manual as an employment contract, the first page of the manual should clearly state that nothing in the manual is intended to be, nor should be construed as, an employment contract. Such statements don't guarantee protection, but they may offer some defense.

Every employee should be required to sign a statement indicating he or she has read the entire manual and each addendum. Generally, employees are asked to return the signed and dated statement within 30 days of receipt.

A typical handbook included the following sections:

- Welcome and introduction. A description of the firm's history and philosophy, perhaps in the form of a welcome letter from the firm's managing partner. The firm's mission and values statement should be included.
- Statement of business hours, including expectations during tax season, and how overtime is authorized.

- Pay, salary, and bonus structure. This section should stipulate the pay schedule and set out when salaries are raised (e.g., at the end of the probationary period; annually). It should also set out the firm's policy on bonuses.
- Benefits:
  — Paid time off. A description of the firm's holiday, vacation, sick leave, FMLA, military leave, and jury duty policies.
  — Medical, dental, and other health insurance. Include how long it takes for the employee to become eligible, how much of the cost is company-paid for the employee as well as for his or her family, and when plan elections are made.
  — Flexible spending, dependent care, and transportation options.
  — Life and disability insurance.
  — 401(k) and other pension options.
- Smoking policy.
- Drug and alcohol abuse policy.
- Sexual harassment zero-tolerance policy.
- Dress policy.
- Safety policies.
- Disciplinary policies.
- Grievance policies.
- Statement of at-will employment.
- Grounds for involuntary termination.
- Process for voluntary termination, including exit interviews.
- Use of firm equipment policies.
- Policies concerning Internet access, IM, social media, etc. on company time.
- Guidelines for employee performance reviews (such as how and when they are conducted).
- Confidentiality agreement to be signed by employee.
- "I agree" form stating they have read and understand the information, and accept the terms of the employee handbook to be signed by employee within ___ days of hire.

As the handbook is prepared, there are two important things to keep in mind. First, no employee handbook can cover every possible situation, and it's prudent to say so in the handbook. This leaves some room for interpretation. Second, laws change, and the manual needs to be updated periodically so it is in compliance. In the same vein, the laws vary between states, so if your firm has offices in more than one state, the handbook needs to be reviewed so it complies in each state in which you operate.

¶ 1220 At-Will Employment: Protecting the Firm from Wrongful Discharge Claims

Sometimes, it is necessary to terminate someone's employment. As a general rule most employees are at-will employees, which means they freely entered into the employment relationship and each party has the right to sever that relationship at any time for any reason or for no reason. Such arrangements are based on the premise that good job performance warrants continued employment unless adverse economic conditions mandate a change in the work-force. If, however, the employee is covered by a written employment contract, civil service rules, a union collective bargaining agreement, or is in a protected class as defined by law, dismissal is governed by either the contract provisions or the relevant statutes and regulations.

Employees have successfully pursued wrongful discharge claims for the following reasons:

- *Implicit employment contract.* Employees who have been on the job for a number of years, have received promotions or raises, or have not received negative work evaluations may be considered to have an implicit employment contract. In the California case that introduced the concept, an employee who was fired after 18 years of employment was found to have an "implied contractual right" to job security and could be fired only for "good cause." The employer had charged the employee with multiple violations of company rules but had failed to follow its own required disciplinary procedures before terminating employment.
- *Violation of public policy.* An Illinois court found that an employee was improperly discharged as a result of filing a workers' compensation claim. The Oregon Supreme Court held that it was improper to fire an employee for serving on a jury despite her employer's request that she be excused. In a California case, the court ruled that an employee was wrongfully fired for not committing perjury as instructed by his employer. All of these decisions are based on the concept that public policies must be protected, and employers cannot fire employees for reasons contrary to these policies.

- *Statements assuring job security.* When job applications, personnel guides, or management personnel make statements promising "permanent" employment or discharge only for "good cause," the courts have found those statements to be binding. In a Michigan case, an employee received an oral promise that he would not be discharged as long as he did his job. The Michigan Supreme Court found that this assurance of job assurance was enforceable by the employee.

- *Breach of good faith.* Employers cannot fire employees to avoid paying pension benefits, earned sales commissions, or other compensation. In a New Jersey case, an employee was terminated with only weeks remaining until his pension benefits would be vested, and he sued the employer. A jury decided in the plaintiff's favor under ERISA, which prohibits employers' interference with employees' pension rights. The court held the employer liable for damages. The jury's decision was based on insufficient evidence to support a "willful" violation of company policy that would warrant termination. Therefore, it was determined that the employer may have been terminating the employee for other reasons relating to the pension.

To avoid potential risks in this area, firms must frequently and consistently document performance problems and ensure that their policies do not discriminate against any employee on the basis of age or pension status.

- *Protected status.* Firms should consider whether the individual has protected status as defined by law. Examples of protected classes include:

  — Coverage by a union contract

  — Race

  — Gender

  — Age

  — Disability

  — Religion

  — National origin

  — Marital status

  — Veteran status

  — Civil service status

  — Sexual orientation

- Other reasons an employer may not fire an at-will employee include:

  — Refusing to commit illegal acts. An employer is not permitted to fire an employee because the employee refuses to commit an act that is illegal.

  — Taking family or medical leave for a reason outlined in the Family and Medical Leave Act.

  — Failing to follow the firm's termination procedures as outlined in the employee handbook or by company policy.

If none of the above situations exist, firms are free to terminate employment. If the employee in question is a member of any group with protected status considered to be a minority within the firm, the employer must be prepared to prove the termination decision was based on legitimate business reasons, such as the employee's failure to satisfactorily fulfill job requirements.

The preceding examples don't cover all of the situations that can give rise to a claim of wrongful discharge. It is advisable for the managing partner, COO, or HR director to periodically attend seminars on updates in personnel law so they can keep abreast of changes in the law. An attorney should be consulted if there is any question about a particular situation.

¶ 1225 Layoffs

These are challenging times, and there may be some situations that require firms to lay off employees. As long as the firm protects itself from claims of wrongful termination by following the above guidelines and checking with an attorney, the firm doesn't have any other duty to the employee other than to provide COBRA. The rules for when COBRA must be provided were changed under the American Recovery and Reinvestment Act of 2009 (ARRA) (P.L. 111-5). While most of the existing provisions of COBRA haven't changed, there are new temporary provisions. An attorney or other specialist should be consulted to ensure you are compliant with the changes.

Employers generally aren't required to pay severance or to pay for unused sick time or vacation time. However, there is an element of good will involved that makes it a good idea to pay these items—the economic situation will change, and the firms that will be left standing are the ones with the foresight to believe that their strength ultimately lies in their people even if they are forced to make some unpleasant decisions in the short term. This is true even for firms who are using the economic downturn as a reason to trim their low-hanging fruit.

¶ 1230 Offers of Employment

Since employment is at-will in most states, it is important that offer of employment letters reflect this. The language in the letter should not in any way imply a contractual situation. (This may not apply if you are in a union environment or in a state that is not employment-at-will.)

It is particularly important to consider the language around a probationary period. According to Richard Paris, president of M&K Executive Search LLC/Melville, N.Y., many employers require new, transferred, and promoted employees to complete an introductory period of employment that allows an evaluation of their skills and compatibility with the organization and their jobs. During this period, the employee also has the opportunity to demonstrate his or her ability to learn the new job and to determine if he or she likes working in the organization. Some employers refer to this time period as a "training period," "orientation period," "initial employment period," or even a "familiarization" period. Other employers use the more traditional phrase "probationary period," although use of this title may create some legal problems.

Here is an example of language that can increase your risk exposure:

> The first 90 days of your employment will be under a probationary period. During this probationary period, both the company and you will determine whether you can perform the requirements of the job you have been assigned to. Near the end of this probation, we will assess your performance and decide whether further employment is warranted.

And here is language that cannot be misconstrued:

> The first 90 days of employment are considered an orientation period that gives you and the company a chance to get to know each other. Your performance will be evaluated during this time to assess your potential for continued employment. This period also provides you with the opportunity to evaluate us as an employer. We encourage you to share your thoughts with your supervisor during your orientation review.

Figure 12.7

Sample Offer of Employment Letter #1

[DATE]

[NAME]

[ADDRESS]

[CITY, STATE ZIP]

Dear [NAME]:

We thoroughly enjoyed meeting with you in our office to discuss the opportunities that Marcum LLP has to offer you. Those of us who met you are extremely impressed with your background and look forward to having you join us. We are pleased to offer you a position as a _____ in the _____ Department of our _____ office starting on or before _____, 2009. Your compensation will be $_____ per pay period (annualized at $_____).

As a manager, you are eligible to participate in our annual bonus pool paid each February. This bonus can be up to a maximum of 20% of your base compensation, depending on your contribution to the firm as well as the firm's profitability during the fiscal year. Managers who join the firm mid-year will participate in the bonus pool on a pro-rata basis. You must be an active employee in good standing at the time of payment of the bonus, which will be paid out each February.

Annual compensation reviews take place on or about September 1st of each year. Performance and evaluation reviews are scheduled semi-annually. Attached is Marcum LLP's summary of benefits for you to review, as well as a business card and name plate form to be completed and returned with your acceptance. Also attached is a Manager Agreement, which all professional staff members sign upon being hired. Please review and sign the agreement, and bring both copies with you on your first day.

Offers of employment with Marcum LLP are contingent upon several factors, including completion of a satisfactory background and reference check. Nothing in any firm document or writing creates a contract for a specific term of employment. No management person is authorized to offer or create a contract of employment for a specific term. Employment is at-will.

This offer remains valid until _____, 2009. If you would like us to extend this offer beyond the expiration date, please call me before the date has expired. Please indicate your acceptance of the terms in this offer letter by signing and returning one copy of this letter to me.

On your first day you will be required to fill out an I-9 form. Please see the attached list of acceptable documentation that you need to bring with you on your first day. Our company dress policy is business casual attire at all times.

We hope that we have been able to show you what our firm has to offer in the way of a promising, exciting, and challenging experience. If you have any questions, please feel free to call me at (631) 414-4010.

Sincerely,

Partner-In-Charge, Human Resources

Enclosure

Accepted by:

_____

Name   Date

Source: Marcum LLP/Melville, N.Y.

Figure 12.8 —————————————————————————————————————

Sample Offer of Employment Letter #2

Date

Name

Address

City, State Zip

Dear _____:

It is my pleasure to extend the following offer of employment to you on behalf of (your company name). This offer is contingent upon your passing our mandatory drug screen, our receipt of your college transcripts, and (any other contingencies you may wish to state).

Title: _____

Reporting Relationship: The position will report to [Name and Title]:

_____

Job Description and Goals or Objectives are attached.

Base Salary: Will be paid in bi-weekly installments of $_____, which is equivalent to $_____ on an annual basis, and subject to deductions for taxes and other withholdings as required by law or the policies of the company.

Bonus (or Commission) Potential: Effective upon satisfactory completion of the first 90 days of employment, and based upon the goals and objectives agreed to in the performance development planning process with your manager, you may be eligible for a bonus. The bonus plan for this year and beyond, should such a plan exist, will be based on the formula determined by the company for that year.

Signing Bonus: $10,000 payable during the first pay period.

Non-Compete Agreement: Our standard non-compete agreement must be signed prior to start.

Benefits: The current, standard company health, life, disability, and dental insurance coverage is generally supplied per company policy. Eligibility for other benefits, including the 401(k) and tuition reimbursement, will generally take place per company policy. Employee contribution to payment for benefit plans is determined annually.

Car Allowance: $500 per month car allowance will generally be provided.

Stock Options: [Spell out any options that may be available for purchase by the executive. Spell out any options or other stock vehicles for which the executive is eligible.]

Stock Buy Back Provisions: [Detail how the executive's stock will be repurchased by the company if the executive leaves the employer for any reason other than cause.]

Severance Pay: If the executive is let go by the company for any reason other than cause (i.e., violence, theft, fraudulent activities, harassment, etc.), the company will pay the executive six months of salary and cover COBRA expenses for the executive's family during the same time period. Payment is due in a lump sum upon termination or is payable in regular pay periods over the six months. [the details of the severance package.]

Expenses: Spell out any moving or other transition expenses the company will pay.

Vacation and Personal Emergency Time Off: Vacation is accrued at x.xx hours per pay period, which is equivalent to four weeks on an annual basis. Personal emergency days are generally accrued per company policy.

Phone/Travel Allowance: Normal and reasonable expenses will be reimbursed on a monthly basis per company policy and upon completion of the appropriate expense request form.

Start Date: _____

Your employment with (Company Name) is at-will and either party can terminate the relationship at any time with or without cause and with or without notice.

¶1230

You acknowledge that this offer letter, along with the final form of any referenced documents (such stock repurchase plan, job description, bonus goals, etc.), represents the entire agreement between you and (Company Name) and that no verbal or written agreements, promises, or representations that are not specifically stated in this offer are or will be binding upon (Company Name).

If you are in agreement with the above outline, please sign below. This offer is in effect for [generally, five business days].

Signatures:

_____

(For the Company: Name)

_____

Date

_____

(Candidate's Name)

_____

Source: Marcum LLP/Melville, N.Y.

¶ 1235 Noncompete Agreements

Noncompete agreements protect employers from losing valuable trade secrets and employees. After losing scores of valuable employees (and trade secrets) to competitors, a growing number of employers are asking, or requiring, employees to sign noncompete agreements. By signing a noncompete agreement, an employee promises not to work for a direct competitor for a specified period of time after he or she leaves the company.

¶ 1240 Procedure to Follow for Just-Cause Discharge

If it becomes necessary to terminate an individual, the firm must be prepared to defend its decision. To do so effectively, the firm should follow these steps:

1. Ensure that all decision makers involved in the management, supervisory, and termination processes are familiar with protected states and just cause laws.

2. Document all job descriptions and review and update the job requirements annually.

3. Make certain that job functions and expected behaviors are job related and in alignment with what is required of other staff members in similar positions in the firm.

4. Review all job requirements thoroughly with new hires as well as with existing staff members who are assigned to new job responsibilities.

5. Issue a written warning to any employee found in violation of the firm's policies and procedures before terminating the individual's employment. Describe the employee's inappropriate or unacceptable behavior in detail, state what the staff member must do to change the behavior, and define the time frame allotted for making the necessary changes (usually 30 days).

6. Clarify management's intended action in the event the required changes aren't made. Communicate this in writing to all employees affected by the policy.

7. Conduct a thorough review of the facts that may lead management to conclude that termination is necessary. Document observable behavior and support the observations with detailed descriptions of incidents perceived to substantiate violations of the firm's policies, procedures, or performance standards. Avoid relying on hearsay or rumors since neither provides an adequate claim defense.

8. Review and communicate performance standards for all members of the firm annually to ensure consistent application of such standards to all employees in similar positions within the firm. Be prepared to justify the firm's standards and support enforcement procedures.

¶ 1245 The Role of the Equal Employment Opportunity Commission (EEOC)

The EEOC oversees the enforcement of federal antidiscrimination legislation. Many states also have laws that prohibit discrimination. Employers also may not pay workers of one gender less than workers of the opposite gender for work on jobs that require equal skill, effort, and responsibility and are performed under the same working conditions. Your firm's equal employment opportunity (EEO) policy must comply with these laws.

You may want to use fairly general wording in your firm's equal opportunity clauses. Changing employment laws and court interpretations may render the clause out of date without your notice. In addition, many state and municipal laws include more protected classes than do federal laws. Contact your attorney or the state department of labor for the most current guidelines.

Although establishing and implementing an EEO policy is required by law, it is also a matter of good business sense for your firm and your employees. By doing so, your firm is assured of the largest possible pool of qualified applicants. Also, each staff member is assured that he or she is on equal footing with others in terms of employment and advancement opportunity.

The EEO laws apply to every aspect of employment: hiring, training, supervision, promotion, and termination. Therefore, it is essential that all supervisors, managers, and partners in your firm are trained in and follow appropriate practices when interviewing and disciplining employees. All criteria for employee selection and evaluation must be job related and nondiscriminatory.

Figure 12.9 ———————————————————————————————————

A Guide to Interview Questions

As a general rule, only questions that specifically relate to the position may be asked. There is a fine line though, and sometimes it is the way a question is asked that causes problems. For example, you may ask whether someone is willing to relocate, but you may not frame the question so that the person must indicate whether he or she is married in their response. Similarly, you may ask whether someone is qualified to work in the United States, but you may not ask where the person was born or whether they are a U.S. citizen.

Keep in mind that any question related to a subject that relates to a protected class (age, gender, race, ethnicity, national origin, religion, and sexual orientation) is a sensitive area. Most states have enacted laws that make certain questions unlawful. Consequently, it is prudent to stay away from any questions concerning whether the prospective employee:

- Has ever worked under a different name.

- Has plans to marry or have children or has made arrangements for child care.

- Is fluent in any languages other than English (unless such fluency is part of the job description.

- Observes any holidays related to a religious organization.

- Belongs to any clubs or fraternities/sororities.

The laws vary by state, so it is a best practice to have your attorney review the questions you plan to include in the interview process.

———

.01 Some Behaviors That Could Be Considered Discriminatory

Any of the following behaviors could be considered discriminatory if they are based on race, color, creed, religion, gender, sexual orientation, marital status, national origin, disability, or other protected status:

- Epithets, slurs, quips, or negative stereotyping.

- Threatening, intimidating, or hostile acts.

- Written or graphic material (including graffiti) that denigrates or shows hostility or aversion to an individual placed on walls, bulletin boards, or elsewhere on the firm's premises or circulated or displayed in the workplace.

- "Jokes," "pranks," or other forms of humor that are demeaning or hostile.

.02 Employer Responsibility

The EEOC's guidelines make it clear that employers are responsible for the acts of their employees "regardless of whether the specific acts complained of were authorized or even forbidden by the employer and regardless of whether the employer knew or should have known of their existence." In addition, the employer may be responsible for claims of sexual harassment by nonemployees in the workplace (e.g., client personnel or outside contractual personnel such as equipment repair people) if "the employer (or its agents or supervisory employees) knows or should have known of the conduct and fails to take immediate and appropriate corrective action."

It is important to keep in mind that different people have different views of what constitutes sexual harassment. The following scenarios illustrate how this can play out in an office situation:

- *Scenario 1.* Amy finds it extremely uncomfortable to be in a group that is telling off-color jokes. She stays, however, because her boss is part of the group and she wants to be seen as a good sport. Amy seemed to have joined in the "fun," and she didn't complain because Mary, her boss, the person she was supposed to complain to, was part of the group. Eventually, she leaves the firm and files a harassment suit.

- *Scenario 2.* Jill, a manager, finds Jack, a staff accountant, attractive. She begins teasing him, often with sexual innuendo. Soon, her remarks become more and more suggestive. Finally, she jokingly propositions him. Jack is new to the firm.

Because of Jill's position, he feels intimidated about reporting her actions to her superiors. Unable to handle the situation, he leaves the firm and files a suit charging sexual harassment.

- *Scenario 3.* While working at a client's office, a female staff member alleges she is the victim of sexual harassment because an employee of the client assigned her a workspace that had explicit sexual material on the wall. She reported the incident to the partner-in-charge of the account, who quickly contacted the client and suggested a joint investigation of the incident. Any other action could have resulted in liability exposure for both the firm and the client.

In each of these examples, the firm could minimize its risk exposure by:

- Having a written policy specifically prohibiting sexual harassment,
- Putting in place a formal procedure for victims of harassment to register complaints, and
- Documenting everything as carefully as possible.

Figure 12.10

Sample Sexual Harassment Policy Involving Use of Electronic Media

Electronic media may not be used for knowingly transmitting, receiving, or storing any communications of a discriminatory or harassing nature or which are derogatory to any individual or group or which are obscene or X-rated communications or are of a defamatory or threatening nature, or for any purpose which is illegal, against firm policy, or contrary to the firm's interest.

Figure 12.11

Sample Equal Opportunity Policy

The firm seeks to provide equal employment opportunities to all employees and applicants for employment without regard to race, color, creed, religion, gender, sexual orientation, marital status, national origin, age, disability, or other protected status. The firm fully complies with all applicable federal, state, and local antidiscrimination laws.

It's the firm's policy to maintain a work environment in which all individuals are treated with respect and dignity. Each individual has the right to work in a professional atmosphere that prohibits discriminatory practices. Harassment, whether verbal, physical or environmental is unacceptable and will not be tolerated by the firm.

This policy covers all firm employees. Any type of harassment, whether engaged in by fellow employees, supervisors, or by nonemployees with whom employees come into contact (e.g., service providers or contractors), is contrary to this policy and will not be tolerated.

All employees are encouraged to report all incidents of unlawful discrimination to their immediate supervisor or the managing partner regardless of who the offender might be. Upon receipt of the complaint, the firm will conduct a prompt investigation and take appropriate corrective action as may be warranted. The firm will endeavor to maintain confidentiality throughout the investigatory process to the extent practical and appropriate under the circumstances.

The firm will not tolerate or permit any employee to suffer retaliation of any kind or any adverse employment action as a result of reporting an unlawful discrimination claim. Any employee who feels he or she has been subject to any acts of retaliation should immediately report such conduct to the managing partner.

Figure 12.12

Sample Complaint Procedure

The firm encourages individuals who believe they are being harassed to firmly and promptly notify the alleged offender that his or her behavior is unwelcome. However, we recognize that perceived power and status disparities between an alleged offender and a victim may make such a confrontation difficult. Therefore, whether or not you discuss the incident with the alleged offender, we ask that individuals who believe they have been subject to harassment to report the incident to the managing partner.

We encourage the prompt reporting of complaints so that rapid and appropriate action may be taken.

The firm will not in any way retaliate against an individual who reports perceived harassment nor will we permit any employee to do so. Retaliation is a serious violation of the firm's harassment policy and anyone who feels he or she has been subject to any acts of retaliation should immediately report such conduct. Any person who retaliates against another individual for reporting any perceived acts of harassment will be subject to disciplinary action up to or including discharge.

All allegations of harassment will be promptly investigated. We will endeavor to maintain confidentiality during the investigation process to the extent practical and appropriate under the circumstances.

If it is found harassment has occurred, the harasser will be subject to appropriate disciplinary action. The specific corrective action taken will be within the firm's discretion. Such actions may include the following:

- Verbal or written reprimand.

- Referral to appropriate counseling.

- Withholding of a promotion or bonus.

- Reassignment.

- Temporary suspension.

- Discharge.

The firm realizes that false accusations of harassment can cause serious harm to innocent persons. If the investigation results in a finding that the complainant knowingly or in a malicious manner falsely accused another person of harassment, the complainant will be subject to disciplinary action up to and including discharge.

The firm has developed this policy to ensure that all employees can work in an environment free from sexual harassment and from harassment based on race, color, creed, religion, gender, sexual orientation, marital status, national origin, disability, or other protected status.

Figure 12.13

Sample Confidentiality Agreement

Privacy and trust are implicit in the accounting profession. As part of my employment, I will be exposed to private client information. My signature acknowledges that I understand I am required to keep such information confidential, both during and after my employment.

_____   _____
[Employees signature]   [Date]